GEORGE MASA'S WILD VISION

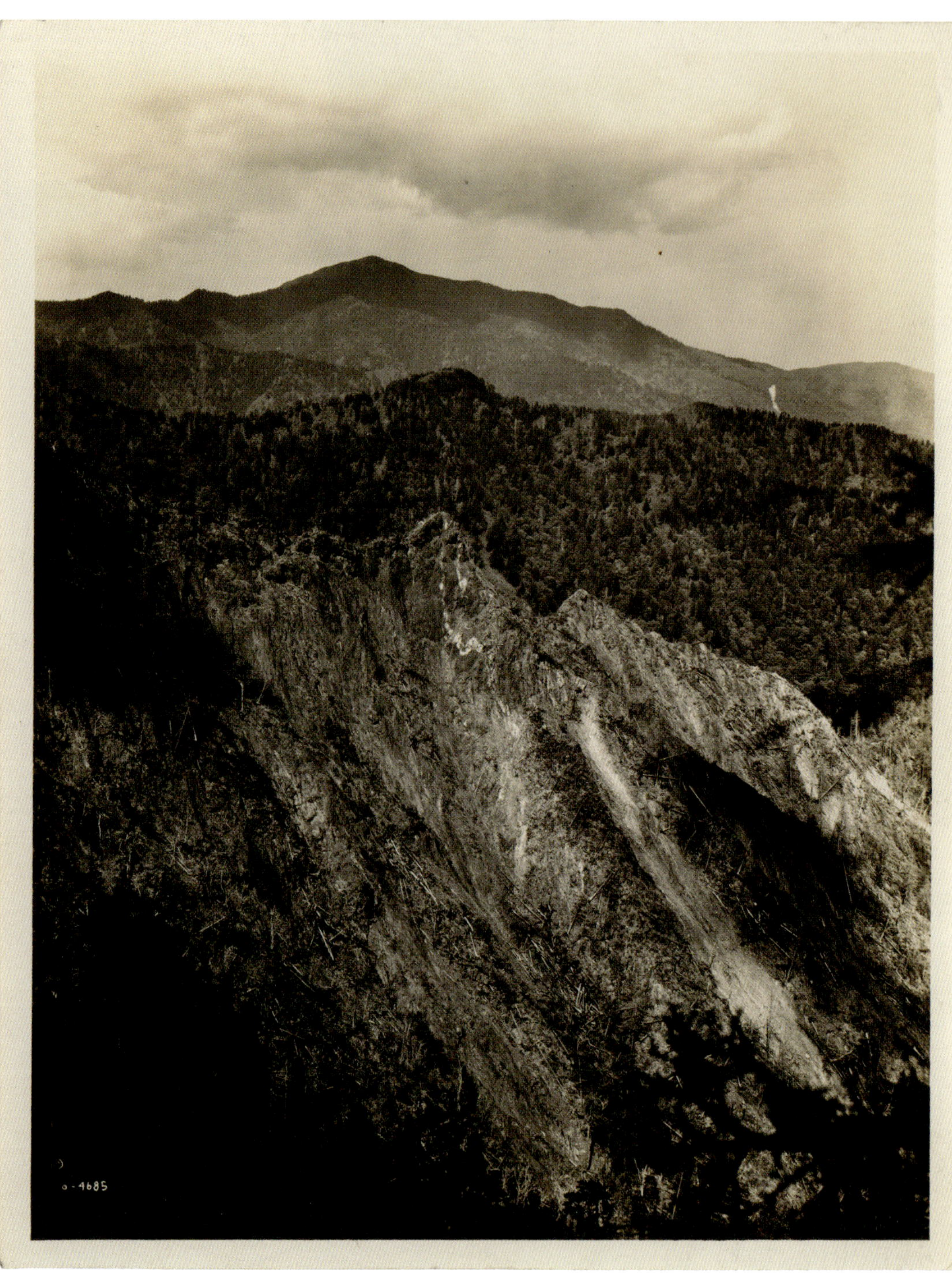
0-4685

GEORGE MASA'S WILD VISION

A Japanese Immigrant Imagines Western North Carolina

BRENT MARTIN

HUB CITY PRESS | 2022

Cover design: Meg Reid
Interior design: Bonnie Campbell
Editor: John Lane
Copy editor: Stephen Kirk
Proofreaders: Kendall Owens, Stephanie Trott

Printed in the United States of America

FRONTIS: *Looking west from Sawtooth to Clingman's Dome (Western Carolina University)*
PAGE X: *George Masa, c. 1920 photographer and location unknown (WCU)*

Library of Congress Cataloging-in-Publication Data

Names: Martin, Brent, author.
Title: George Masa's wild vision : a Japanese American imagines Western
   North Carolina / Brent Martin.
Description: Spartanburg : Hub City Press, 2022. | Includes bibliographical references.
Identifiers: LCCN 2022004541 | ISBN 9781938235931 (hardback)
Subjects: LCSH: Masa, George, 1881-1933. | Photographers—United States—Biography.
Mountains—North Carolina—Pictorial works. | Japanese Americans—Biography.
Landscape photography—North Carolina.
Classification:
LCC TR140.M367 M37 2022
DDC 770.92 [B]—dc23/eng/20220406
LC record available at https://lccn.loc.gov/2022004541

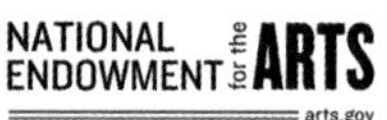 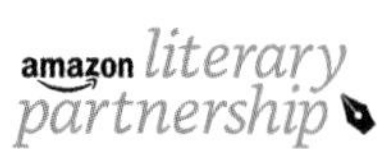 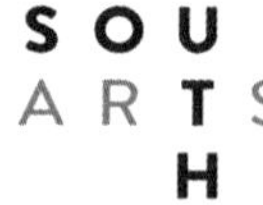 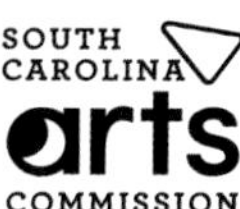

Hub City Press gratefully acknowledges support from the National Endowment for the Arts, the Amazon Literary Partnership, South Arts, and the South Carolina Arts Commission.

Manufactured in the United States of America
First Edition

HUB CITY PRESS
200 Ezell Street
Spartanburg, SC 29306
864.577.9349 | www.hubcity.org

Dedicated to the millions of immigrants who took risks pursuing their dreams to enter this country, and to those who continue to do so

CONTENTS

INTRODUCTION
I

CHAPTER ONE
Great Smoky Mountains National Park
15

CHAPTER TWO
Highlands Plateau
35

CHAPTER THREE
Mount Mitchell/Black Mountains
63

CHAPTER FOUR
Chimney Rock/Hickory Nut Gorge
83

CHAPTER FIVE
Outliers
99

CONCLUSION/CODA
119

ACKNOWLEDGMENTS
131

REFERENCES
133

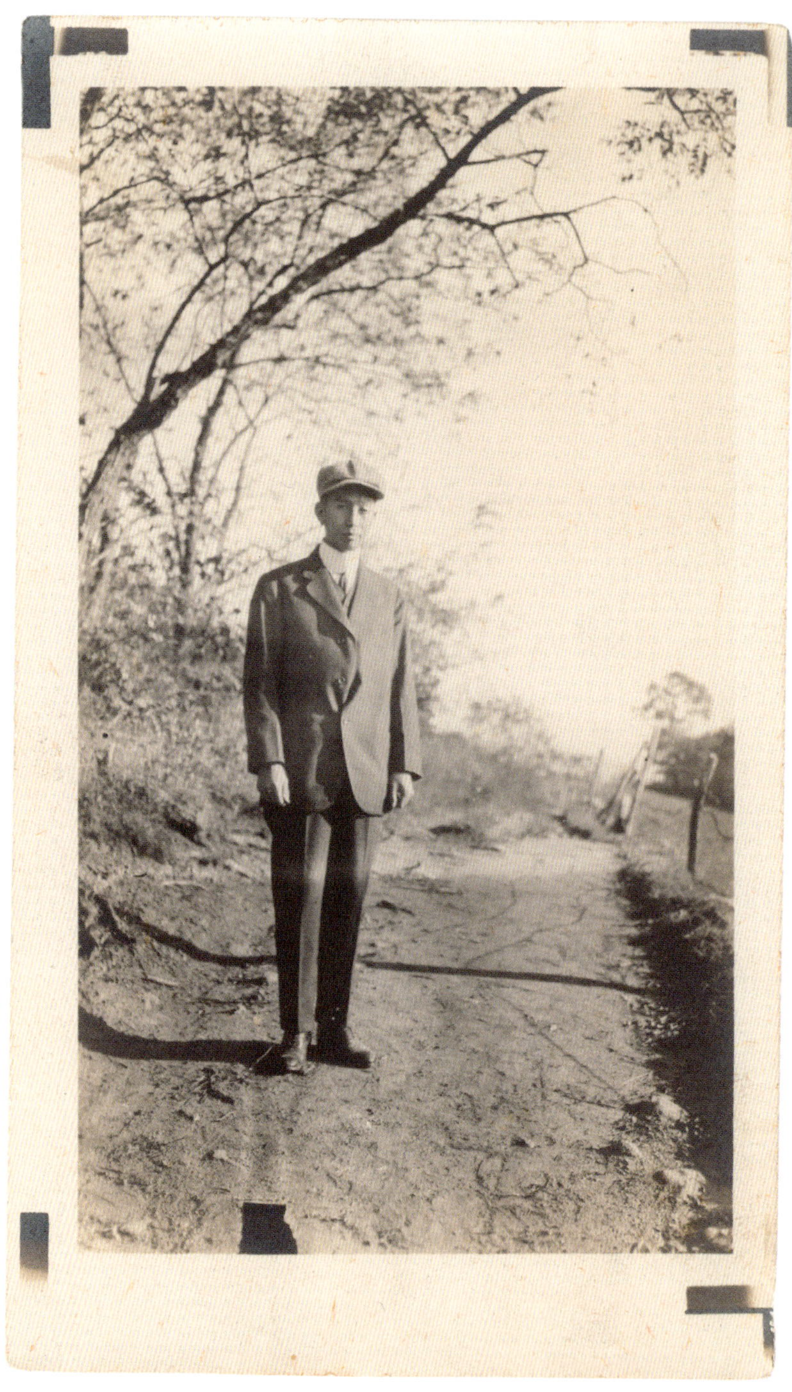

INTRODUCTION

WHEN THE YOUNG Masahara Iizuka stepped onto the California shore in the early 1900s, could he have imagined that within the next twenty-five years he would emerge on the other side of the country as one of southern Appalachia's greatest photographers, along with being one of its most significant advocates for protection of its wild places? By all accounts, this was not his original intent. He was in the United States to study and pursue a career in engineering, and had laid groundwork for this already, having ostensibly spent time at Meiji University in Tokyo in this pursuit. He was twenty-six years old, according to the scant information available. What instead lay ahead for the young George Masa, as he was to rename himself, was an artistic and visionary journey into the soul of the some of the oldest mountains on earth—a creative rendering of their light, their magnificence, their lushness, and their need for a voice to ensure their protection for generations to come. It was a love affair of place. Masa fought like a madman to capture their light and beauty, a trait of his noted by many friends and customers. He cared little for comforts or accumulation of wealth, to the point of asceticism, and his desire for perfection and connection was legendary. Self-denial in the pursuit of beauty was *de rigeur*. And as anyone knows who has spent time much time in the southern Appalachians—particularly in the rugged backcountry—they can be fickle and turn on you with harsh impunity, challenging loyalty with raw indifference. Masa's photographs are statements to this.

Most of what we know about George Masa is thanks to the research of documentary filmmaker Paul Bonesteel and writers George Ellison, William Hart, Janet McCue, and Susan Shumaker. Bonesteel's 2002 film, *The Mystery of George Masa,* was the first effort to compile Masa's life and photographs into a coherent visual presentation. What biographical information exists was first gathered and written into a full-length essay by historian William Hart for the two-volume set of Appalachian

best reference; reasonable. Send postal, GOLDMAN, 1958 Bush st.

JAPANESE first class butler, bright and gentle, wants a position in a good family; good reference. GEORGE MASA, box 1972, Call office, 1651 Fillmore st.

COOK—Situation wanted by competent Japanese in hotel or family; first class all around man; references; $40 up. MIYABARA, care Kumano, 1723 Post st.

CHAUFFEUR, careful, reliable driver and first

The San Francisco Call, December 17, 1907

history, *May We All Remember Well* (1997)—an effort that inspired and informed Bonesteel's production. George Ellison and Janet McCue's *Back of Beyond: A Horace Kephart Biography* (2019) includes the most current and comprehensive history of Masa's life, particularly as it relates to his friendship and collaboration with Kephart on the Great Smokies park movement and the creation of the southern route of the Appalachian Trail. Painstaking research among this group has led to a comprehensive narrative of his life upon his arrival in Asheville, yet nothing is known of his childhood or his years as a young adult. Bonesteel and McCue are currently collaborating on a full biography of Masa's life. Historical information on Masa in this publication draws heavily from all of the above and is what informs me as I travel in Masa's photographic footsteps, reflecting upon his life and work in a twenty-first-century context.

Masa perhaps arrived here in 1906 or 1907. My own research discovered what is possibly one of the earliest records of him here in the States—an advertisement placed by Masa in 1907 as a Japanese first-class butler, "bright and gentle," looking for a position with a good family, and with a reference. If this is our George Masa, he lived at 1651 Fillmore Street, San Francisco, which somewhat ironically today is a Goodwill store. "Bright and gentle"—a humble assessment of self, and characteristics that others would attribute to him later, along with his intensity of being. How rare those characteristics are in today's polarized, overwrought society. In correspondence with Bonesteel about this possibility, many questions are raised. Bonesteel's current research raises the possibility that Masa might have returned to Japan for a time during this period, as there are no known records for the years he is assumed to have spent here prior to his father's death in 1913. We know he made his way east eventually, leaving California in January 1915 and arriving in Asheville in July, after a stay in New Orleans. Asheville's opulent Grove Park Inn had recently opened, and Masa gained employment there in the laundry room.

Masa's love affair with Appalachia was yet to blossom, however, and he left Asheville and backtracked to the American West in 1917, perhaps to pursue a career in photography or mining. By this point, he had already begun dabbling in photography, taking and developing photos of guests at the inn and exploring the possibilities of a career in the business. Masa returned after a few months, out of cash but with a new passion and commitment to photography, perhaps born from his western experience, or perhaps from some mystical intuition telling him this was *the place*—the place where his dreams and art would flourish, and where his albeit brief but productive life would unfold.

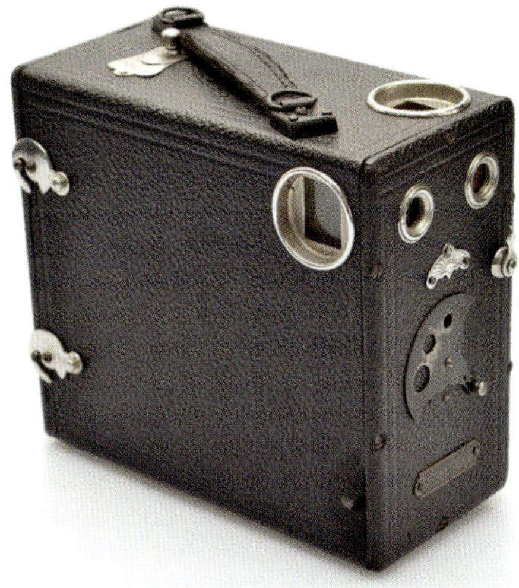

The Cherry Camera,
manufactured in Japan, 1903

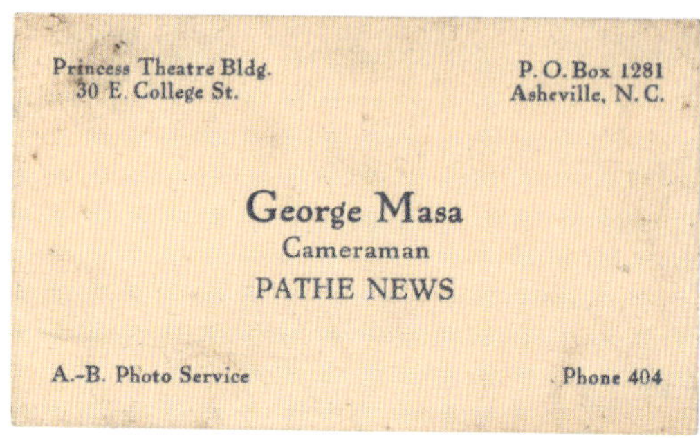

One is left to wonder upon Masa's influences, early years, and where and how this passion was born. The latest research by William Hart suggests that Masa was so smart and talented that he could have very well learned on his own, or through instructional publications he ordered. Lola Love of the *Asheville Citizen* interviewed Masa in 1929 and concluded that he "brought to his new art all the painstaking care and the inward eye for a truly artistic production which made notable the works of the old Japanese painters." One can speculate, and it is worth considering the development of photography in Japan in the context of Masa's youth there. When George Masa was born in 1881—if that was indeed his birth year—photography in Japan was barely three decades old. The first camera believed to have been brought into the country was through a Dutch trading settlement in Nagasaki in 1848. The American photographer Eliphalet Brown Jr., who participated in the Commodore Perry expedition (1852–54), is generally attributed with the earliest photographs taken in Japan. Perry negotiated America's first trade agreements with the Japanese and opened ports where Brown was able to set up shop. Curious Japanese subjects sat patiently for him as he painstakingly implemented the daguerreotype process.

The American photographer Edward Edgerton attended U.S. naval expeditions to Japan in the 1850s, serving as photographer and sketch artist of the coastlines. He also accompanied the first Japanese embassy to America in 1860, traveling on the Japanese ship *Kanrin Muru*, which had as its senior interpreter Nakamura Manjiro, with whom American artist, photographer, and explorer Edward Kern would have communicated. Manjiro returned to Japan with a daguerreotype camera, and it is possible that Kern could have provided him with instruction. However, the earliest photograph in the country to be attributed to a Japanese photographer dates to 1857.

Other cameras entered Japan via the Dutch during this period. Dutch photographers engaged Japanese students in courses that included photographic processes theory, with limited results. Many other European photographers and artists entered Japan during the latter half of the nineteenth century, some creating large-format albumen prints and stereoviews of Japanese landscapes, architecture, officers, royalty, and more, often starting studios in ports recently opened by the Japanese to foreign trade. Japan's first professional photographer was Ukai Gyoksusen (1807–87), who opened a studio in Edo in 1860 or 1861. Ueno Hikoma (1838–1904) is one of the most famous pioneers in Japanese photography and was the first to embrace the new improved gelatin dry-slate photography, beginning his experiments with it in 1881. Hikoma found commercial success with his Nagasaki river landscapes, selling them to foreign travelers, who also sat for his portraits.

Masa may have been exposed to this recent phenomenon of Japanese photography, one which was growing in geographical and artistic scope. As a young man, he potentially would have been exposed to the Japanese photographic journal *Shashin*

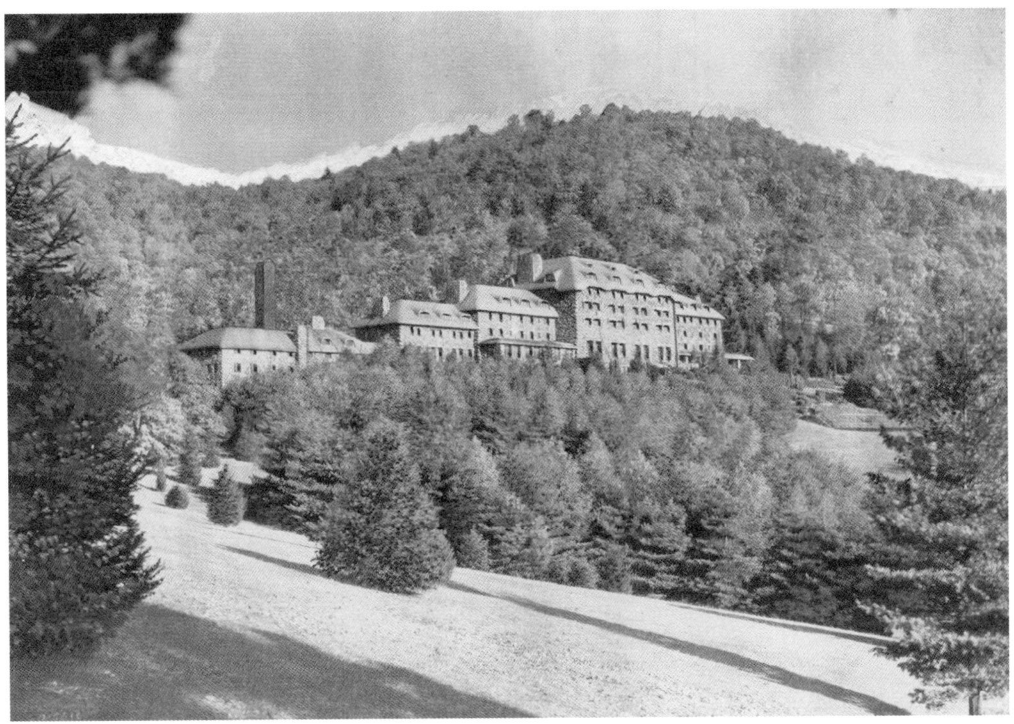

Grove Park Inn, c. 1929 (Pack Memorial Library)

Sowa, or would have been familiar with the photographic tours of Japan made by American and Japanese photographers in the early twentieth century. The picture postcard was introduced into Japan in 1900, and in 1905 architect Frank Lloyd Wright traveled there to photograph Kyoto and Kobe. Maybe Masa saw these post-cards and collected ideas. He did create quite a postcard business during his life in western North Carolina. Regardless, Japanese aesthetics were ancient, and one can draw lines from them to his photography. The Japanese concept of *ma* should be considered when thinking about his creative process. As Japanese scholar Ken Rodgers describes the Japanese character for *ma*, it is an amalgamation of the characters for *gate* and *sun*, representing light entering as through an aperture—a spiritually opportune moment of illumination that could be filled with harmonious and awe-inspiring nature. Japanese architect Isozaki Arata defines *ma* as a Japanese space-time concept of "things fading, flowers falling, flickering movements of mind, shadows falling on water and ground"—phenomena he considers having most impressed the Japanese. We will likely never know what motivated Masa, but one must wonder upon these cultural attributes within his work. The mystery of George Masa lives on.

Regardless, Masa dove in upon his return to Asheville, and for the next fifteen years until his death in 1933 he was productive, prolific, and indefatigable. He left the Grove Park Inn in 1918 to join Pelton Studios in Asheville as a partner, then took over the studio a year later, renaming it Plateau Studios. Throughout the 1920s, he performed a wide range of work, including newsreels, promotional pieces, film processing, and postcard production, and also served as a photographer for the *Asheville Citizen* and the *New York Times.* But although these projects paid the bills, Masa's heart was in the nearby mountains, and he would abandon all commitments for long photographic sojourns into the Smokies, often for weeks at a time and alone.

He became active in the movement to establish the Great Smoky Mountains National Park during the early 1920s, having met the well-established outdoor writer and ethnographer Horace Kephart. Masa and Kephart became fast friends, and their collaboration as writer and photographer was instrumental in the park's establishment. Both were members of the Smokies North Carolina Nomenclature Committee, which required an intimate knowledge of the proposed park landscape, a knowledge that they acquired through their collective years of exploring the future park's backcountry. The National Park Service's Nomenclature Committee was appointed and was charged with mapping the park and its features, utilizing available place-based knowledge, folklore, Cherokee history, and the committee members'

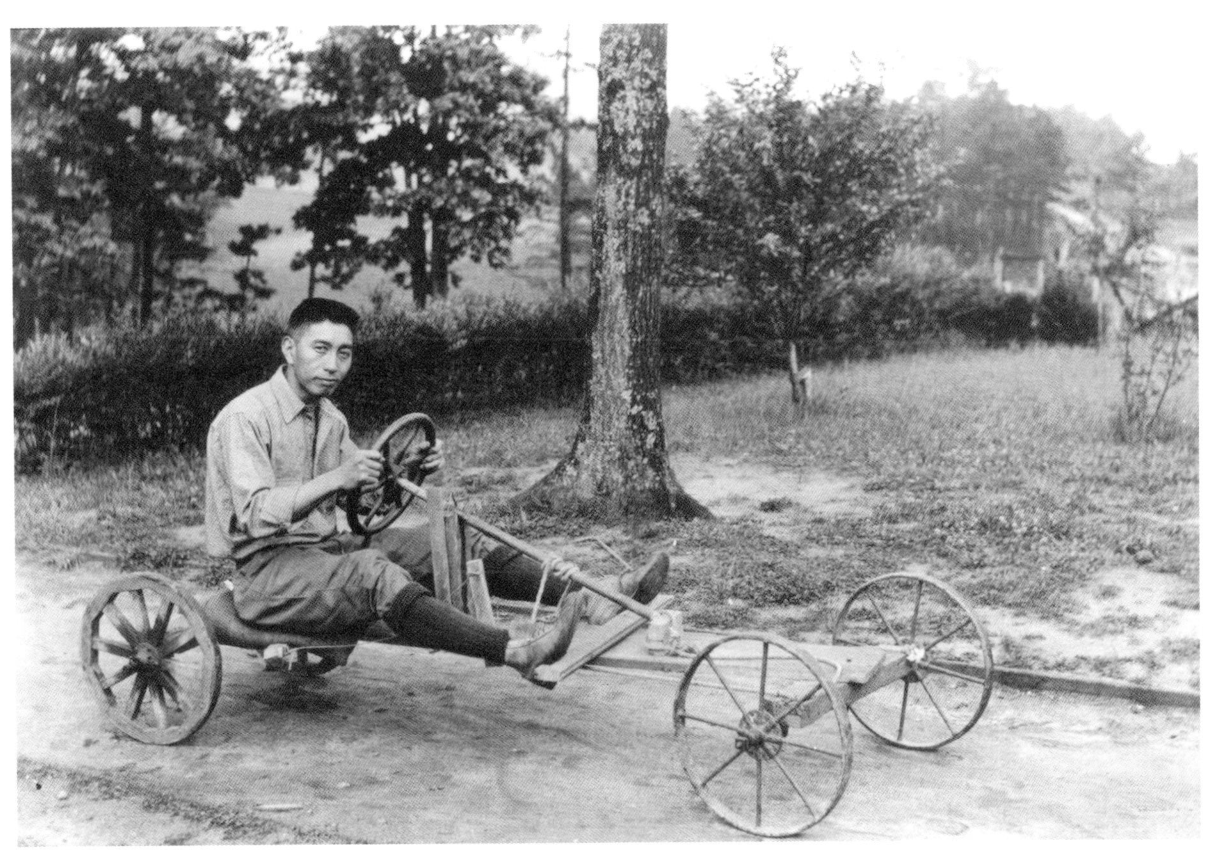

Masa at the Creasman House. Masa appears to be in his late twenties or early thirties. Masa lived with the Creasmans for a few years between 1915 and 1920. Oscar Creasman was a cabinet maker at the Biltmore House and Masa was in his business with his brother Blake in the late twenties. (GSMA)

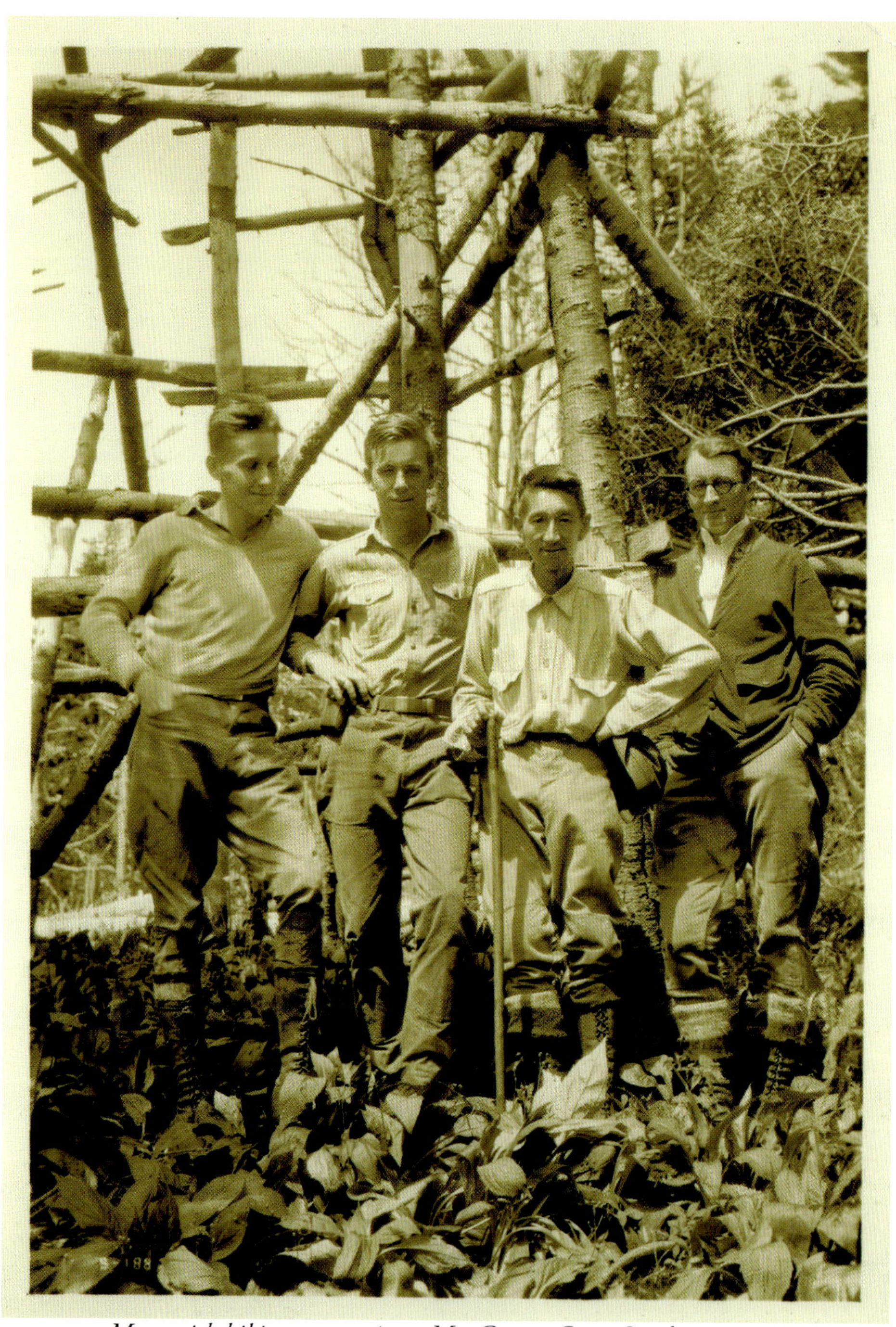

*Masa with hiking companions, Mt. Guyot, Great Smokies, c. 1930
(Great Smoky Mountains Association)*

own direct experience with the vast acreage. There could not have been two more apt and capable appointees. They were a formidable and scrappy pair, with Kephart's local popularity and national recognition as a consummate woodsman and Masa's well-established reputation as one of western North Carolina's most respected photographers. Kephart and Masa tramped through the Smokies for nearly a decade, two unlikely comrades, Kephart exercising his prowess as a backcountry gear guy and cook and Masa lugging his heavy box cameras with a few tins of caviar and a blanket, pushing his characteristic bicycle measuring wheel, making highly detailed maps, and logging place names. It's impossible not to smile, thinking about these moments of them together.

And it's also impossible to imagine how Masa balanced his business life with his passion for the outdoors and his love of place during this period. The twenties were an incredibly productive decade for Masa. In addition to their feverish work on the park, he and Kephart worked to determine the southern route of the Appalachian Trail, a project that allowed Masa to photograph the North Georgia mountains, the Smokies, and the Nantahala and Snowbird mountains. Masa also traveled and photographed for the Asheville Chamber of Commerce, the Asheville Postcard Company, the Highlands Inn, the Carolina Mountain Club, the Georgia Appalachian Trail Club, and other groups, rendering the most remarkable photographs of western North Carolina from that era. The end of this decade, however, as was true for many Americans, brought hardship to Masa and his business, resulting in several years of financial struggle until his death from tuberculosis on June 21, 1933. Although the years were financially trying, perhaps nothing was more difficult for Masa to bear than the loss of his close friend Kephart on April 2, 1931. Masa wrote to his friend, outdoor writer Paul Fink, "I never experience such feeling in my life." Such tragedies often create indelible wounds in a person. This is one event in Masa's life that may have weakened his spirit to an unrecoverable low.

Nonetheless, Masa, in collaboration with *Asheville Citizen* reporter George McCoy, produced the first-ever *Guide to the Great Smoky Mountains National Park* during this period. He also filmed and produced a promotional film on Blowing Rock for Warner Brothers. He attended annual meetings of the Appalachian Trail Conference and worked on the southern route of the trail, continued his nomenclature work and photographic promotion of the park, and organized a well-attended hike to the newly designated Mount Kephart, a poignant reminder of the many journeys he and Kephart had made into this rugged and spectacular location in the Smokies.

Masa had lost almost everything by the time of his death from tuberculosis in 1933. Two earlier hospitalizations, personal financial ruin from the American National Bank's failure, the Depression-era struggle with his business—particularly after his partner, Don Topping, walked away, leaving Masa with the debt—and the theft of his automobile all took their toll on him. He attempted to borrow money from friends and acquaintances. His car was stolen and found in a condition he could not afford to repair, and the Smokies park project was demanding more and more of his time. The Carolina Mountain Club voted to acquire his collection of negatives for not more than one hundred dollars, but in August the Asheville photographer Elliot Lyman Fisher made a successful offer of fifty dollars for all of Masa's mountain photos and unsold commercial negatives. Two years later, an *Asheville Citizen-Times* story on Fisher noted his Masa collection and quoted him on the recent rise of tourist interest in photography. The degree to which Fisher claimed Masa's photos as his own is unknown, but he often stamped his name on the backs of Masa photographs, and possibly sold them as his own. In a 1953 advertisement in the same paper, Fisher was hawking mountain photographs at six for five dollars, but the provenance is not part of the advertisement.

Masa was buried in an unmarked grave at Asheville's Riverside Cemetery, his expenses paid for by the Carolina Mountain Club. Pallbearer George Stephens, an Asheville civic leader, raised funds for a steel casket with the hope that Masa's body would eventually be moved to the Smokies and interred adjacent to Kephart. Kephart biographers George Ellison and Janet McCue have noted the irony in the State Department's letter to Stephens thanking him for his efforts to honor Masa, when less than two decades earlier they had investigated him for un-American activities. As they further note, "There were still mysteries about his background, but no longer suspicions about the man."

The Carolina Mountain Club eventually raised the funds for a proper headstone, but Masa's dying wish to be buried next to Kephart would not transpire. And as much as Masa was loved by his close friends and hiking companions, one cannot help speculating upon the persistent and rising anti-Japanese sentiments at the local and national levels when considering such rejections then, and in later acknowledging his contributions to the Smokies park movement. He and Kephart went to their graves without seeing the formal opening of the Great Smoky Mountains National Park in 1934. These were difficult times, and there was no concerted effort

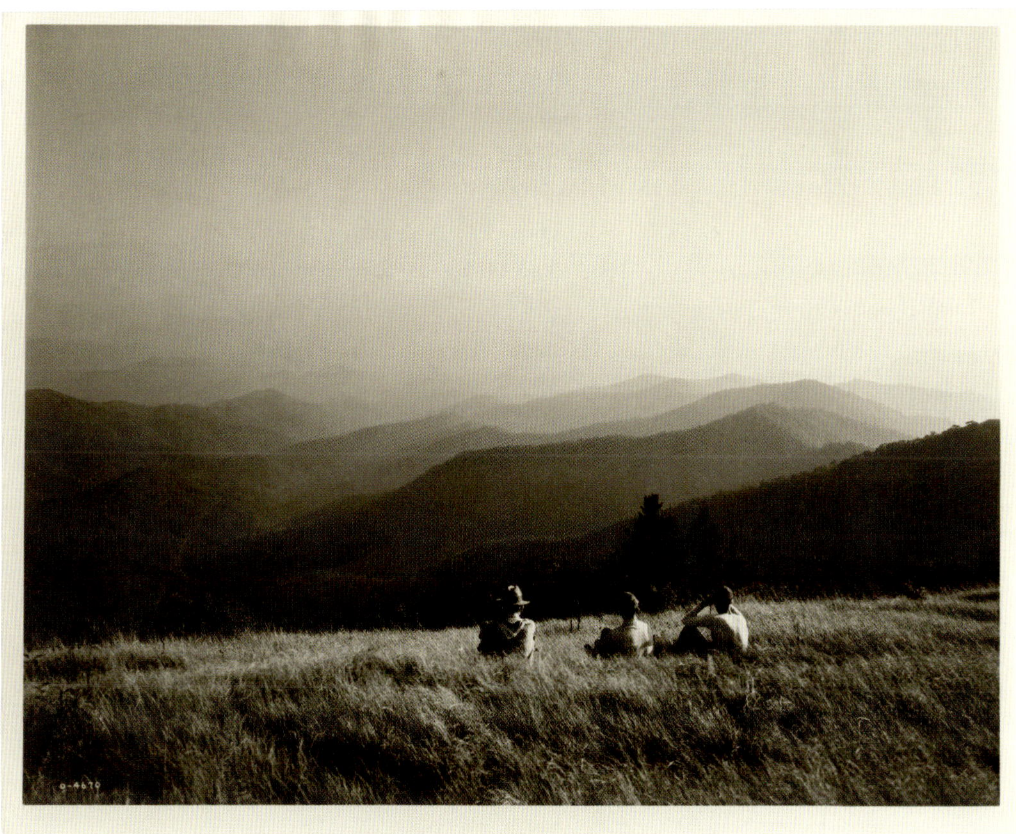

View from Andrews Bald into the Noland Creek watershed (GSMA)

to rescue Masa's enormous oeuvre. Though the bulk of his work was scattered far and wide, hundreds—if not thousands—of his photographs reside with the Great Smoky Mountains Association, Western Carolina University, the University of North Carolina Asheville, Pack Memorial Library, the Highlands Historical Society, and elsewhere. It is hard to conceive of this now, but Masa might have been cast into the dustbin of history had the Carolina Mountain Club and a handful of journalists not kept his memory alive in the decades following his death. The second edition of *Guide to the Great Smoky Mountains National Park* omitted his credits, and his photographs were increasingly hijacked and used without mention of his name. Park officials resisted efforts by the Carolina Mountain Club to have a peak in the park named for him, and success in this endeavor took almost three decades.

Just fifteen years after Masa's death, noted photographer Ansel Adams visited the Great Smokies in 1948 to photograph for a project documenting America's national parks. He wrote to a friend that "the Smokys [*sic*] are ok in their way, but they are going to be devilish hard to photograph." Adams produced just four photos from his brief time in the park, and likely had no knowledge of George Masa, who had died after pursuing those "devilish hard" mountains for almost two decades with a fierce passion like no other before or since—there is certainly no reference to Masa in Adams's writings that I can find. But Masa's photographs reveal an eye for light that Adams would surely have admired and respected. Masa has often been called the Ansel Adams of the Smokies, but I think it should be the other way around. Adams should be referred to as the George Masa of the American West.

The southern Appalachians of Masa's time were a region of great transition. In the early twentieth century, railroads were hauling out the remaining old-growth timber with total abandon, new roads were being blasted into and through hillsides, rivers were being dammed, and activists were emerging to fight these trajectories through the creation of a national park and a southern Appalachian national forest system. George Masa captured this transition like no other photographer of his day, and his images serve as stunning windows into this period of great flux. In many ways, this transition has never stopped, and looking at the landscape of his photographs today is bittersweet. Though much was gained during the rising era of conservation when he took his photographs, much is now being lost. The Masa images juxtaposed a century later with the modern world make for a powerful statement. Climate change, fragmentation and development of the rural southern Appalachian landscape, invasive exotic pests, and public lands being loved to death are some of the major factors, and approaching these through the lens of Masa's early-twentieth-century documentation is one of the reasons for this book. Masa's photographs are stunning windows into a period of great change in the southern Appalachian Mountains.

This collection represents an exploration of Masa's photographic vision through my own direct experience of living in the western North Carolina mountains. In my twenty years here, I have seen great changes inflicted upon this ancient and resilient landscape. I have also seen epic conservation efforts to protect and restore it. And during the strange and challenging pandemic year of 2020, I also saw more people descend upon this place at once than I could have ever imagined. It became impossible to visit and reflect upon Masa's old haunts during such sickness, upheaval, and widespread societal return to nature without having an emotional response. This response varied in range from gratitude and hope to outright despair. What emerged became an attempt to compare, lament, and exalt the condition of the landscape he so well loved and worked to interpret and protect. I could not help reflecting upon the environmental writer Edward Abbey and his thoughts on the Smokies landscape that provided the text for photographer Eliot Porter's collection, *Appalachian Wilderness: The Great Smoky Mountains*. Much like Masa, Porter captured the magic of Appalachian light and landscape with brilliant sensitivity, while Abbey provided humorous and critical commentary on the apparent human disregard and disrespect for what made this mountainous region uniquely spectacular and wild. That was almost fifty years ago, and since that time western North Carolina has become one of the most visited recreational destinations in North America, due in part to its proximity to rapidly growing urban centers, its increased accessibility, and what was, at one point, its affordability for second-home owners and retirees.

That Masa, an enigmatic immigrant, captured this essence of these mountains so that a case was made for their preservation in the halls of our nation's capital is compelling. How, through poverty, extremity, and sickness, could such a svelte man contain such range as to move among the wealthy and powerful of his day, and to navigate the privations of solo trekking in forbidding terrain in a country not of his origin and a language not his own? His legacy challenges the notions of the typical white conservationist of his day and disproves that our "purple mountain majesties" know any human profile defined by race or creed. But perhaps most importantly, what will be the fate of this storied and fragile place?

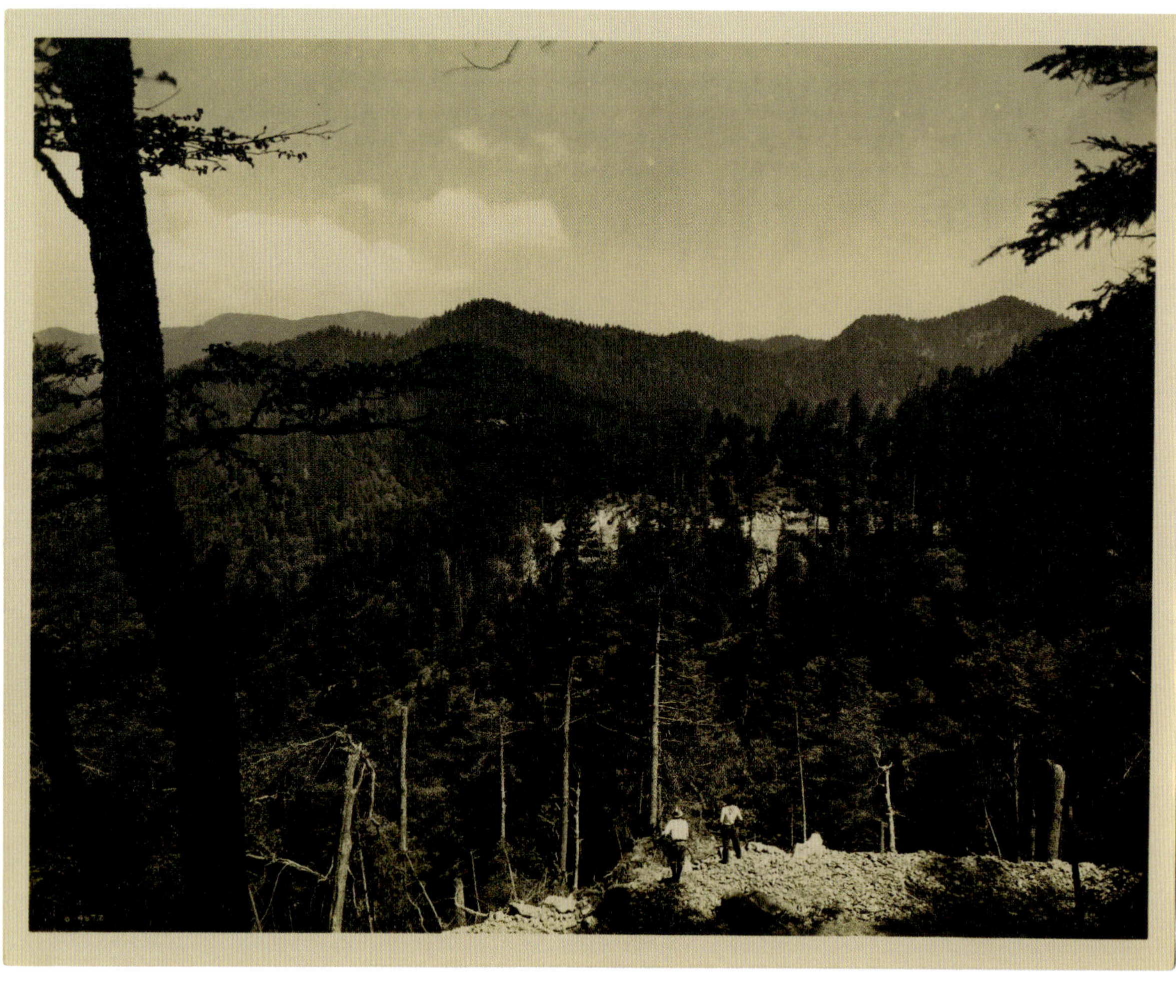

The "Great Smokies Highway" at Newfound Gap, now State Highway 441 and one of the most highly traveled roads in the National Park System. Masa and Kephart traveled the road in the twenties, describing it as a difficult single-lane unmaintained gravel road; they were once stuck there once upon a return trip.

CHAPTER ONE

GREAT SMOKY MOUNTAINS NATIONAL PARK

MASA KNOB

THE PARKING AREA at Newfound Gap is packed on this sunny, clear pandemic July Wednesday, and I park far down at the end, where there are few vehicles and groups milling about. George Masa's image of this spot in the twenties shows two companions, one of them perhaps Horace Kephart, looking east from what was then no more than a gravel pullout on a primitive road that is now State Highway 441. In June 1930, he and Kephart attempted to traverse the park by automobile, concluding that it was advisable to keep automobiles out until the roads were improved. In an *Asheville Times* article regarding the adventure, Kephart tells of how they made it to Gatlinburg by taking a route near Mount Sterling on the eastern side of the Smokies, then traveled toward the gap on graded road, part of it already surfaced. At the gap, Kephart describes the road stopping, and the road down to Smokemont near Cherokee as not much more than an old trail. The two of them proceeded and got the vehicle stuck, abandoned it, and walked to a Champion Fiber lumber camp for help getting it out. This is now one of the busiest national park thoroughfares in America, largely due to 441 being the only corridor between the two tourist towns of Gatlinburg, Tennessee, and Cherokee, North Carolina. People travel it for its outstanding scenic quality and recreational opportunities, but its record as a route through America's most visited national park can largely be attributed to the fact that it's a tourist commuter route to either of the two heavily developed and crowded destinations. In February 2021, almost one hundred years after Masa and Kephart attempted the route, it was bestowed with the designation of All-American Road, an honorific given to those national scenic byways that are considered the best of the best.

Masa and Kephart also located the Appalachian Trail across this high ridgeline of the park, a trail that many of these out-of-state tourists are anxious to set foot on today. I'm looking for my companions for the day, Jess Riddle and Rachel Granade, who have agreed to bushwhack with me to the top of Masa Knob. Loud Harleys with leather-clad Rebel flag-bearing drivers pound the atmosphere, and three crows perched in a nearby dead balsam fly off and drift about, watching the show. Peering from a distance through the crowd that is gathered at the interpretive kiosk and overlook, I see that the majority of people are unmasked—families, groups of friends, and one large group of young men from a boys' outdoor camp near Lookout Mountain, Tennessee—and I think I see Jess and Rachel standing above the group on the stone platform above the kiosk. I navigate the scene as carefully as I can, masked and distancing, until they see me and walk the steps down to the crowd where I am waiting. We take off on the Appalachian Trail in hopes that in a mile or so we will lose most of the tourists and be able to relax a bit and catch up.

Masa would have enjoyed my companions for the day. Jess is executive director of Georgia ForestWatch and a forest savant, someone I first met when he was a young teenager, and who at the time knew as much about Appalachian forests as any expert. Much as Masa searched for the perfect images of these mountains, Jess has spent most of his life in search of its remaining old-growth forests—a good bit of them in this park—and from my numerous times out in the woods with Jess I know I'll have a hard time keeping up with him. Rachel is a 50k trail runner, and after five minutes I feel I'm already lagging behind these two as we proceed toward Charlies Bunion.

The trail is crowded starting out, and we step to the side often or wait off the trail for others to pass. It's startling that almost a century ago Masa and Horace Kephart began painstakingly determining the location of this trail, bushwhacking through precarious terrain on one of the most rugged state lines in America. Masa's photographs from this period—less than a decade before the park's creation—reveal a remote, untraveled landscape, a stark contrast to what was to become America's most visited national park within the next fifty years. After the first mile, we still see a constant stream of hikers coming at us, and I'm starting to think this will be the pattern for the day. Pathless Masa Knob will be our refuge, and I'm looking forward

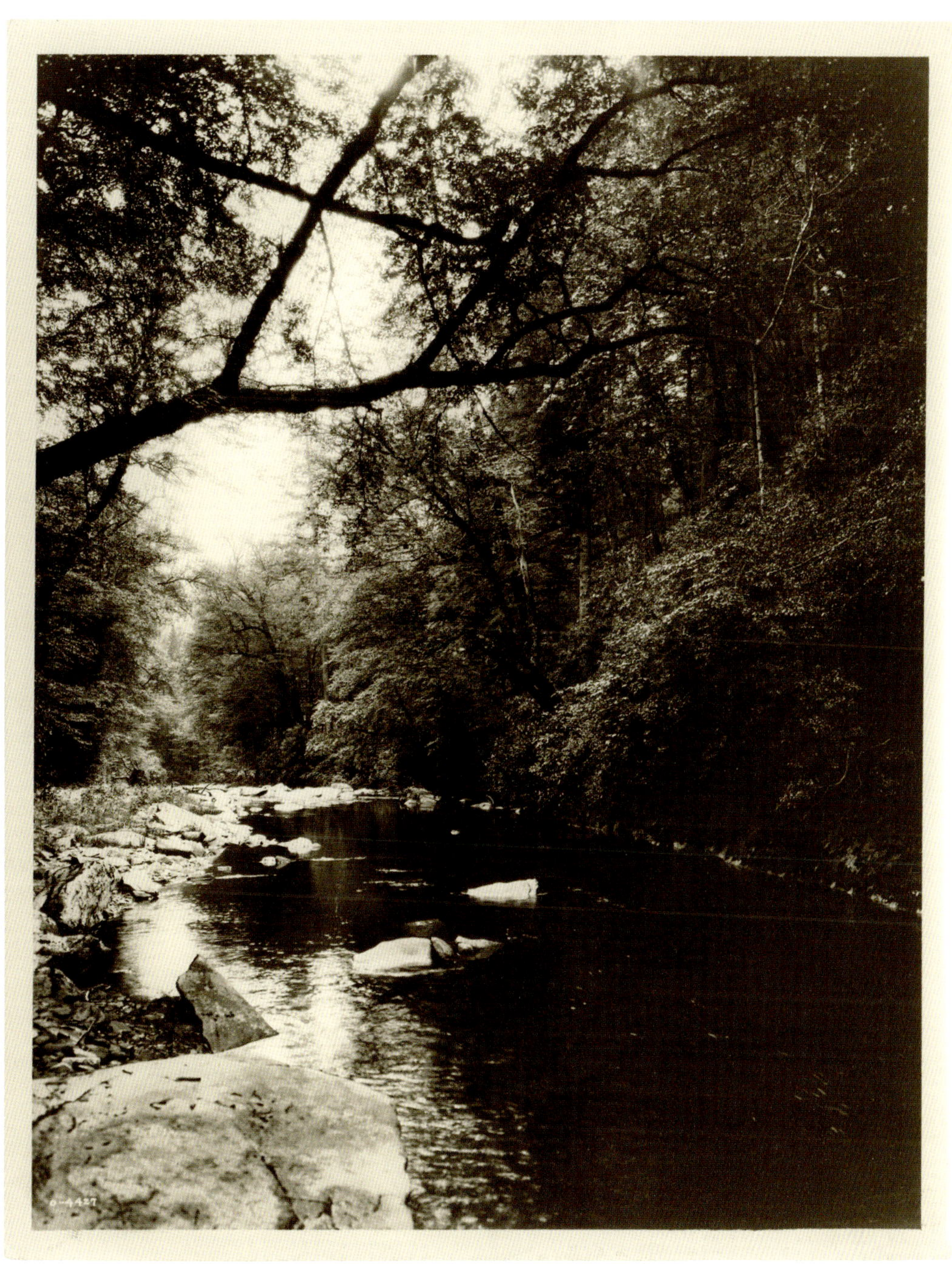

Raven Fork, downstream of Three Forks

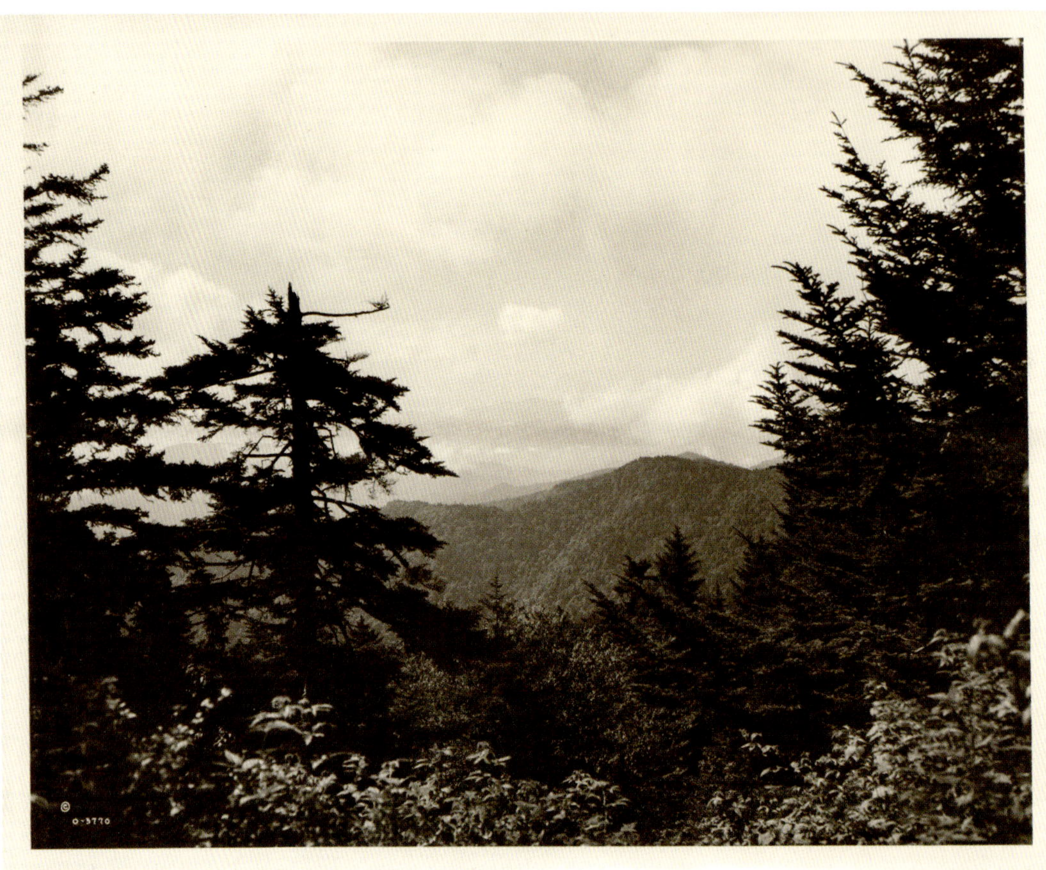

Outlook from the Summit of Mt. Kephart

to bushwhacking through whatever lies ahead. The knob sits to the southeast of Mount Kephart and just to the southwest of Charlies Bunion, an iconic destination for most of the people on the trail today, with its sheer cliffs and rock outcrops. We pass three women in hijabs, what we think is a sorority outing of maybe twenty young women, multiple couples of various ages and ethnicities, and families of various ages and numbers. The country is still reeling from the murder of George Floyd, with Black Lives Matter demonstrations occurring in many of the small mountain towns around the park, accompanied by Confederate monument worshippers and proud, outlandish bigots determined to keep racism on the ventilator of a past that should have been dead and buried long ago. The diversity here on this trail reflects America's tormented soul at this moment, and the sweet respect and smiles that I collect as we move along provide me with a measure of hope in the face of this tension.

The pandemic has heightened my anxiety in recent weeks, though, and I feel a few surges of it as we pass large, unmasked groups and attempt to distance ourselves. We at least see the knob from a distance and begin looking for an access point that is not choked with Appalachian shrubs and thick herbaceous understory. At last, we settle on a point where we can see into the dense stands of red spruce and balsam. Gazelle-like, Jess and Rachel push ahead, and I forge on behind them, ducking and stretching and remembering days spent chasing Jess on such afternoons over twenty years ago, surveying for old growth in the Chattahoochee National Forest. Did Masa ever make this ascent? Would he appreciate the knob that now bears his name, unnoticeable by most who pass by on their way to the Bunion, or on their way to any of the park's other more popular destinations? If the ghost of Masahara Iizuka haunts these mountains, this is surely one of his favorite abodes.

We reach the 5,685-foot summit after twenty minutes of struggling through spruce-fir forest full of hobblebush and a few large yellow birches, accompanied by golden-crowned kinglets, blue-headed vireos, and veeries singing us along, a melodious thread as we stitch our way up the mountain. The small, distinct knob is open enough for us to spread out and have lunch. White-striped black moths are thick in the sky, descending to feed on jewelweed. *Rugelia nudicaulis,* a high-elevation Great Smokies endemic commonly known as Rugel's ragwort, is abundant and blooming here. Dark-eyed juncos are now singing along with the others. This is our lush and verdant context for lunch, and as Rachel's and Jess's knowledge on Masa is scant, we talk about his efforts to establish the park and to promote the Appalachian Trail and Mount Mitchell State Park.

When Masa first discovered the Smokies is a good question. Likely, it was while photographing for the Grove Park Inn, schmoozing the tourists, snapping photos, and obsessing over quality and light. Rachel is curious about Masa's obscurity and speculates about the potential racism of his day that could have consigned him to the dustbin of history. This is a valid observation and not surprising, given that the country is erupting with the Black Lives Matter movement and America's racist legacy. In 1905, around the time of Masa's arrival in the United States, the Asiatic Exclusion League was founded in San Francisco, marking the official beginning of the anti-Japanese movement. A year later, Japanese schoolchildren were segregated from white students by the San Francisco school board. The rise in anti-Japanese prejudice led

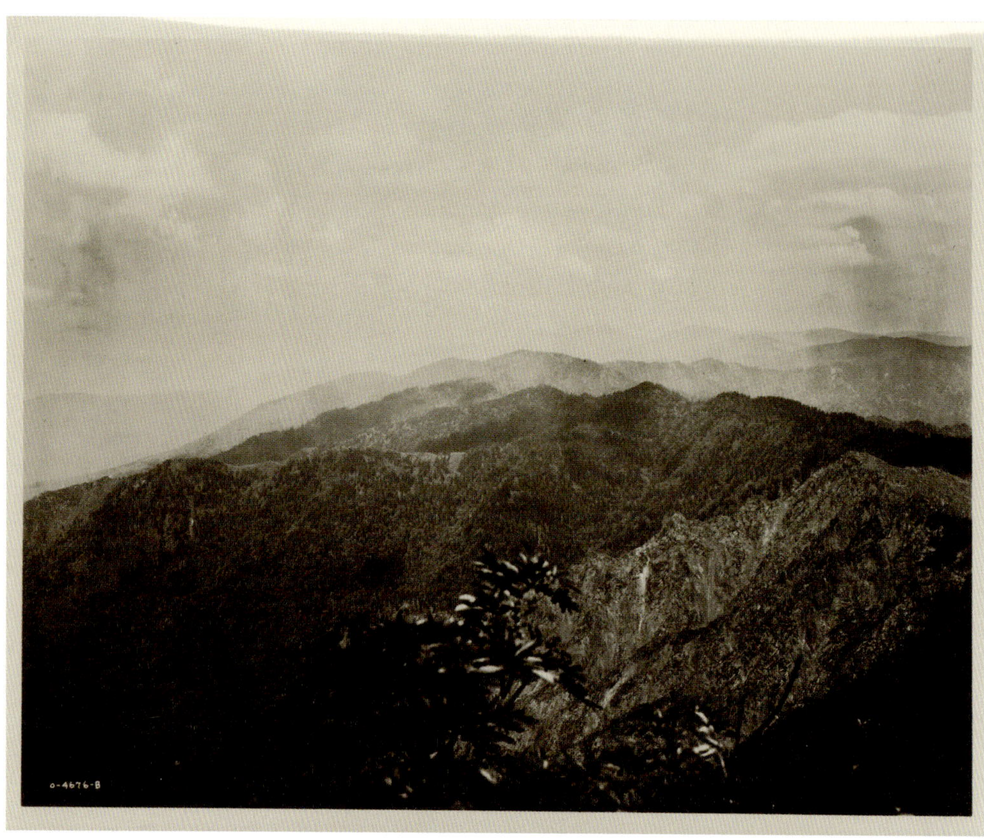

View of Charlies Bunion, Mt. Black, Mt. Guyot, Laurel Top

President Theodore Roosevelt to negotiate a gentlemen's agreement with Japan in 1907. The government of Japan agreed to stop issuing passports to laborers, thus slowing Japanese immigration to the United States. During Masa's first known year after his arrival, Congress approved amendments to anti-immigrant legislation that allowed Roosevelt to stop the migration of Japanese laborers from Hawai'i and Mexico. This action ended labor immigration to the United States and put labor contractors out of business.

Fred Seely, Grove Park Inn manager and son-in-law of E. W. Grove, wrote to the head of the FBI in 1916 regarding his concern that Masa was a spy, noting Masa's extensive journaling while at the same time praising Masa's brilliance and photographic abilities. He later urged the matter to be dropped, based on Masa's plans to remain under his employment. In 1924, President Calvin Coolidge signed an immigration bill into law that effectively ended Japanese immigration to the United States. George Masa is nothing short of a miracle.

The country in general experienced a wave of xenophobia upon the outbreak of World War I, with anti-immigration legislation passed against East Asians in 1917, a fact that is somehow apropos to the conversation here in Trump-era America. Surely, Masa would have felt the sting of racism in these southern mountains. At the outbreak of World War II, less than a decade since Masa's death in 1933, Japanese diplomats and Japanese Americans would be placed in internment camps. Masa's old employer, the Grove Park Inn, would serve as a temporary internment location for Japanese diplomats. One of his closest friends and hiking companions, Barbara Ambler Thorne, claimed that she and the other hikers in Masa's life never considered his ethnicity in their relationships, but I've wondered why it took thirty years of Carolina Mountain Club advocacy to get this little knob dedicated to his legacy. Park service officials and superintendents certainly knew that his efforts were as significant and as noble as Horace Kephart's in many ways. Early attempts were rebuffed, though Masa himself had served on the state Nomenclature Committee to provide names for streams, peaks, and other geographical features in what was to become the park. Kephart himself said Masa deserved a monument.

AFTER LUNCH, we descend the north side of the knob to the busy Appalachian Trail and go back to dodging our fellow pandemic refugees, all of us seeking asylum in this vast restorative place. At Charlies Bunion, designated in 1929 after Masa and Kephart's hiking companion, Charlie Connor, I choose not to ascend the large outcrop with Jess and Rachel and its numerous visitors drinking in the view and snapping smart-phone photos. Once again, I can't help thinking that Masa's much less iconic knob took thirty-one more years to garner a place name, though he was known among all involved as one of the most tireless promoters of the national park designation. I ease off the trail a bit and watch white-striped black moths thick in the sky, never lighting on any of the numerous flowering plants. I write in my journal and stare at the knob while the others contemplate the view from the Bunion. Hundreds of thousands of the most biologically diverse acres on earth surround me—thank you, Horace Kephart and George Masa. We're in the midst of global chaos today, but I rest in a sanctuary of wildly diverse and indifferent forest. After ten or so minutes, the crowd subsides, and I ease out to the outcrop. My view is to the north. Mount Kephart lies just to the west. To the southwest, Masa Knob, diminutive in comparison to the higher, more prominent Mount Kephart, lies softer, more rounded, and unobtrusive. Just to the southeast are the Sawteeth, a jagged length of ridgetop outcrop that Masa captured in power and light. His wish for his final resting place to be next to his close friend Horace Kephart was never realized, but perhaps this is close enough.

THREE FORKS

At Three Forks, the Left Fork of Raven Fork seems relatively gentle and benign, but by the time it gets there it has descended through some of the most forbidding wilderness in the eastern United States from its source under Tricorner Knob, on the backbone of the Smokies.

—TOM ALEXANDER, timber cruiser and fishing guide, from *Mountain Fever*, his 1920s account of working in the Raven Fork watershed

GEORGE MASA PERHAPS knew the Smokies more intimately than anyone of his day, and his journeys into the Three Forks area are testimony to this. Three Forks lies in the eastern part of the park and is rugged, remote, and unlogged, all due to its inaccessibility. To this day, it remains one of the wildest places in the East. I am humbled by his photography and cartography now as I stand in cold rain on this fog-drenched September morning, pushing through pathless terrain crisscrossed with hemlock ghosts. I had never seen a handheld GPS unit go haywire, but there it is, making no sense as we stand in pouring rain and lightning somewhere along a spine of mountain aptly titled Breakneck Ridge.

My friend and I left this morning out of Three Forks, bushwhacking up what remains of the old manway cleared by George Masa and Tom Alexander in the early thirties, when the two were coming here often with Asheville tourists and whoever else wanted to experience and fish unspoiled terrain and catch the abundant brook trout. Virgin spruce forest unlike any that remains anywhere is found here in this rugged eastern corner of the Great Smoky Mountains National Park, where we spent the last two nights. Though overnight camping is not allowed in this area, the park service granted us permission due to my friend's reputation and credentials as a forest ecologist, along with his interest in documenting the area's old-growth

CAROLINA MOUNTAIN CLUB

TRIP REPORT

Trip Name ___Andrews Bald & Clingmans Dome.___________ Date___________

Mileage of round trip; By car__________miles; Afoot__________miles; **X By wheel** / By Pedo / Estimated

Time required: By car_______hours one way; Afoot_______hours (total)

Departure: From Asheville___________ From car ___________

Arrival: At car___________ At Asheville___________

Members __4__ Visitors __6__

Trip register: (get signature if possible) LEADER ___*George Masa.*___

1 *Etta M. Wills*   *O C Barker* ___________
2 *Doris Matthews*   *Jno. R C Barker* ___________
3 *Geraldine Gilchrist*   *Marcus Book* ___________
4 *Alfred H Wills*   *Charles H Beck* ___________
5 *Fred M. Davis* ___________

1 to 5 member of Natural Bridge Appalachian Trail Club, Lynchburg, Va.

Motor Log: (Asheville to point of leaving car)

Follow N.C. No. 10 West to Bryson City(70.7 m.) at the Square,
Court House at right turn to right cross Tuckaseegee River Bridge
after crossing Railroad turn to left follow N.C.288, at 77.7 m
just this side of Noland Creek Bridge turn right on dirt road
follow East bank of Noland Creek, to Clingmans Dome Camp at

Trail Log: Set wheel at forks of Noland Creek Road, 0.2 m. below Clingmans Dome
Camp, Mill Creek School behind on top of the hill, follow wagon road
At 0.35 road forks, take right, left road goes up old Jenkins House;
At 0.6 m. cross Mill Creek Bridge and turn to right, follow Mill Creek;
At 1.0 m. Tulip tree at right; At 1.1 m. trail forks, close watch be
taken, the trail sharp turn to right very dim and weeds over grow and
straight trail more distinct but further up trail, bridge washed out
so turn to right and cross Creek at 1.13 m.; Cross Creek at 1.18 m.
At 1.26 m. trail forks take left, cross Creek at 1.64 m. cross branch
at 1.65 m. 2 mile marker on birch tree at left; At 2.05 cross branch,
swing side of ridge then steep grade, at 2.8 m. cross branch, 3 mile
marker on Birch tree at left; 3.35 m. at the Gap where Bald Creek trail
comes up, sharp turn to left; At 3.8 m. Eastern edge of Andrews Bald

characteristics. Becoming more anxious and hypothermic by the moment, we at last find the small saddle of land that will take us over to Hyatt Ridge, where we can walk our remaining soggy miles on a somewhat established trail.

Tom Alexander was a timber cruiser and fisherman who had surveyed the area's timber for Ravensford Lumber Company. The year was 1931 and the country was in economic turmoil, and Masa struggling to make it as a photographer. His best friend, Horace Kephart, had died that spring, and Masa was likely still in grief and shock. Perhaps he never recovered from the blow, and with his will weakened and pockets empty, he succumbed as many did to the overall economic despair and poverty. Given the terrain and the stamina required to navigate it, it is hard to believe that in less than two years Masa would be taken down by tuberculosis, penniless and alone. Alexander knew he was in the midst of something special. Masa did as well. Alexander knew the watershed's remoteness and beauty from his time spent determining the value of its timber, and when the economy tanked, leaving Ravensford Lumber owing him money, he arranged for rights to the area for a fishing camp. There is no record of how Masa and Alexander met, but the two made numerous trips into the area together. Masa took photos of the majestic old-growth forest and its rugged beauty, along with photos of Alexander's customers and friends. It is one of the few places I can visit that remains unchanged by humans and where Masa's images sync with the modern landscape.

Nothing remains of the old camp where Masa stayed. Those who venture into this part of the park today must do so by bushwhacking over and under downed hemlocks and pushing through the densest rhododendron on earth. What tiny portions of the trail remain are meaningless, nothing more than artifacts to give explorers some sense of confidence from knowing that others have gone before them. Perched within a high-elevation valley and cut off from the more established visitor locations and trails by a rugged and narrow gorge, Three Forks is a hydrological and forested wonder. Its name derives from the fact that three streams come together at a shared terminus, forming a long, deep pool and the beginning of Raven Fork, one of many large and iconic streams that characterize the Great Smokies. Though indigenous Americans likely accessed Three Forks for thousands of years, the first documented exploration of the area began in 1799, when crews surveying the Tennessee-North Carolina state line attempted to enter it, only to abandon their efforts after becoming entangled in the dense rhododendron, spruce, and fir. Another failed attempt occurred in 1821, and it was not until 1858, when Swiss-born geographer Arnold Guyot

Proposal To Name Peak For Masa To Be Pushed

The George Masa Memorial Committee of Carolina Mountain Club will request the N. C. National Park, Parkway and Forests Development Commission to support the club's proposal to have an unnamed peak in t h e vicinity of Mount Kephart in the Great Smoky Mountains National Park named as a memorial to Masa.

Masa, Japanese mountaineer and scenic photographer, w i t h his pictures was among the first to tell the world of the wonders of the Great Smoky Mountains.

Club representatives will a t tend the quarterly meeting of the Commission at 10 a. m. Tuesday at the Commission headquarters in Waynesville.

Masa, (real name, Masahara Iisuka), who died in 1933 at the age of 51, came to the United States from Japan at the turn of the century to study mining engineering at the University of California. His college career terminated with the death of his father in Japan.

After engaging for some time in engineering work in Colorado, he came to Asheville in 1915 with a group of foreigners recruited by the late Fred Seely for service at Grove Park Inn. Masa took extensive mountain tours with this group.

To capture views afforded on his trips he became perfected in the details of scenic photography. He opened a photographic studio known as The Plateau S t u d i o in downtown Asheville.

The Craggies and the Smokies were his favorite subjects and he joined forces with H o r a c e

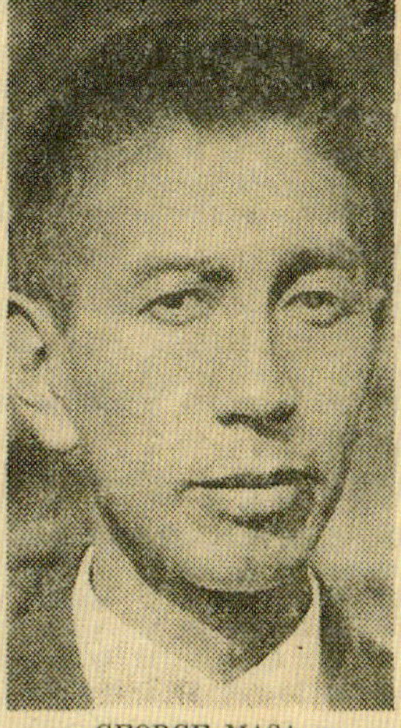

GEORGE MASA

Kephart, Bryson City author, on many expeditions into the Smokies. The partnership of Kephart and Masa was a potent influence in drawing nationwide attention to the establishment of G r e a t Smoky Mountains National Park.

Masa was a charter member and moving spirit in activities of Carolina Mountain Club, which has been studying the project of commemorating his work in a suitable manner for some 20 years. Last May a resolution was adopted proposing a peak in the Park area be named in his memory in a similar manner as Kephart, memorialized by the naming of Mount Kephart.

The resolution was presented as a petition to the Board on Geographic Names, Department of the Interior. The request w a s then referred to the National Park Service and assigned to Fred J. Overly, park superintendent, to conduct a field study.

At its October meeting, t h e Western North Carolina Associated Communities adopted unanimously resolutions endorsing the project.

George Masa Memorial C o m mittee members are Dr. Samuel Robinson, chairman; F. Piercy Carter, club president; and Henry Arch Nichols, Roger Morrow and George M. Stephens.

ASHEVILLE CITIZEN-TIMES, Asheville, N. C. A **3**
Sunday, January 22, 1961

THE ASHEVILLE CITIZEN, ASHEVILLE, N. C. **5**
Tuesday, February 7, 1961

Club To Pinpoint, Measure Proposed George Masa Peak

The council of Carolina Mountain Club Monday night voted to set Sunday, March 5, as the date on which to measure and pinpoint the location of a peak in the Smoky Mountains National Park, for which the club is proposing the name of George Masa.

Photographs will be made of the club's project operations on that date, Dr. Samuel Robinson, committee chairman, reported to the council at its monthly meeting, held in the home of Mr. and Mrs. Piercy Carter on Edgewood Road.

Arch Nichols was appointed chairman of the hiking committee composed of Dr. Edgar Lyngholm, Hal Reed, Roger Morrow and Dr. Robinson.

Other committee chairmen appointed by Carter, president, included: Carroll Cromwell, trails; Jerome Dykeman, historian; Miss Nina Forbes, entertainment; and Roger Morrow, membership.

Dr. Robinson was named chairman of the photograph committee comprised of Bill Kirkman and Miss Elizabeth Parker.

A committee was chosen to investigate the feasibility of building a cabin for club members. Members are Arch Nichols, Dr. Lyngholm and Cromwell.

Carolina Mountain Club's push for Masa Knob in the Great Smokies

explored the area, that some accuracy was provided as to the location of the state line. But as Ravensford timber cruiser Alexander noted while exploring the area in the 1920s, even Guyot made mistakes mapping the Smokies' main range in the area, as did subsequent U.S. Geological Survey attempts.

Much like the survey crew of 1799, my first attempt to enter Three Forks failed for the exact same reasons. My wife and I camped at McGee Springs, thinking we would bushwhack out Breakneck Ridge and descend along the old manway that Tom Alexander and George Masa forged almost ninety years ago. Unable to find even a remnant of this path, we retreated after hours of entanglement in dense rhododendron and ancient fallen spruce and hemlock. Beaten and bruised but undeterred, we decided that night around our campfire at McGee that we would return with more determination and preparation for our next attempt.

When we finally made it to Three Forks on our second attempt, I felt a sense of timelessness like I had never experienced before—the forest primeval, untouched by senseless modern human hands. The place was fairy tale-like in its appearance, Jurassic in its feel. We had found a bit of the old manway and had crawled, slid, and prayed our way down it over several hours, wondering how we were going to turn around and crawl our way back out after making our destination, since we had again decided to day-trip the excursion. At last reaching the great confluence of the three streams, we enjoyed a brisk swim and brief exploration of the area before making the brutal climb out and returning to camp, racing against sunset.

The only early descriptions we have of the Three Forks area are from Alexander's journals and Masa's exquisite maps, and the only early photographs are from Masa. Alexander explored the area as a timber cruiser in the 1920s for the James D. Lacey Company and its client, Ravensford Lumber Company, tallying the commercial value of the ancient forest prior to its sale to the Department of the Interior and the establishment of the Great Smoky Mountains National Park. Ravensford owned thirty-five thousand acres in the high-elevation basin, and Alexander fell in love with it, so when the Lacey Company went broke in 1929, owing him six hundred dollars in back salary, he quickly seized the opportunity by negotiating the use of the camp at Three Forks and all of its gear as a settlement.

Alexander referred to Three Forks as one of the "finest trout streams in the southern Appalachians even if only the most dedicated fishermen could actually get to it." He quickly established a tourist fishing camp there, hiring a cook and declaring that

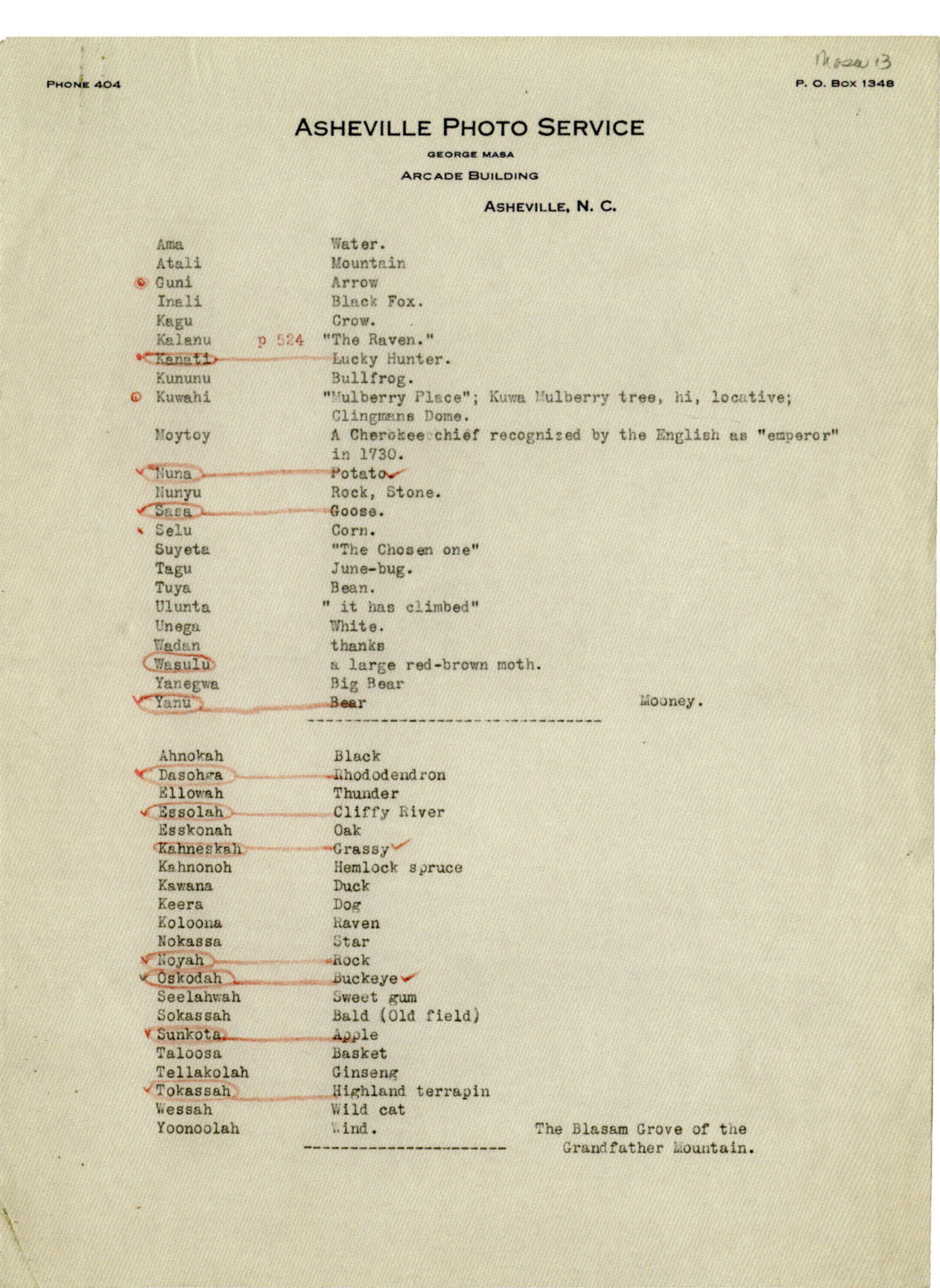

Masa's notes on Cherokee place names

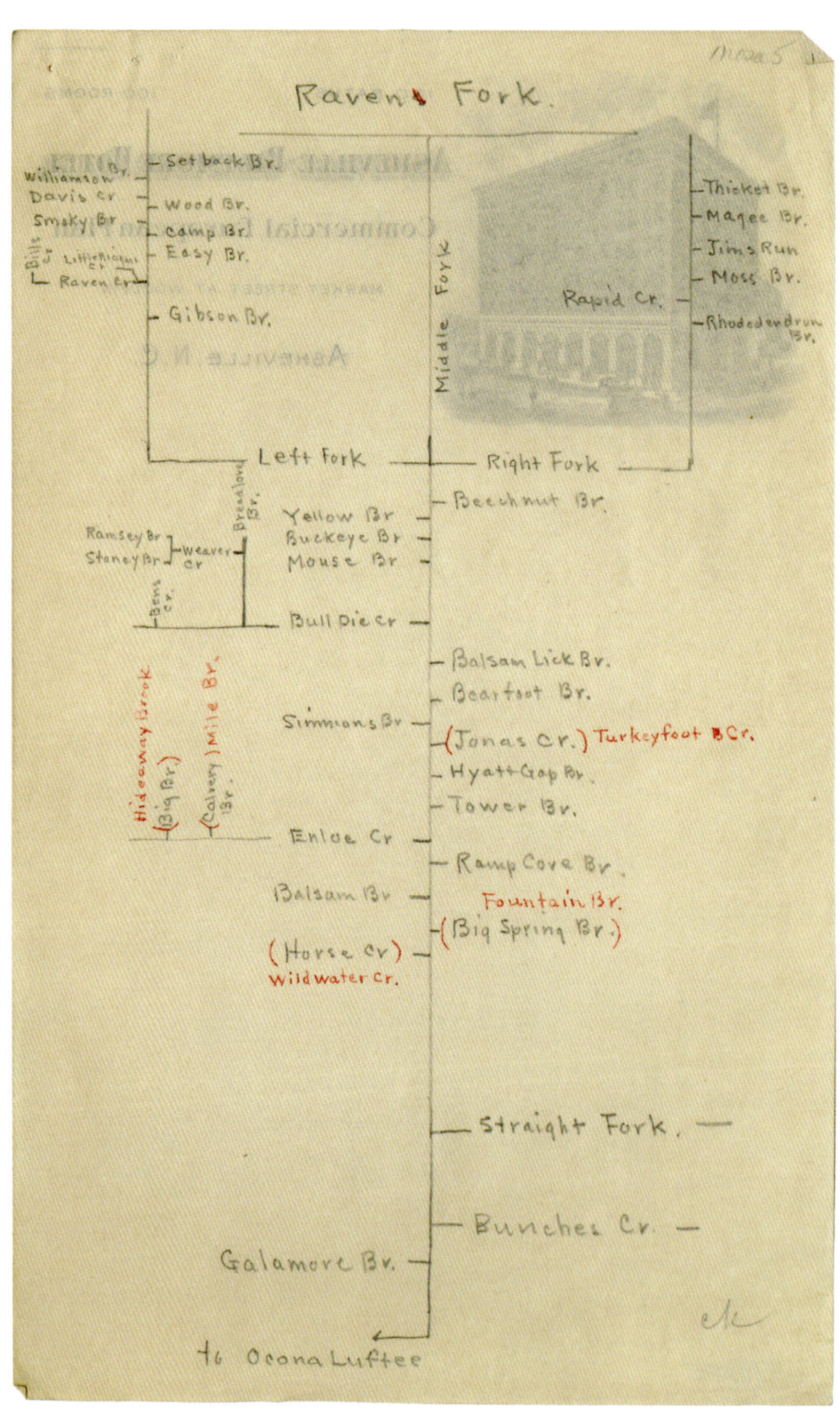

Masa's schematic of the Raven Fork Watershed (WCU)

if fishermen "had any trout fishing skill at all, we could practically guarantee them all the fish they wanted." Almost a hundred years later, I have fished these waters and caught between forty and fifty brook trout a day with little effort. There was an old hunters' cabin at Three Forks at the time of Alexander's explorations, and he soon added a few canvas-wall tents and a cook shed to accommodate his many visitors willing to make the rugged nine-mile walk in from Smokemont.

Masa became close friends with Alexander, traveling to Three Forks to photograph the stunning beauty of the area. Like all great photographers, he captured the spirit of the place, and I refer to his images in Alexander's book when conjuring up my own memories. Masa photographed Alexander's fishing camp often, and in one of his last photographs, taken in 1931, a large group of Asheville men and women is huddled around a campfire with Masa's famous converted bicycle measuring wheel leaning against a tent pole. The camp is large and hospitable in appearance, and camp cook Avery Gouge stands in a professional-looking apron with buttoned-up collared shirt.

I find no remains of Alexander's camp today, only Masa's photographs of it, though someone did make it in at some point with some large sheets of plastic tarp that lie rolled on the ground in a miserable state of decay. Unless we can pack it out, this ugly desecration will likely be here a hundred years before vanishing from human sight, so we roll it up in the rain, strap it to our packs, and add its weight and awkwardness to our already ridiculous climb out. There is also an old wooden picnic table made from rough-cut logs and lashed to two stout young spruce trees. Who are those who enter such a place to pillage and defile? There are some who believe they saw the fugitive bomber Eric Rudolph downstream from here, and perhaps that is true, with this being the remnants of his camp.

George Masa would likely be startled at the park's high visitation and overcrowded trails and parking areas today, much as he would the highly overused and overrun Appalachian Trail, particularly in this pandemic year, when so many Americans are discovering the great outdoors. Yet the most visited national park in America remains one of the wildest and most unroaded places in the Southeast, though diminished by surrounding development and overuse. It has over four hundred thousand acres of federally inventoried roadless areas, and was even recommended for wilderness status after the passage of the 1964 Wilderness Act. Three Forks likely feels wilder and less accessible today than it did when Masa and Alexander were running trips in with tourists to fish and camp. How many places remain on this planet that are wilder now than they were a hundred years ago?

MASA's PHOTOGRAPHS of the Great Smokies can be considered his best and most abundant, as it was an obsession with him through the twenties and early thirties. The park movement consumed him, and his efforts and explorations during this time are legendary. His countless solo journeys into the area and multiple trips with Horace Kephart, the Carolina Mountain Club, and political and press delegations all led to what his friend and *Asheville Citizen* reporter Lola Love described as a "very intimate and correct knowledge of the territory he covered." Masa kept a map of the Smokies on his wall that Love said was covered with pins for places he had been and places he would go. Her description of his passion for the Smokies reveals the side of Masa that made his work so powerful and profound: "If everything were taken from him, he says, there would still be beauty and contemplations enough—set free by study of that map, to fill all the days, and to console." Horace Kephart expressed Masa's intimacy and experience with the Smokies in an *Asheville Times* article in September 1929:

> During the past summer, George Masa, the Japanese photographer of
> Asheville[,] has been exploring the wildest and most remote parts of
> the Great Smoky Mountains, charting the trails through the prime-
> val forest of the National Park area, where there aren't any trails, and
> often boring his way through untracked jungles, scaling precipitious
> [sic] mountain sides, delving in rocky defiles, where no sign has been
> left by man. On all of his trips George has carried an 8 x 10 view cam-
> era. By judicious use of various ray filters, and an uncanny skill in
> timing exposures, he has overcome the difficulties of haze and cloudy
> weather which often balk an amateur photographer in the Smokies.
> The result is a series of about fifty views of wild mountains and gorges,
> deep forests and naked crags, trout streams and waterfalls, camp scenes,
> "close ups" of blooming shrubs and wilderness flowers, the like of
> which is not to be found elsewhere than in Masa's collection.

Masa wrote to his and Kephart's close friend Margaret Gooch in September 1931, following Kephart's death, on how important the Smokies were to replenishing his spirit whenever he was down, telling her that "when I make trip these things don't bother me I just leave office and go into woods get fresh Balsam air then come back start strong fight, no use to worry, that's the way I do, may I am wrong, but it good to me all time." Tragically, he never saw the national park come to its congressionally chartered fruition in 1934, a year after his death.

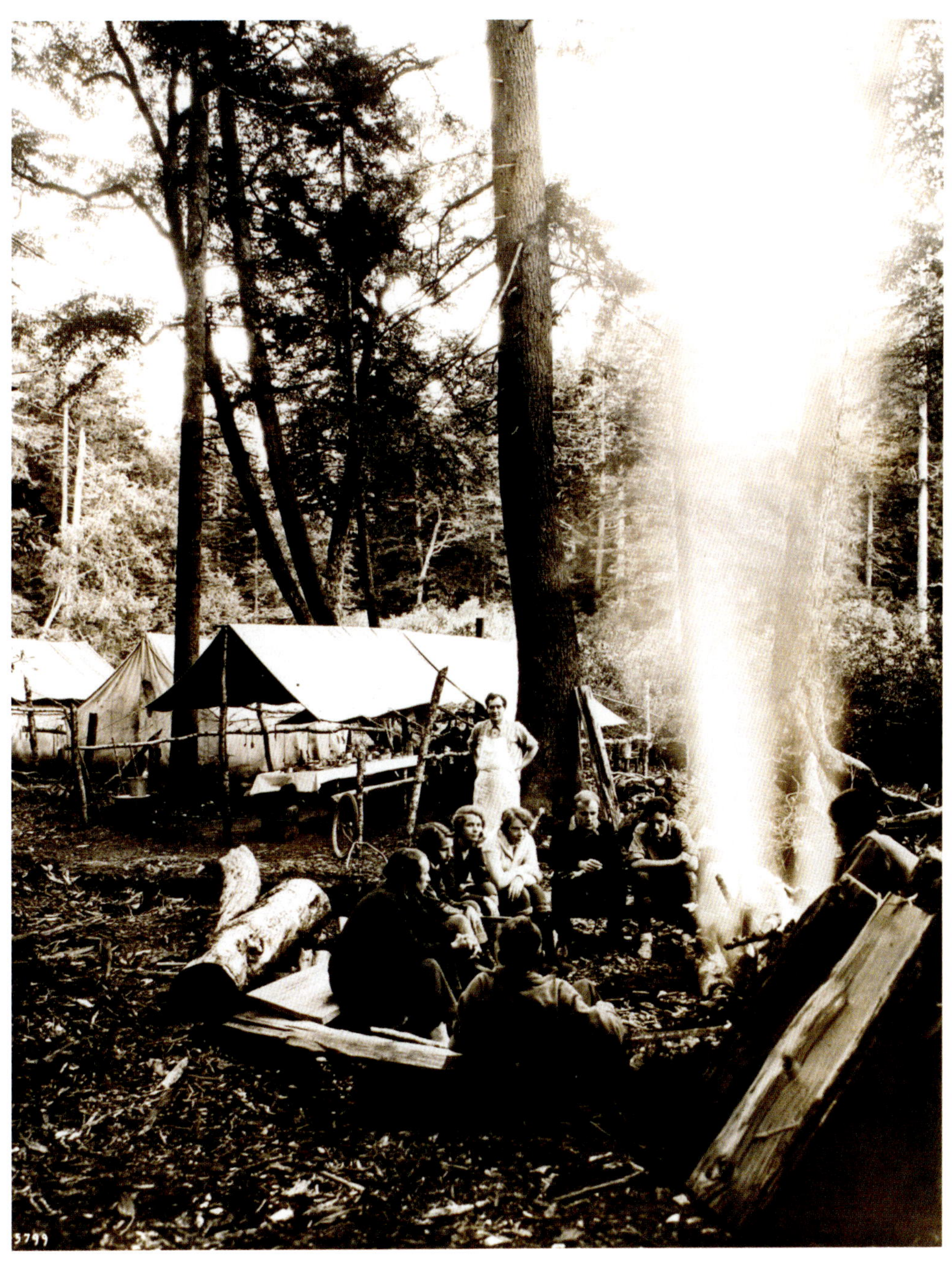

Tom Alexander's Three Forks Camp

TRIP REPORT

Trip Name   Camp Three Forks & Mt. Guyot   Date July 2-3-4, 1932

Mileage of round trip; By car 160   miles; Afoot 34½   miles;   By wheel

Time required: By car 2½ hours one way; Afoot_____ hours (total)   By Pedo Estimated

See trail log

Departure: From Asheville 6:30   From car _______

Arrival: At car 12-30   At Asheville _______

Members 6   Visitors 2

Trip register: (get signature if possible) LEADER   Barbara Ambler

| George Masa | Dr. O. C. Barker | Pauline Smathers |
| Roger Morrow | Dr. S. Weizenblatt | |

Visitors

Mrs. George Cushing

Mrs. Tom Alexander

Motor Log: (Asheville to point of leaving car)   Left Federal Building Saturday
morning at 6:30 followed Highway #10 through Canton, Waynesville,
Sylva and Dillsboro, turned right at Highway # 112 passed the
Cherokee Indian Reservation to Smokemount, turn right at Smokemount
over bridge and follow road # 107 until you come to Swan's place
about 2 miles above Smokemount, where you can park cars and also
leave them in a garage.

Trail Log: To Camp Three Forks from Swan's Place.

Left parked cars at 9:30 A. M. Hiked up road ¾ of a mile turned
right on to trail, going up the side of the mountain, 1/8 mile
further trail forks - take left trail -¼ mile more, and can see
Hughes Ridge ahead and to the right. Chasteen Creek is on the left.
Three miles from cars, look west to see Clingmans Dome - and ¼
mile further to spring. Hughes ridge next point of interest -
four hard miles from the cars and one should arrange not to go over
this area in the middle of the day, as it is mostly cut over land
and very hot. Turn left at top of ridge and follow top of ridge
for about ½ mile, then drop down on the other side for Enloe Creek,
where we reached at 12:00, which is a good place for lunch. 5½ miles
from cars. One mile to the top of Highlands ridge, elevation
4990, drop down off of the ridge to Ocunaluffty river. (Be sure to
cross river on foot log) Trail from the river to vamp is very good
and no more climbing, we re ched Camp Three Forks at 2:25. 9½ miles

32

Sunday - Trip to Mr. Guyot

This trip being much harder than going into Three Forks, only George Masa, Roger Morrow and Doc Barker went.

Left camp 7:15 A. M. Proceeded north up Middle Fork Ridge 1¾ miles to a spring 50 feet to left of trail. At 9:15 reached tree used as lookout, near the top of Cams Knob 2¾ miles from Camp. elevation 5834. Cams Knob 6140 - encounted a bad wind fall (trail very hard to follow) 10:00 A. m. 4 miles - ruff going. Next Mr. Hardison ¾ mile from Cams Knob, 6148 Elevation. Then down into "Hell no-a-Gap (named by George Masa) 10:50 A. M. Up again to Mt. Yonagusta 5½ miles from Camp. elevation 6183. Mt. Sterling lies about eight miles east of here. Turn left on ridge to Three Corners ¾ miles away - 11:20. At this point we came on to the N. C.-Tenn. State Line and Appalachian Trail. Turn right on same and advance up to Mt. Guyot. A stiff climb to top of ridge - the left trail to tower 1/8 mile away. Elevation of Guyot is 6621. Totat distance from camp 7½ miles. But what miles.

The day was very clear and two hours were spent on the top of the tower. The entire Mitchell range 60 miles away, was quite clear - Pisgah and Ledge - Cold Mountain, Narrows, Steps and Shinning Rock, Lickstone Bald, Cold Spring Knob, Richland Balsams, Nantahalas, Andrews Bald, Clingmans Dome, Mingus, Kephart, Le Conte and even Thunder Head stood out clearly.

Returning- Back tracked 1½ miles, then left trail and plunged into a beautiful forest to right and down 3/4 mile to south where we reached the headquarters of Left fork of Onunaluffty. Followed stream into tCamp - very picturesque, but hard and wet. Arriced camp 6:00 P. M. Total distance round trip 16¼ miles.

Monday.

Returned to Swan's Place by same trail and reached cards about 12:00 and Asheville 3:30

OPPOSITE AND ABOVE: *Three Forks trip report, Carolina Mountain Club*

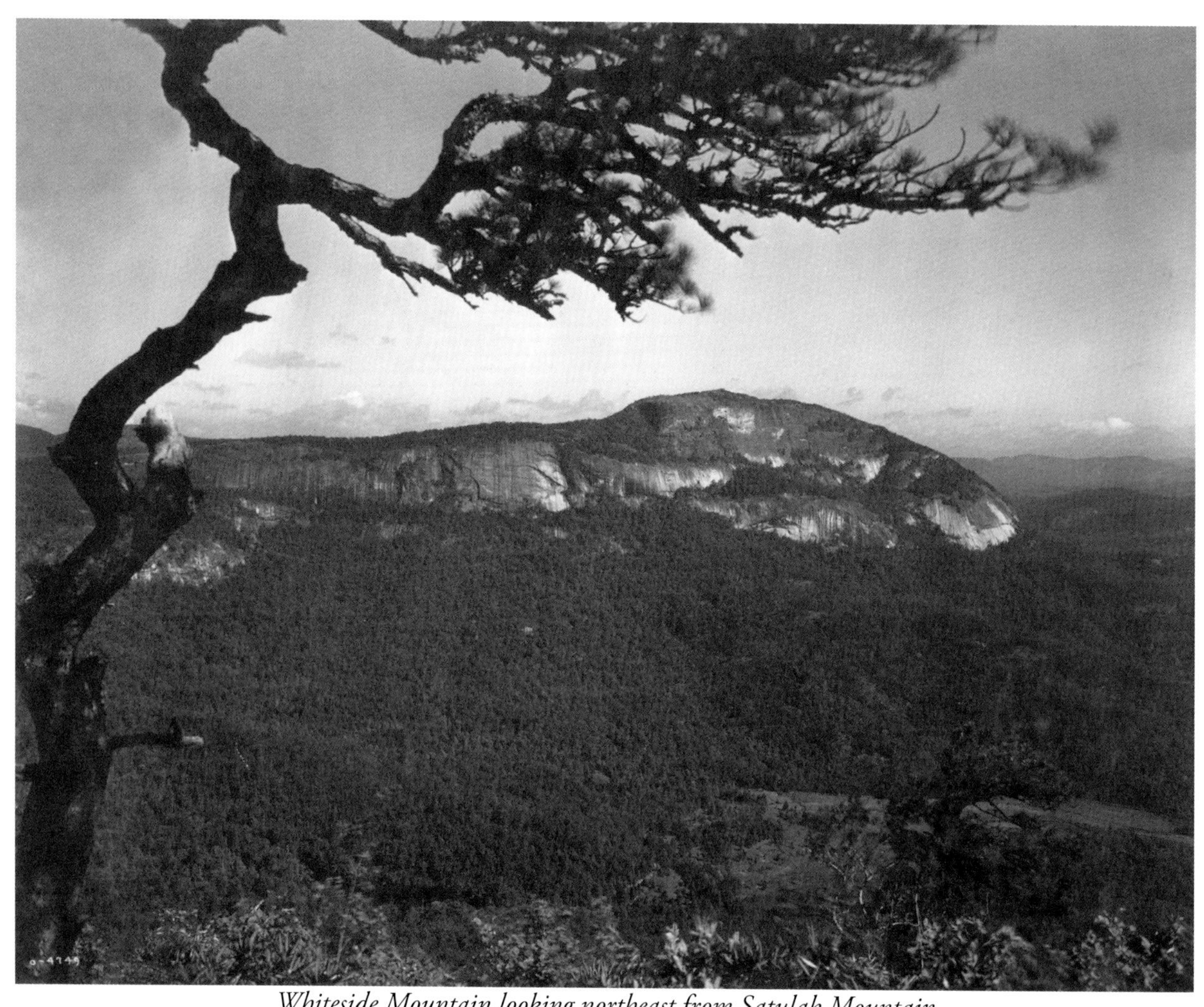

Whiteside Mountain looking northeast from Satulah Mountain
(Highlands Historical Society)

CHAPTER TWO

HIGHLANDS PLATEAU

IN 1929, on the eve of the Great Depression, the town boosters of Highlands, North Carolina, were feeling the need for a promotional piece. The highest city in the eastern United States was itching for development and better access, and local inn owner Frank Cook hired George Masa to assist in the promotion. The first car had arrived in 1917 on a wagon road out of Georgia, and improved automobile access had been an obsession ever since. People played horseshoes on Main Street on July 4. There was one golf course, a post office, the freshly minted Highlands Country Club, and several manors of genteel largesse—and a lot of true mountain people still struggling to make a living from logging and subsistence agriculture. No one-percenters then, lounging about gated communities and country clubs, kicking back at the third home for a weekend of shopping for designer clothing, dining at five-star restaurants, and staying at thousand-dollar-a-night hotels. No, just a starry-eyed Masa kicking about the Highlands Plateau with his camera and Frank Cook, sans the decadence and opulence. Masa was here for two weeks, shooting some of the plateau's most iconic scenes for a promotional brochure that Cook was after, with the adventure costing Cook more than he thought it would. Per his reputation, Masa refused to photograph anything unless the light was perfect.

Some residents were already concerned that the town was attracting visitors and occupants who had little regard for the area's growing significance as a biological hotspot. The creation of the Highlands Museum and Biological Laboratory, soon to become the Highlands Biological Station, was under way at the time of Masa's visit.

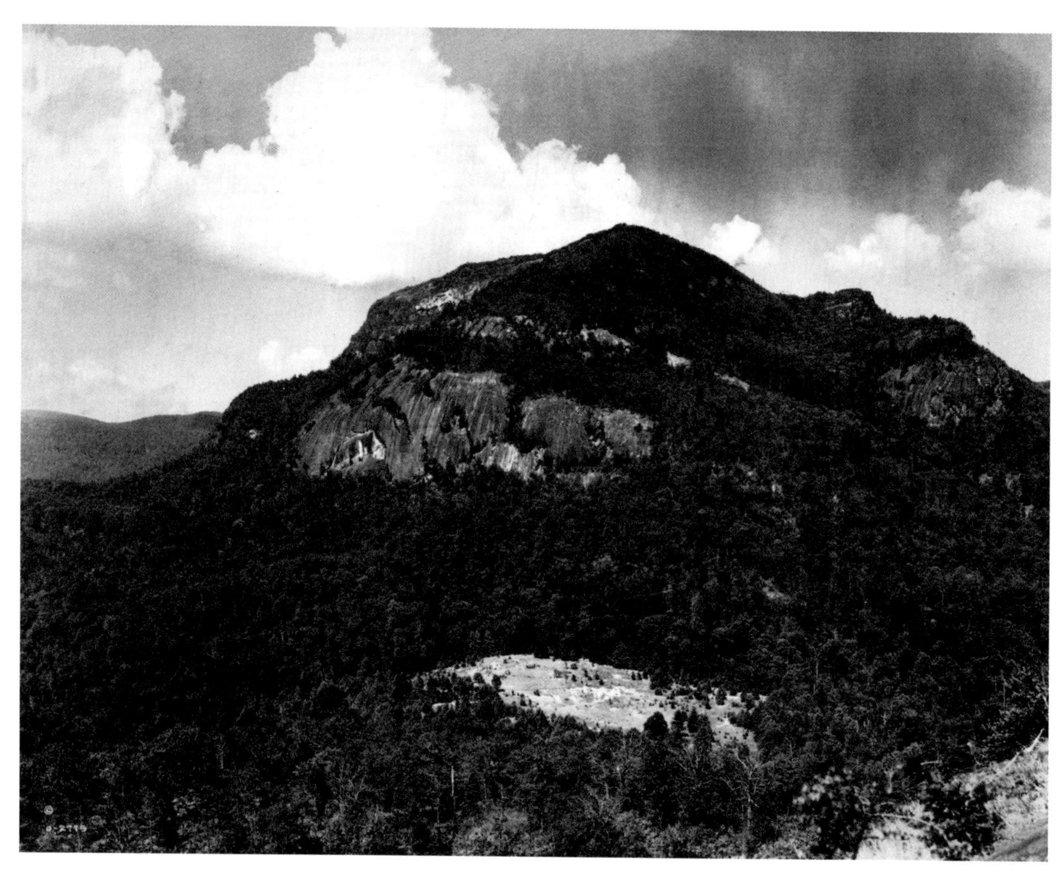

Whiteside Mountain from Turkey Ridge (HHS)

It was an institution born from the region's scientific community's awareness of the plateau's importance for research and the need for conservation. Masa's promotional photos are of the area's incomparable waterfalls, escarpment faces, and old-growth forests, but also of the town's first golf course, Highlands Country Club, its significant historic homes and structures, and road construction in the Cullasaja Gorge. The iconic waterfalls and mountains he photographed were brimming with hemlocks and poplars as wide as automobiles, though the chestnuts were then all but dead and a suite of new invasive pests was on the horizon and bearing down fast. What would Masa think now, with the skies trashed by all-night vapor lights, adelgid-infested hemlocks, four more golf courses in Highlands and eighteen more within twenty miles, the landscape loaded with starter mansions and multi-million-dollar homes?

CULLASAJA GORGE

ON THE WAY UP the Cullasaja Gorge on this cold January day, I stop at Dry Falls. Masa's photo of the falls from 1929 is empty of humans and infrastructure, but it is the same falls I see today. It may have a heavier sediment load and more fecal coliform, but nothing changes about falling water in such places. As Toni Morrison says, "All water has a perfect memory," and though the hydrology upstream is altered by lakes and roads, this rapidly dropping and cascading river has an ancient memory, protected by sheer rock walls and national forest. It is as wild looking today as it was when Masa photographed it. This tourist- and commuter-packed gorge road was then under construction, an engineering feat of that era that rivaled the TVA dams that would soon clog the area's free-flowing rivers. To accomplish the photo, Masa must have climbed high above the falls into the forest. This afternoon, the Cullasaja River is raging with winter rains, and this could be another year for record rainfall and winter temperatures. The U.S. Forest Service recently completed a large, shiny, new parking area, which is still inadequate for the high volume of tourists who circle through today, waiting for someone to leave. Visitors must now pay three dollars to park and walk to the falls or, for some, to park and use the spartan toilets on their way up the gorge to Highlands, which at 4,118 feet is the highest city east of the Mississippi River. The lot is packed with tourists and out-of-state vehicles on this first weekend of 2020, and within two months this will become the year none of us will ever forget. Highlands will post guards to prevent outsiders from entering, and the parking lot will be vacant. But today, the paved path down to the falls is a long line of new Christmas fleece and down jackets. It's freezing cold, and I'd rather hold on until we reach our Highlands lunch spot, but my wife heads for the toilet line, stoic and determined. Cook and Masa would have parked on what was then becoming State Highway 64, as the road up the gorge was just being built. Masa's photos of the gorge road's construction reveal the enormity of the engineering feat—ancient and sheer granite walls being blasted out and the riverbed filled with sediment and mechanical debris. I take my chances on the three-dollar parking fee, and we head to the large accessible viewing platform with my ninety-six-year-old friend, Bob Kibler, who has not seen the falls in some years. We ask one of the tourists to take a photo of us together, and it occurs to me that Masa's promotional photos from almost one hundred years ago were obviously used quite well in those early days.

Earlier this week, I had spoken with Frank Cook's daughter, Beverly, who had no stories of Masa when he was in Highlands with her father. She told me that Masa's ninety-seven photos were in a box stuffed under her father's bed and were rescued after his death. They're now owned by the Highlands Historical Society, which brings them out occasionally for exhibits, most recently at Highlands' Bascom Gallery. The exhibit was just a sampling of the photos in their collection, but it provided viewers with a sense of Masa's artistic eye and a window into the plateau before it became a mecca for millionaires. We'll never know what Masa was thinking as he wandered the area in 1929, but I doubt he could have imagined the future looking quite like this. What was to become one of the most scenic drives in the southern Appalachians—the Cullasaja Gorge road—was under construction when Masa was here, an engineering feat that required blasting and gouging through granite to hang a road off the gorge's rugged cliff faces. Masa saw and photographed the construction, and the fact that he took the time to get the shots suggests his astonishment at the feat. Was he also astonished at the destruction?

The Cullasaja River in his photos is a wounded gash of a landscape, heavy equipment and machinery perched about it like vultures picking away at a carcass. The gorge's forests would have been filled with old-growth hemlocks and dying American chestnuts. In places still, if one is looking, large old-growth tulip trees lie just off the roadside. The gorge today is full of dead hemlocks and struggling young American chestnuts, stumps sprouting and waiting for a cure. It is also now full of tourists snapping selfies and shinning up to the gorge's numerous waterfalls, struggling for parking spaces as they creep around the unfamiliar mountainous twists and turns.

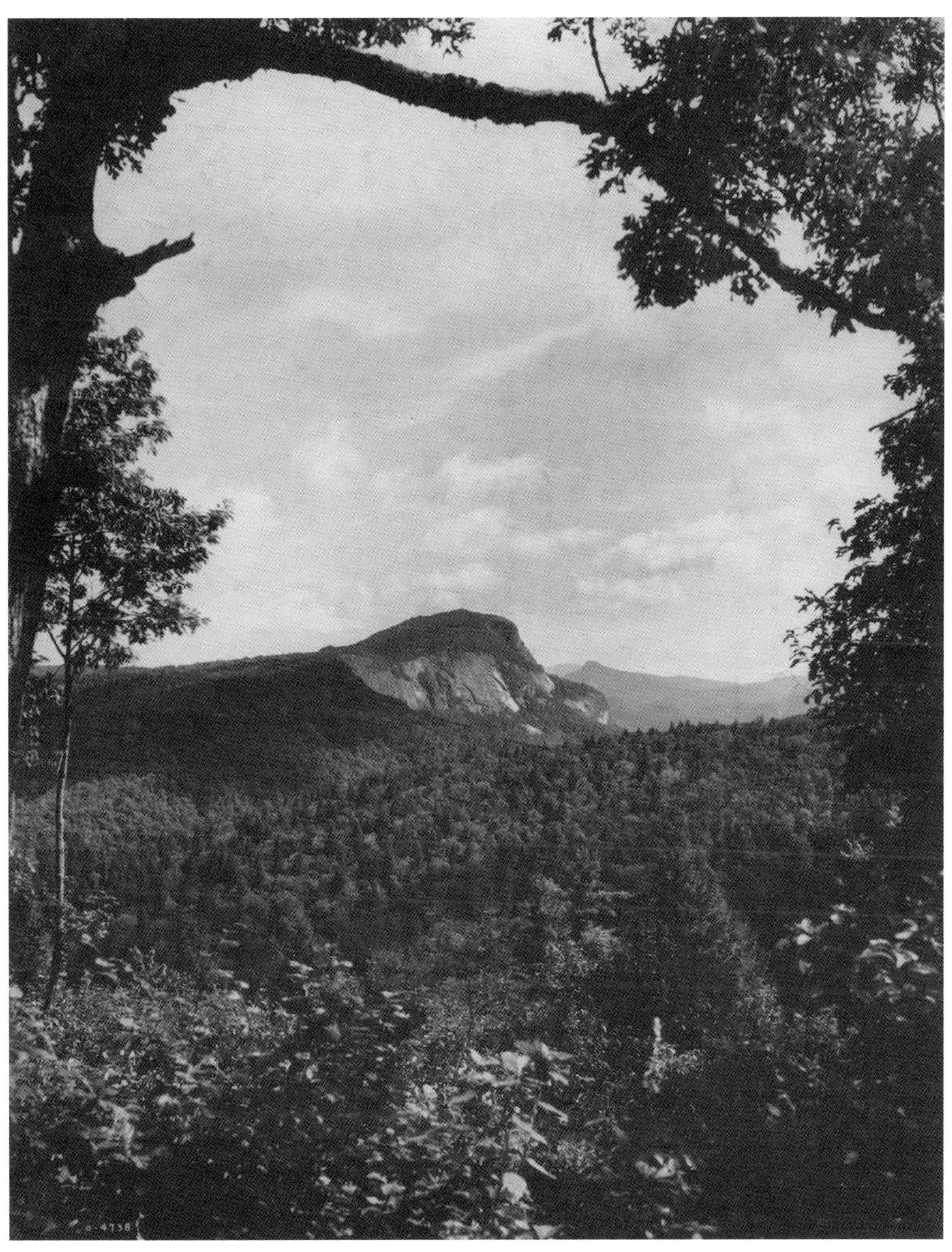

View of Whiteside Mountain from Bear Pen subdivision. Bear Pen was advertised as a potential 42-acre subdivision in the April 12th, 1925, edition of the Palm Beach Post for $5,000 per lot and was one Highlands' first. (HHS)

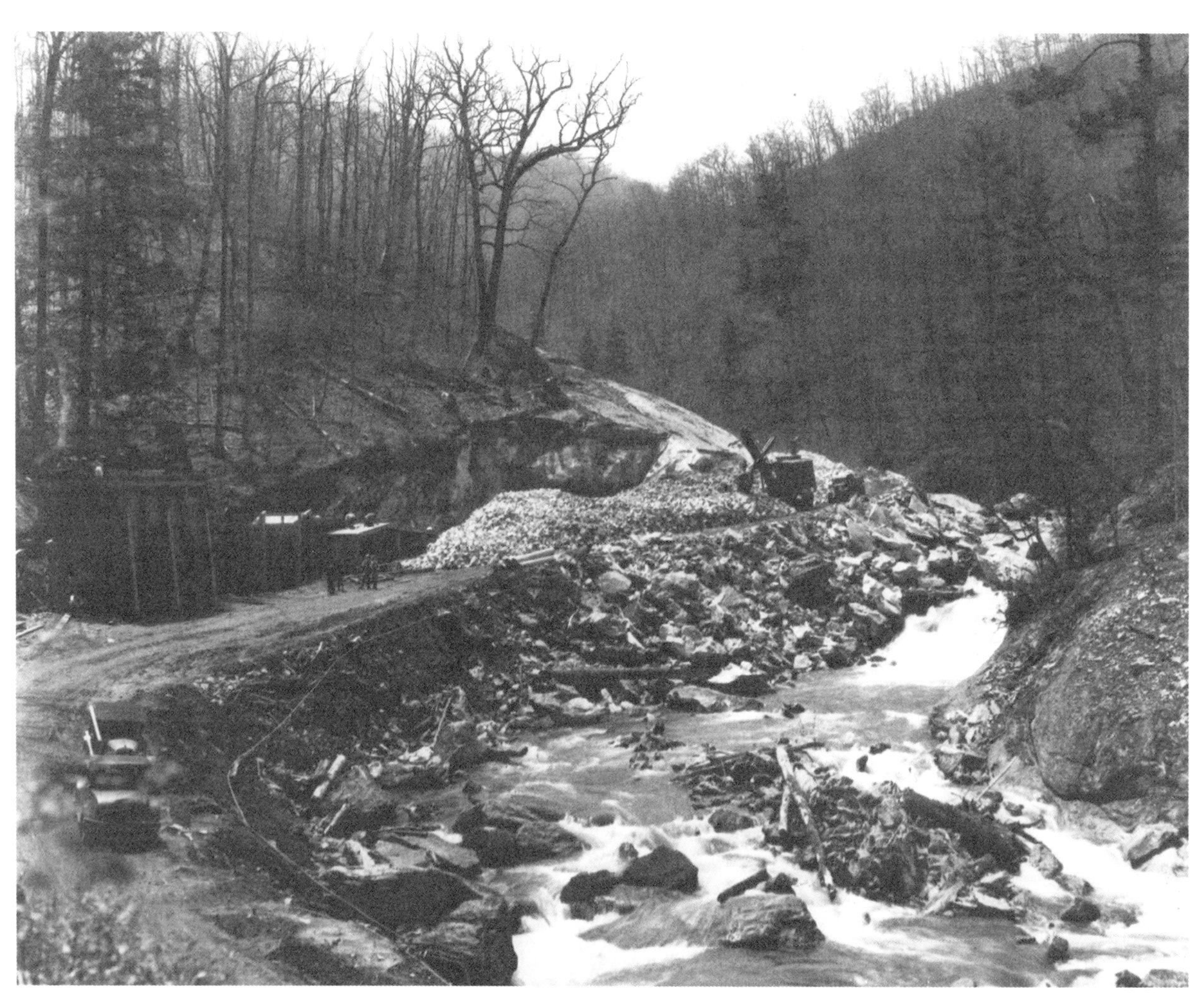

Construction of the Cullasaja Gorge Road, now State Highway 64 (HHS)

A MONTH LATER, IN February, I arrange to meet Obie Oakley, president of the Highlands Historical Society, at their museum in Highlands. There is a room to the right upon entering where Masa's photographs line the walls. It's cold, as the heat has been off since the building's closing for the winter months, when the plateau is empty of tourists and second-home owners. Obie brings out three-ring binders of their collection for me to peruse, and I settle in as best I can. The photos of Highlands are those of a place in great transition. Only one country club then, the views of Whiteside Mountain unobscured and stunning. No high-end clothing boutiques or Persian rug dealers. The Cullasaja Gorge road out of Franklin was being built during Masa's brief tenure, and his photos reflect what must have been his marvel at the project. The gorge itself is spectacular, the sheer rock walls so thick with multicolored lichens that from a distance they appear as paintings. The road bends around granite walls that would have been death defying to workers blasting their way around them. Masa, too, must have been amazed by it. Photos of workers and machinery were not his genre, yet he captured the scene perhaps because he sensed the historical prescience. I leave with a phone full of photos and notes, not knowing that in less than a month the world will turn upside down. The project goes on hold.

ONLY ONE EASTERN HEMLOCK of this size survives on the planet, and I am standing before it, squinting through its branches into late-afternoon sunlight. The hemlock is a miracle. We're six months into the pandemic, and it's somewhat of a miracle that I'm here, too, given the scope of the outbreak and the restrictions placed on travel and interactions. Some years ago, before the hemlock pandemic could decimate it, thoughtful people at the Highlands-Cashiers Land Trust treated this tree and the ones around it so that they might survive extinction. I have signed a waiver to be here, swearing secrecy to its location. I have also signed the waiver so that I can collect leaf litter for a climate scientist working out of Lund University in Sweden. She has ninety-one such sites globally and has chosen the Highlands Plateau for this unique stand of old-growth and for the fact that the Highlands Biological Station can provide lab space for our drying, sorting, and scanning of leaves. My two companions, Morgan and Liam, are recent college graduates with environmental studies degrees and, like me, almost forty years their senior, are working in the gig economy. Yesterday, we walked almost twelve miles in rugged terrain in the Joyce

Kilmer-Slickrock Wilderness collecting from sixty plots for the same project, and my legs are screaming. Morgan and Liam seem unfazed. I drag behind them as we push down the cove through rhododendron, trying not to think about the steep climb back out. The former owner of this tract, Henry Wright, spared it from the blade as Powell Lumber cut all the surrounding timber owned by the Ravenel family. In Masa's photo, Wright is standing next to an enormous white oak, and I wonder about its fate and location. I want to think Masa has been here, has stood in this spot before this stupefying example of an Appalachian icon.

We wrap up after a couple of hours and make the arduous climb back to the cars. Morgan is starting a new job next week in Asheville, and Liam is trying to make it to France this month for a teaching gig he has landed. I've enjoyed their company, and next month I'll be making these same treks alone. We say our goodbyes, and I stop down the road at one of Highlands' upscale convenience stores for a beer while I load the collection into one of the Highlands Biological Station's laboratory dryers. The town has a mask mandate, and the streets are full of masked high-fashion travelers wandering in and out of the clothing and jewelry stores, looking like billionaire bandits. It's quite a contrast from where I have just emerged a few miles down the road. The clerk takes the beer, then looks behind me and tells a woman that she has to have a mask on to enter. A young man who has just gotten off one of the local construction sites and has already had a few tells the woman he has a mask she can have. She looks nervous and leaves the store. Then, in his thick mountain accent, he tells another man in line that he wants to buy his mask, saying, "I've got to have it." The mask the other man is wearing says, "Trump 2020." The other man doesn't respond at first but eventually says, "You can get them on Amazon." On and on and on they go now. I leave the store with my beer and look at the busy streets, Masa's promotional photos in their twenty-first-century fruition. Most of the old, historic Highlands homes he photographed have now been bulldozed, replaced by opulent modern monstrosities with no connection to history or place.

IT'S MARCH 2021, AND it's been over a year since I visited the Highlands Historical Society to examine their Masa photographs. So much has happened since that cold week in February, to all of us. I have arranged with the Highlands Biological Station to stay here in one of their duplexes for five nights, to do nothing but pursue the ghost of George Masa and render it into words. Two months ago, I severely injured

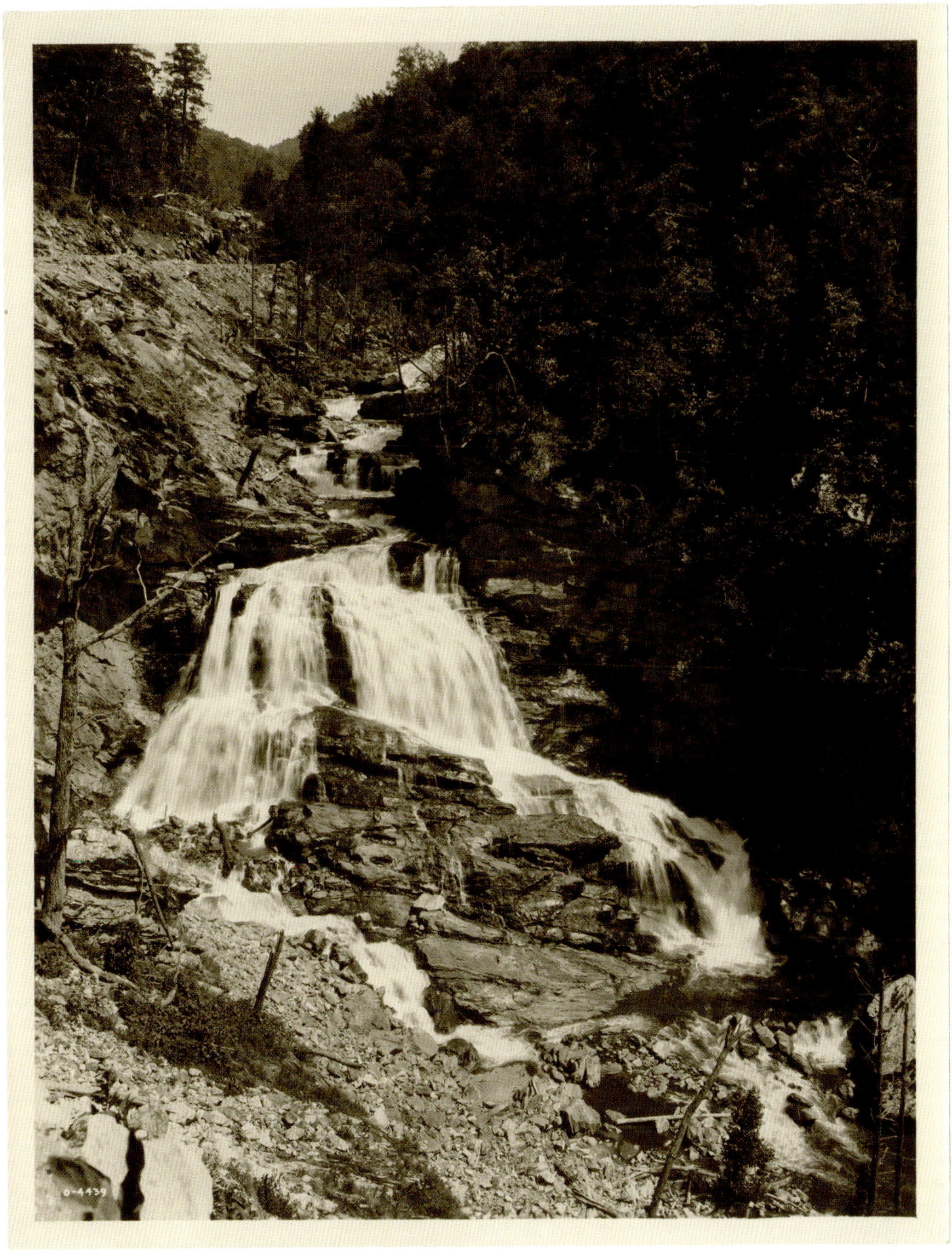

Cullasaja Falls, 1929. Blasting debris from the road cut can be seen down the slope and into the ravine. A visitor to the area in July of 1883 described her journey to the falls in the Highlands newspaper, Blue Ridge Enterprise, *as a trip from Highlands on an old cart path. (GSMA)*

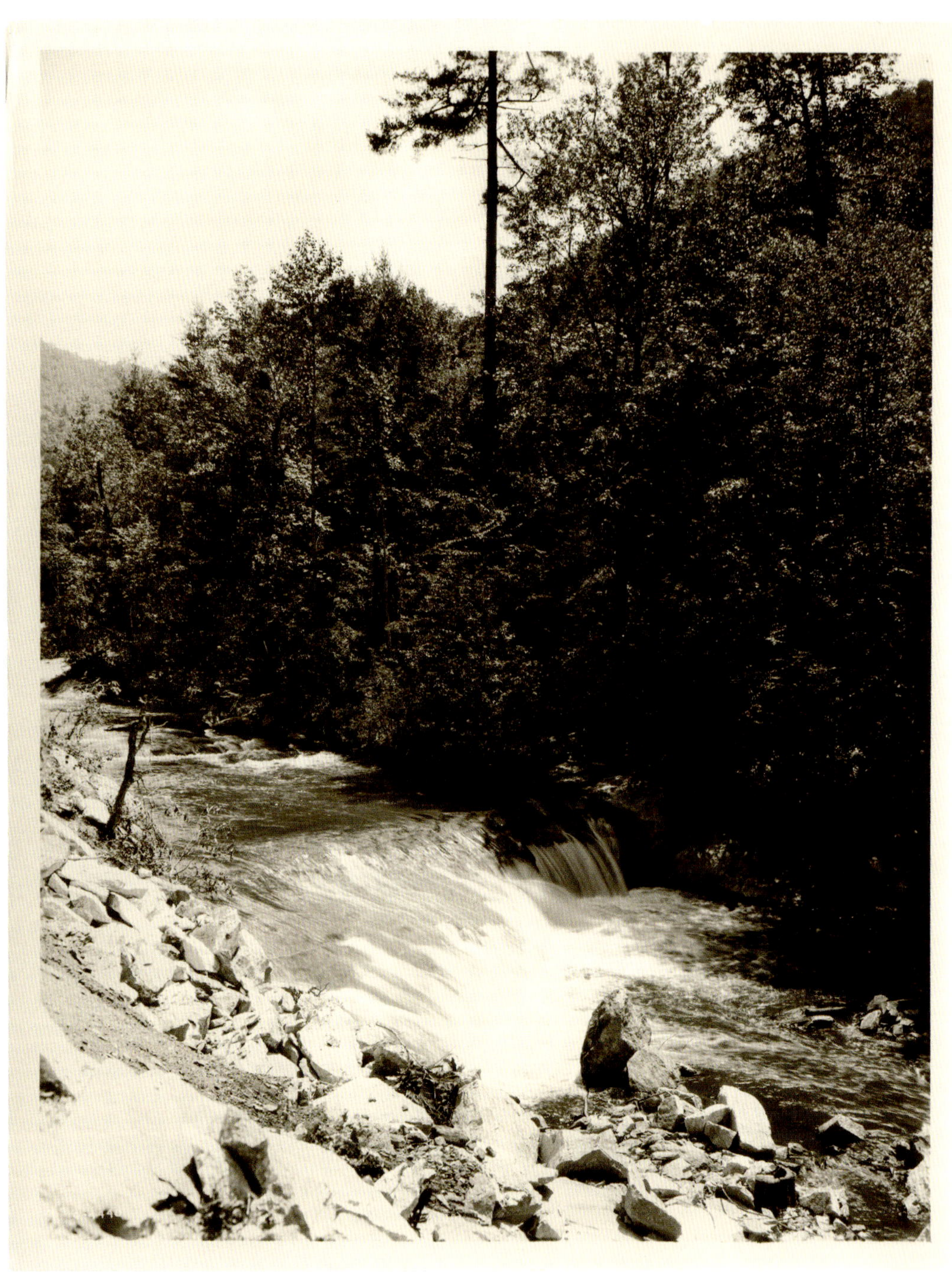

Upper Cullasaja River, 1929 (GSMA)

my left hand, requiring surgery and physical therapy. The injury limits my typing ability, and I feel the urgency of an upcoming deadline and the need for isolation in order to focus. This past year has been a trying one, and I'm feeling deep sympathy for, and connections to, George Masa, his struggle in the face of great difficulties to accomplish his grand, wild vision. The station is empty of students and researchers due to COVID-19, and the town is mostly empty as well. Most of the station staff are here, though, so I have a little company at times. The station has twenty-four forested acres and a small lake, along with several miles of trails. I write, I walk, I look for Masa. I would really like to know the fate of the Richardson Oak, which Masa photographed with Henry Wright. And how to get to Granite City.

The associate director of the station has been to Granite City and tells me how to get there. It's down Horse Cove, past where the paved road turns to gravel, near an unmarked pulloff where the national forest boundary begins. My wife drives up from Cowee to join me, and we embark upon a Masa journey. The trip down into Horse Cove is the same one Masa would have taken. This was the main route from Atlanta for years, before State Road 107 was built out of Dillard. And before that, this was an ancient trade path. We meander down the cove, winding past a few old homes uncharacteristic of those around town, past new ones, and onto the gravel road. We find the pulloff and follow a steep, deeply rutted trail for an eighth of a mile or so.

Suddenly, we are in a different world. This is the first scramble of this type I've been on since injuring my hand, but I feel prepared. I have a mitten on it, and a stiff splint that covers my wrist and hand. The rock rises up before us in a jigsaw puzzle jumble, ancient, covered in crustose lichens and pale green bryophytes. I recognize the spot where Masa took his photo. We climb on through rusty quartz seams and fallen ochre slabs until we reach the highest of the jumble's dark crevices, at a point just below the summit. My wife pushes on, but I stop to observe for a moment and consider the risks. Above me is a brow of rock covered in bright yellow crustose lichens. Rhododendron protrudes from the shallow cracks, and a large sweet birch has created a life for itself by spreading a web of roots across a bare ledge, gripping with gnarled fingers and leaning out over the crevasse. It's a bit more rugged here and entails a higher likelihood of tripping and damaging my recovering hand, but I move carefully and pick my way toward the mountain laurel stretched along the summit. I am happy that George Masa and I have shared this place. I am amazed at the absence of graffiti, beer cans, and garbage. The forest is young but for one old white oak leaning out from the ridge. It looks out of place and is. We find an alternate route down, past the remains of a springhouse, and end up a short distance down the road from where we parked. Across the road is a sprawling vacation home with a For Sale sign out front. We look closer. It's listed with Berkshire Hathaway as part of their "Luxury Services Collection," and the contact is "Great Smokys [*sic*] Realty." Poor George Masa, rolling over in his grave. Still, I'd live in this very spot in a second if I could. We're all complicit in this wholesale twenty-first-century settling and relocating, and who wouldn't want such a place? My own move here twenty years ago was part of a high-growth era in mountain development. And this pandemic year, the mountains are filling up in a rapid urban and suburban diaspora as people flee for more open and less-settled spaces to feel safer in.

The side of this remote section of road is littered with beer cans, likely from disgruntled workers sick of the disparity of wealth within which they must live and labor. We drive back to the station, get takeout pizza, and dream of seeing the Highlands Plateau before any of us, native or otherwise, arrived with our insatiable needs and ideas.

MASA'S PHOTO of the Richardson Oak with Highlands icon Henry Wright is one that I have wondered over for some time. I'm familiar with most of the remaining old-growth forest in the area, but I hoped this mammoth specimen might be standing somewhere on the edge of a golf course or within the confines of a gated community. Yesterday, I emailed Ran Shaffner, author of *Heart of the Blue Ridge: Highlands, North Carolina,* who wrote me back last night about the Richardson Oak. Ran tells me that the oak was on Henry Richardson's property, which Thomas Harbison tried to preserve before Richardson's death in 1938. Richardson agreed to hold the property and sell it to Harbison for twenty dollars an acre, an agreement that never came to fruition. Wilton Cobb purchased the 289 acres of Richardson's primeval forest north of Bear Pen and developed it as Lake Primeval. This property changed hands again, and the place where the oak stood is now Highlands Falls Country Club. Masa's photo of the forest in 1929 is simply titled "Primeval Forest with Rhodo." The oak is gone. On to plan B for the day.

I leave early for physical therapy in Franklin, get a redeye at Mountain Fresh, and head down the Cullasaja Gorge on the state highway Masa photographed while it was being blasted. The road, in addition to being a tourist attraction, is a major commuter route between the towns of Franklin and Highlands. An hour earlier, I would have

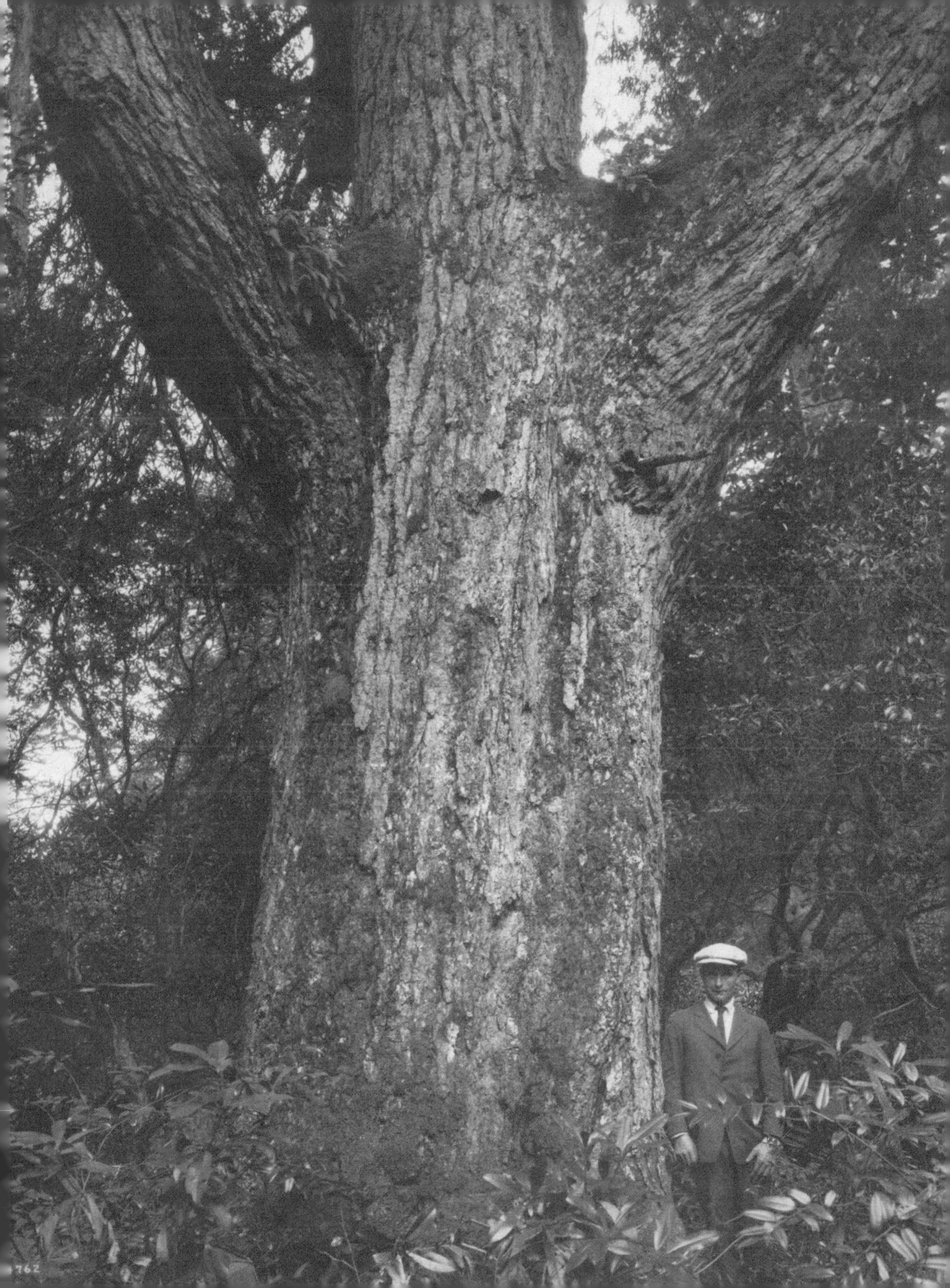

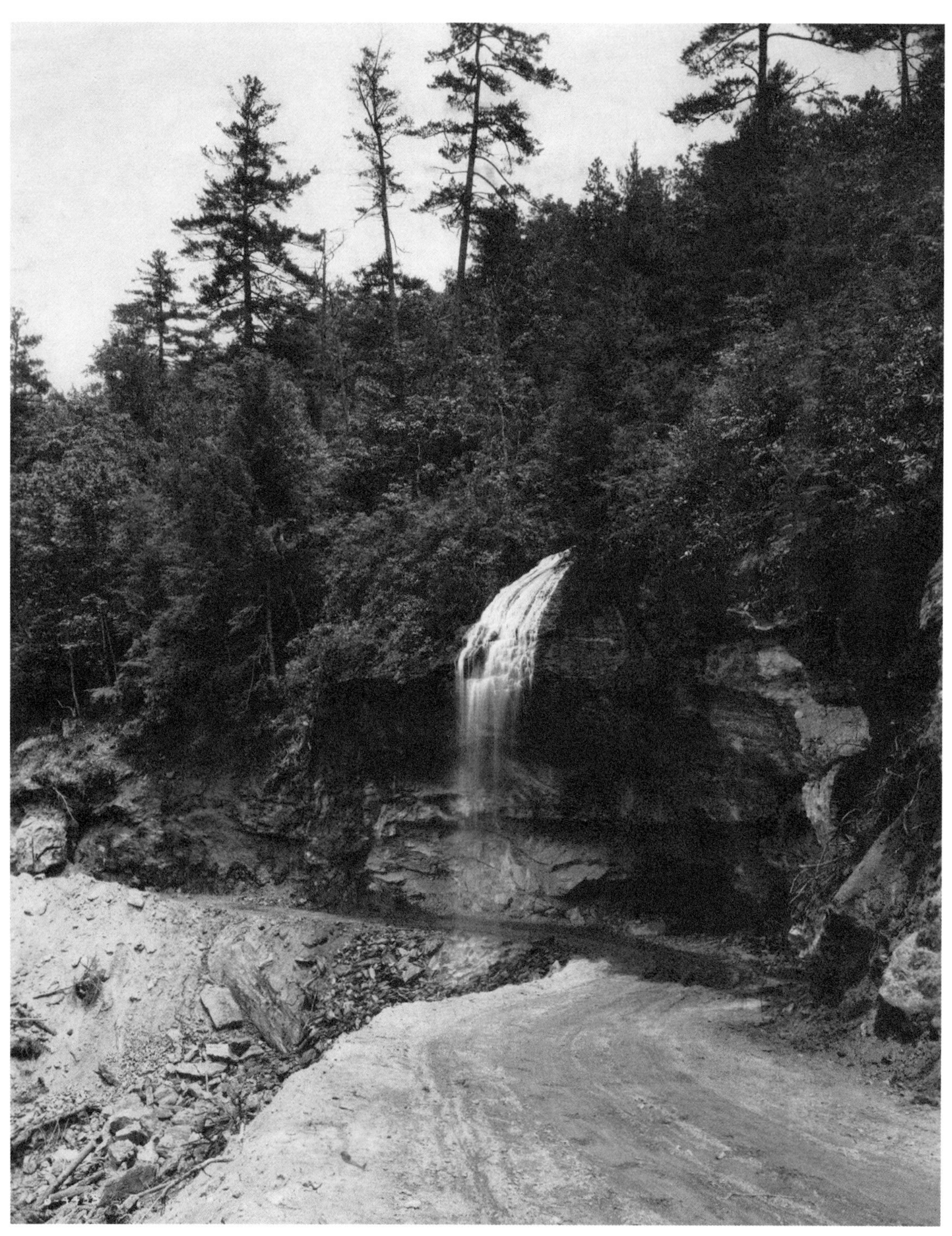

Bridal Veil Falls, 1929 (HHS)

encountered the NASCAR race of Franklin's working class speeding up the gorge to work at the numerous restaurants, hotels, and gift shops in Highlands. That race is surpassed only by the insane dash down the gorge after four o'clock every afternoon of the week. I pass several Masa photo landmarks—Bridal Veil Falls, Dry Falls, and the blasted notch that he photographed when the road was being built in 1929—then pass the pullout for Cullasaja Falls. All of these normally packed parking areas are empty in this tourist off-season. The river looks wild and pristine, but like the Nantahala and any other number of Appalachian rivers, it's altered. Masa's photos show a Cullasaja under assault by heavy equipment, the evidence of which remains to this day. But it looks wild and to a great degree *is* wild, despite the damming of the river in Highlands for Lake Sequoyah, the discharges from the Highlands water treatment plant, and the multitude of RV parks and septic systems along its shores.

I head back up the gorge after physical therapy and decide to spend the afternoon in search of Masa at Satulah Mountain. Satulah Mountain is a significant part of local history, having been saved by the Highlands Improvement Association under the leadership of Marguerite Ravenel, who swore that the thirty-two-acre tract would never be developed. It is now owned by the association's descendant, the Highlands-Cashiers Land Trust, and according to their website I must walk 1.7 miles from downtown to access the property. I last climbed Satulah a decade ago with Jess Riddle, to see a rare occurrence of *Juniperus communis* that is found on its southern edge, and I don't remember having walked there from downtown. I drive up Satulah Road and am greeted by two stone pillars that say, "Satulah Mountain Historic District." Signs farther on say, HIKERS WELCOME, but there are also No Parking signs everywhere. I don't remember any of this. I drive on toward the summit, but I'm less and less convinced I can park anywhere, given the plethora of signs. No one is here in these empty and opulent homes, and I mean *no one*. Nonetheless, I imagine that private security must patrol the area, so I turn around and head back to town to park.

The streets in town are also empty, so I find a place close to Satulah Road and start walking. The original road up this mountain was built by Captain Prioleau Ravenel in the 1890s, and I wonder how much of this road still lies within its footprint. It's uphill the entire way, steep and on pavement with no shoulders. At the road's end is an empty cul-de-sac with plenty of room to park. A woman drives up in a large white SUV with a dog, gets out, and starts walking. I'm confused, since it's so clear that hikers have to park in town, but it seems perfectly normal to her. She probably knows that no one is going to stop her, and I wish I'd spared myself the long walk and parked here as well.

After another half-mile of walking, I reach the open and rocky summit. My first impression, after studying Masa's photograph from ninety-two years ago, is that the summit has revegetated along its edges. The next impression is of the houses along the rim of Whiteside Mountain. That rim was a prominent feature in Masa's photograph. Today, houses line it like a hundred-million-dollar string of Christmas lights. Masa's image has a family of five on horseback, looking south toward South Carolina. They seem content. Was Masa? A line of trees is behind them, and I believe it is this same family of pitch pines whose shade I'm enjoying at the moment. The pitch pines and white oaks on this windswept ridge are all in the two-hundred-year age category, stunted and bonsaied from two centuries of wind and harsh weather. It's warm and clear, like no other day of this year, and I fall sound asleep on the pine straw looking toward Whiteside. I sleep for almost an hour and wake up a bit chilled. I wander out to the juniper, then back to a spot on the mountain that someone on the internet claims is an old Confederate lookout. It's actually the remains of a stone shelter built by the Ravenels for overnighters many years ago. The rocks are mortared and form a distinct wall complete with a fireplace. I hear voices and see a young couple and their child above me coming down the trail. I don't want to startle them, so I move back up and into the trail, stepping aside when they see me. I head back down, stopping at one of the empty homes that has a For Sale sign out front with a brochure box. It's all mine for $1.3 million, but there is some issue with the septic system. Well, that's a deal killer.

I return to my spartan little duplex at the biological station, rest, drink a beer, and decide to hike up to Sunset Rock for, well, sunset. I put another beer in my coat pocket, cross the road, and walk a half-mile up through a sad and dying hemlock forest to this popular Highlands icon.

The next morning after writing, I load up and head for Whiteside Mountain. Tomorrow is my last day here, and I've agreed to volunteer, to the degree I can with my injured hand, at the station. They're treating the hemlocks, and I'll help however possible. Masa took more photos of Whiteside, either directly or indirectly, than any other place on the Highlands Plateau. It's easy to see why. Whiteside is 4,931 feet in elevation, part of the Eastern Continental Divide, with a stunning granite face on its southern exposure. If there were to be one natural landmark to define the area, Whiteside would be it. It also attracts more tourists than anywhere in the Highlands area, and I'm sure Frank Cook had this in mind when he hired Masa. Today, the parking lot is far from full, with twelve vehicles, including mine. I encounter nineteen people on the loop trail around the mountain's summit and remember a visit this past fall during the peak leaf season when there were likely ten times that many on the same hike. I stop at the overlook platform at the summit and am alone for a few minutes. It's another brilliant, cloudless day, cool but comfortable. I hear voices after a few minutes, and a middle-aged couple joins me. They're here from Philadelphia, staying in Highlands and looking for hikes. I tell them how to get to Satulah Mountain. We talk a little about Philadelphia's Bartram's Garden, and then I see a splash of blue-gray dart out from the cliff far below. It's a peregrine falcon dropping down for something. I hope they understand the significance of this moment. I hike back to my truck, double-check the falcon's cry on my bird app, and drive back to the station.

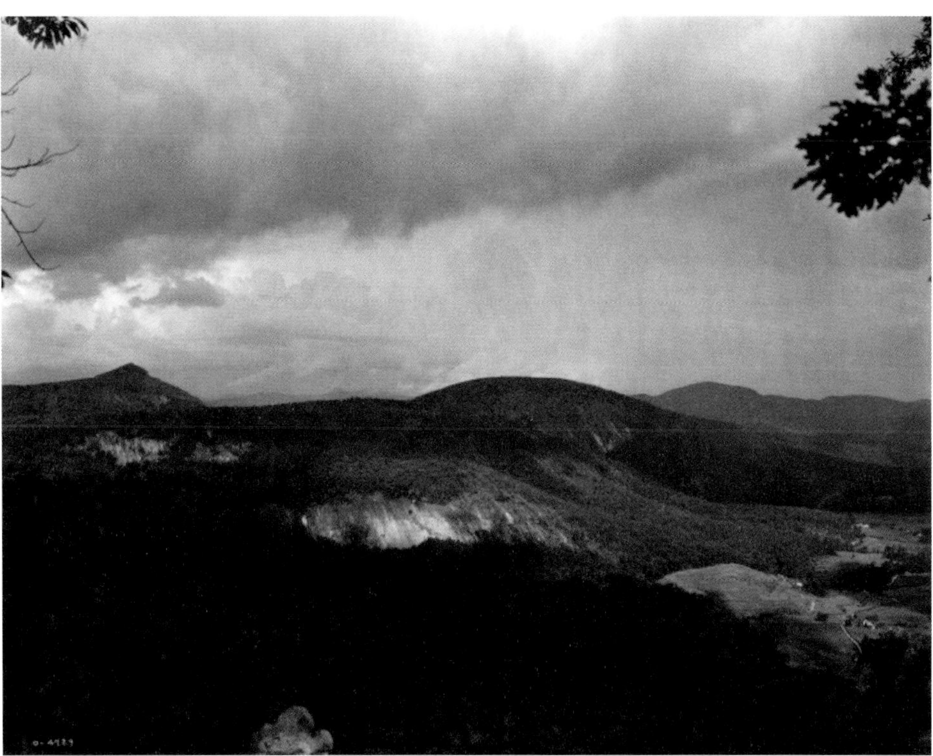

View from Sunrise Rock, east of Sunset Rock, 1929 (HHS)

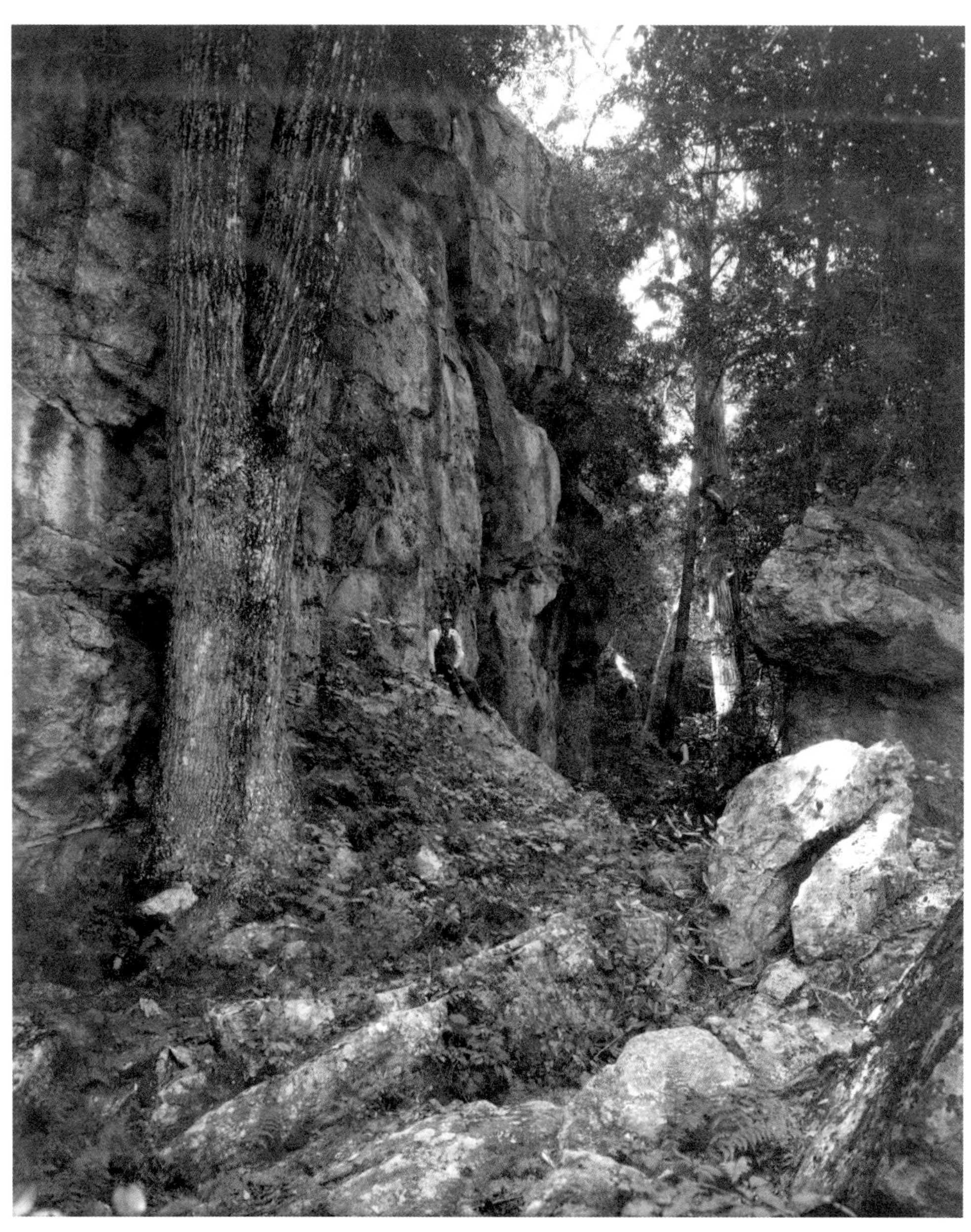

Granite City, 1929 (HHS).

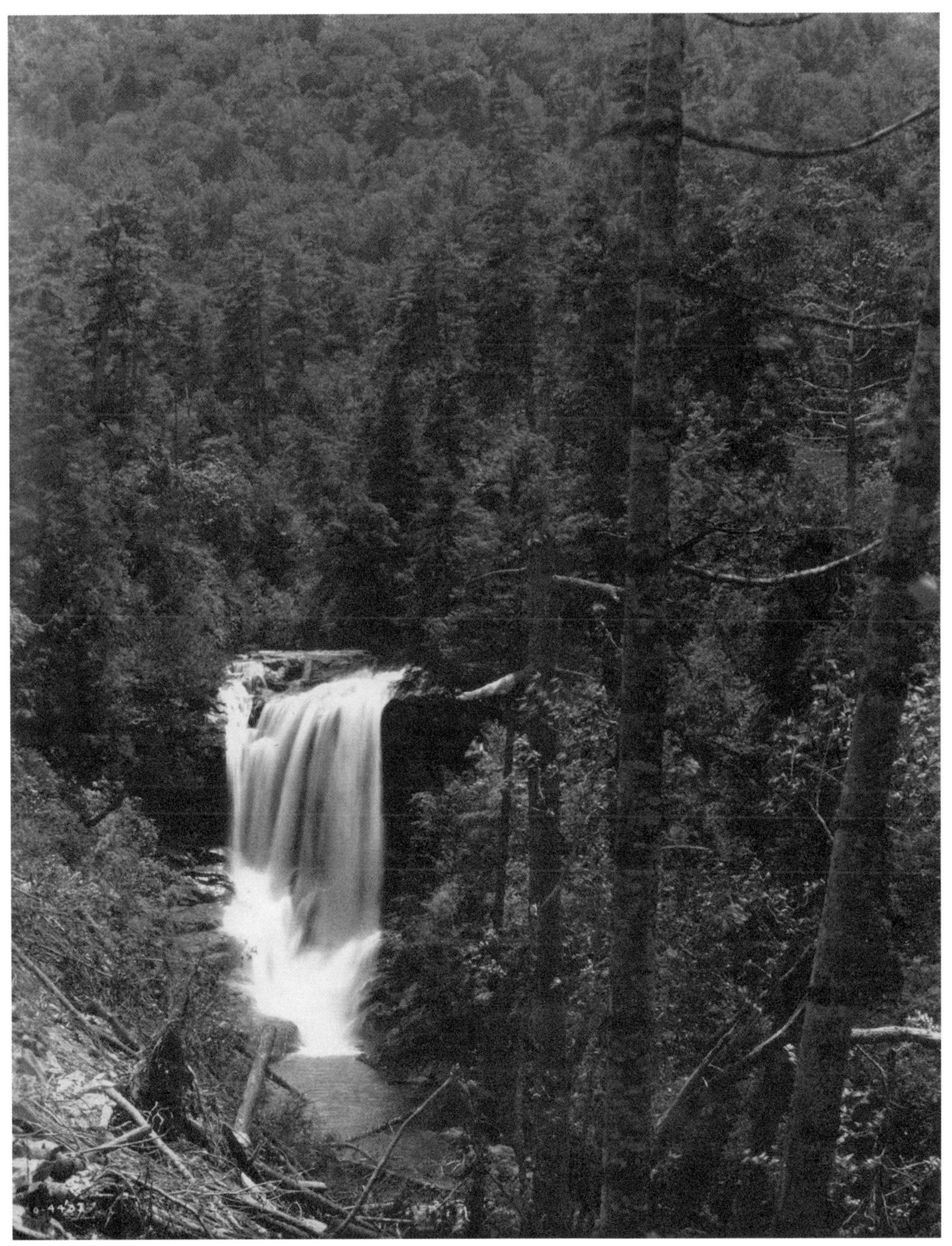

Dry Falls, 1929 (HHS)

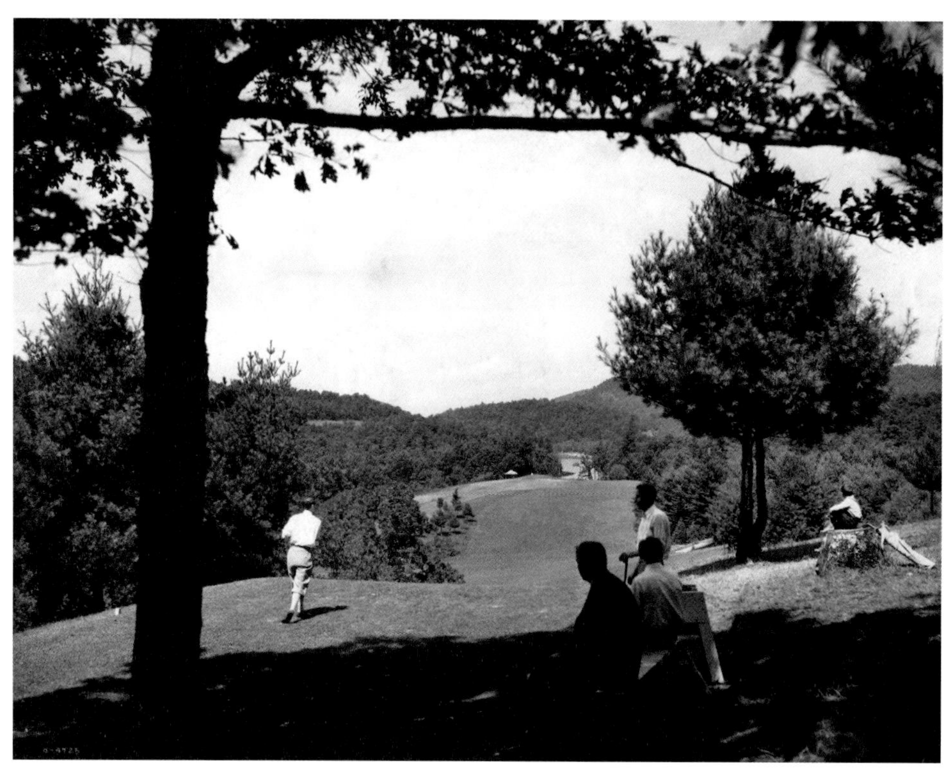

Highlands Estates tee no.5 and fairway, 1929 (HHS). OPPOSITE: *What was known as Highlands Primeval Forest, pre-development, 1929 (HHS)*

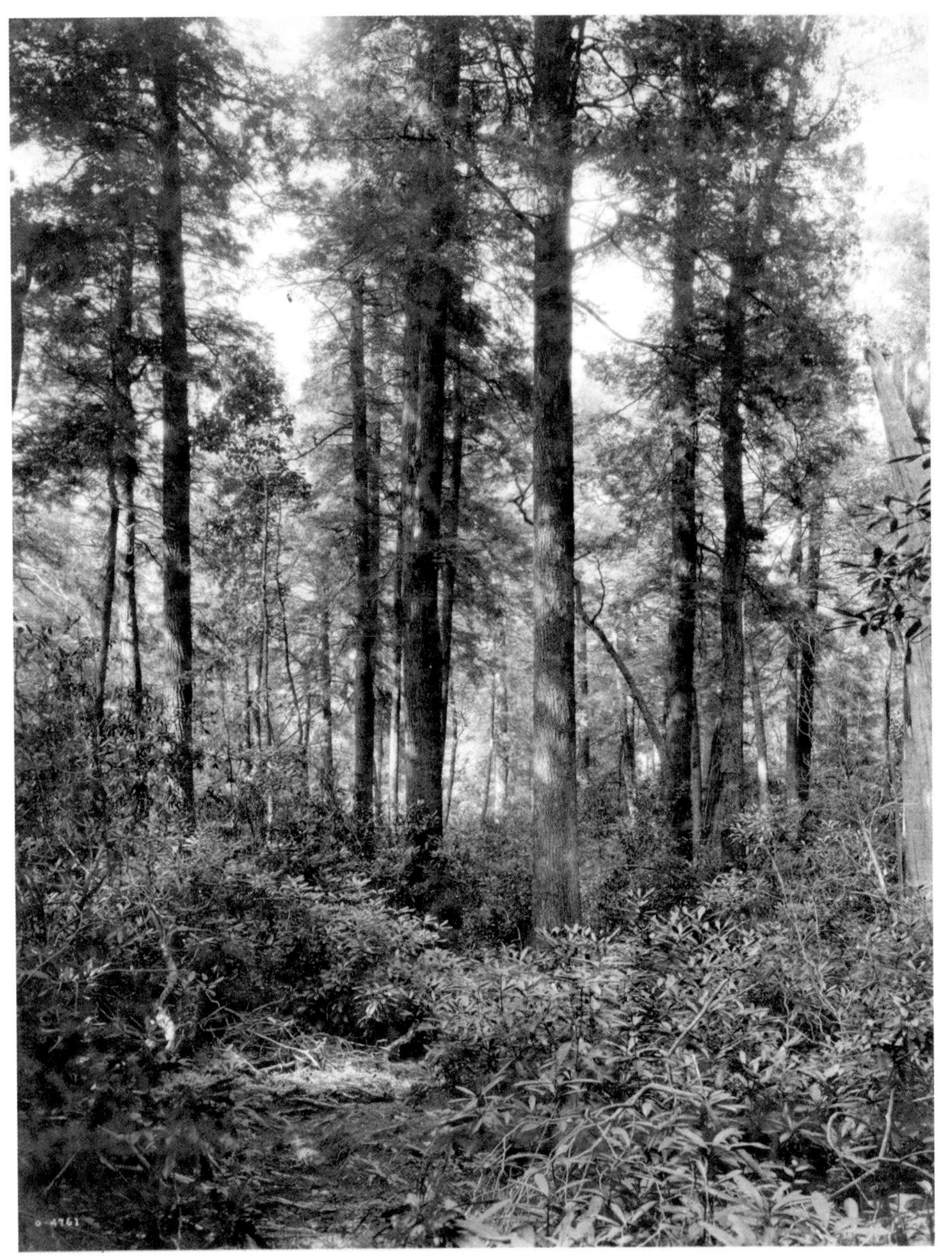

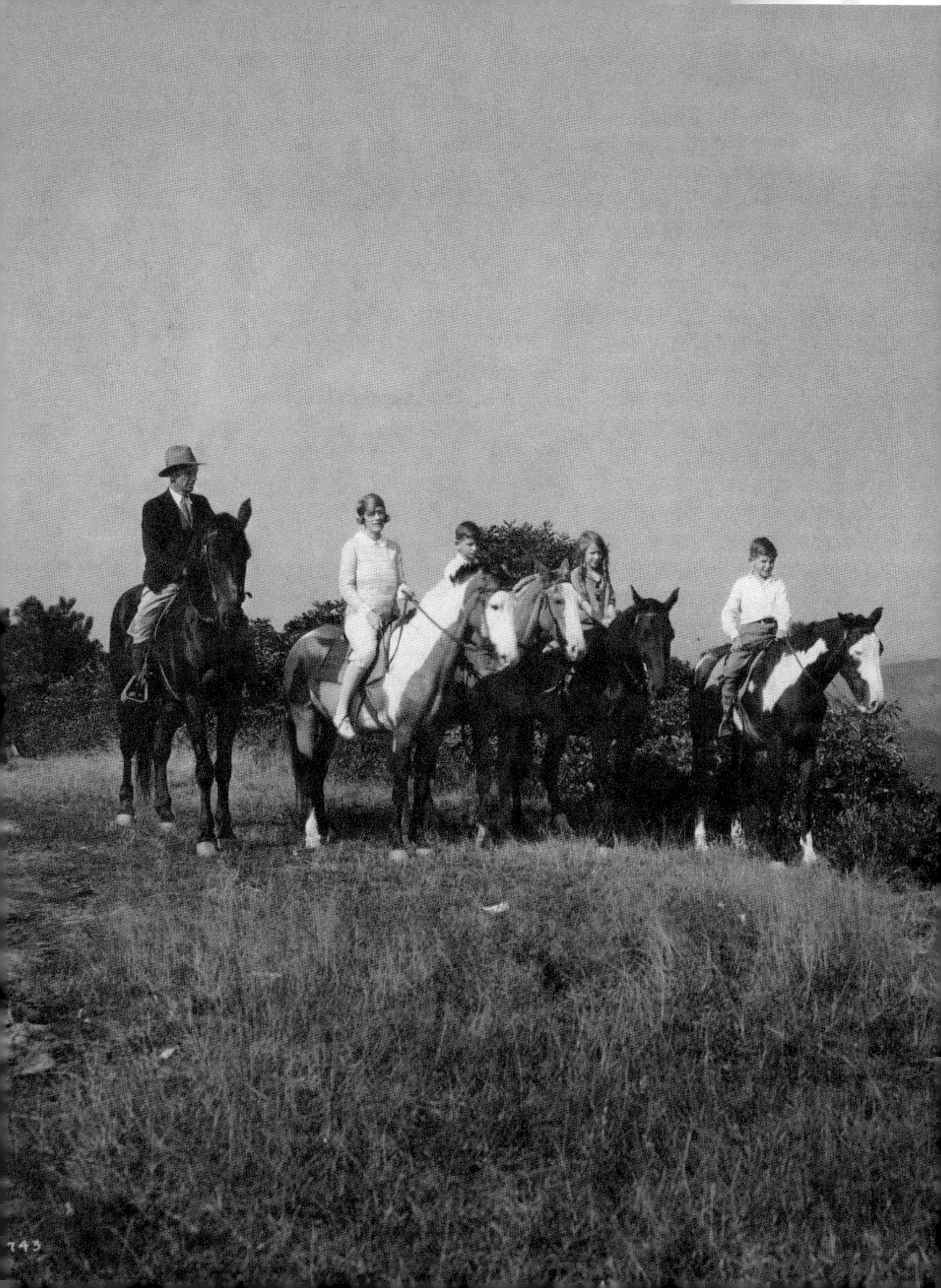

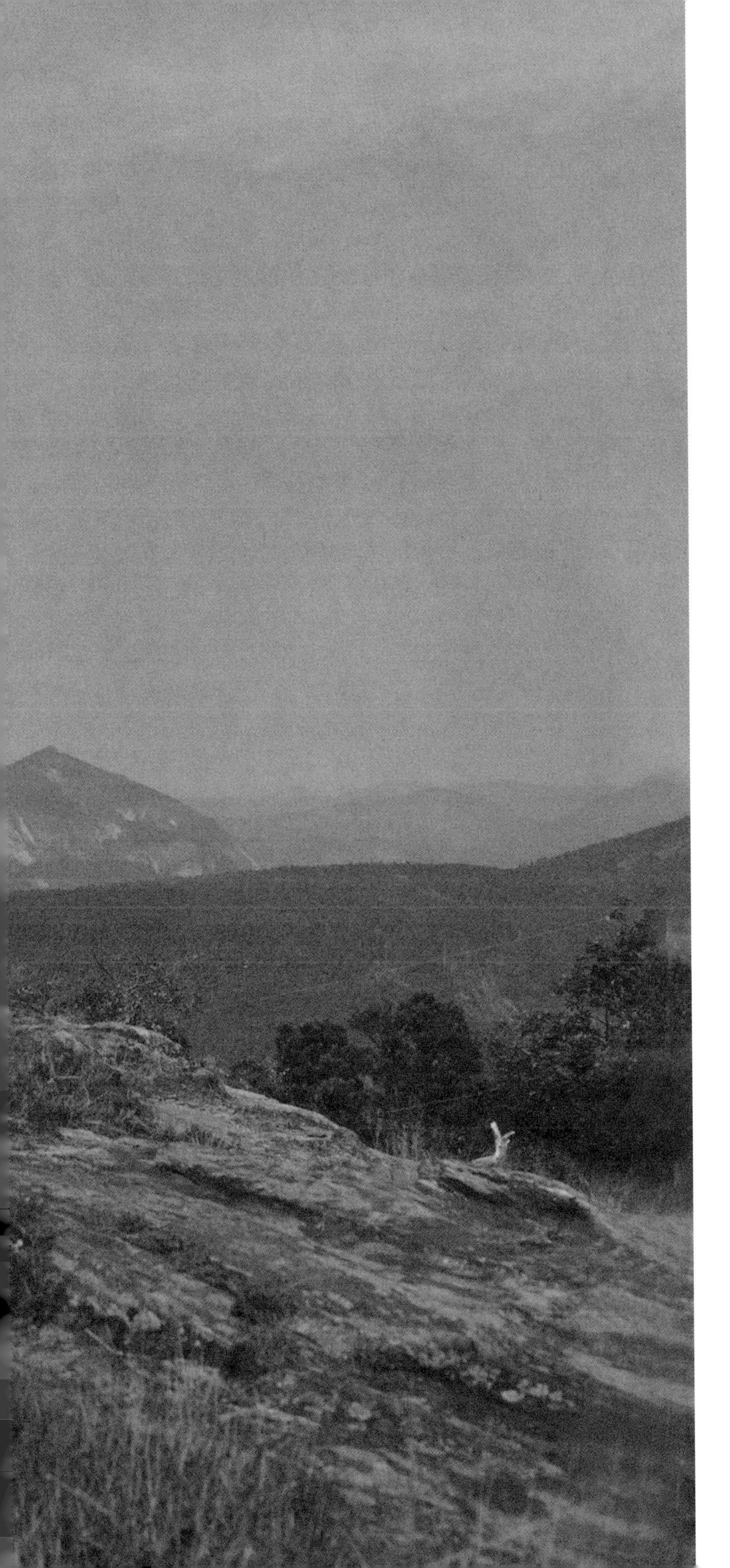

Family horseback outing,
Satulah Mountain, 1929.
Whiteside Mountain in
background (HHS)

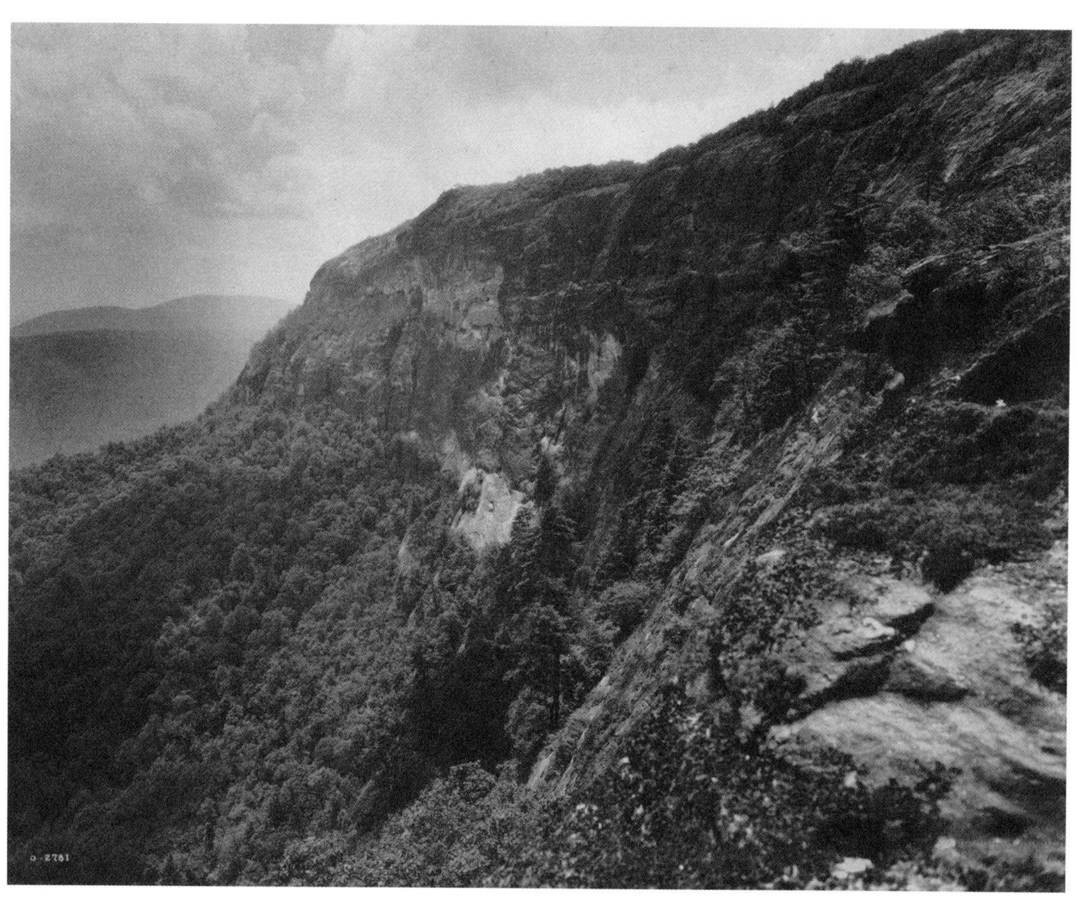

Escarpment Cliffs of Whiteside Mountain, 1929 (HHS). OPPOSITE: *Dry Falls, 1929 (HHS).*
OVER: *Looking south from Satulah Mountain into the Chattooga River watershed and to
Rabun Bald, Georgia's second highest peak (HHS).*

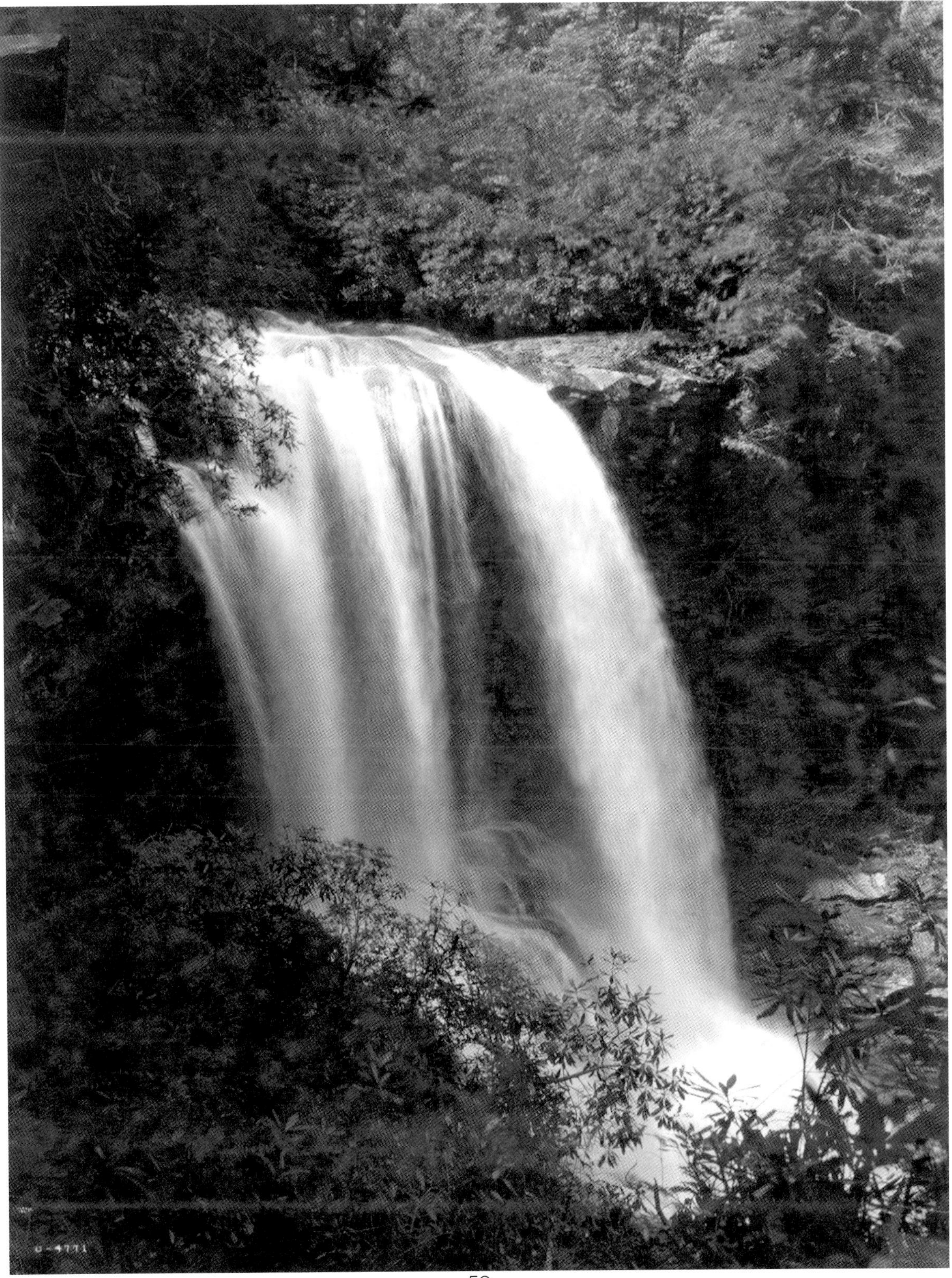

O-4719

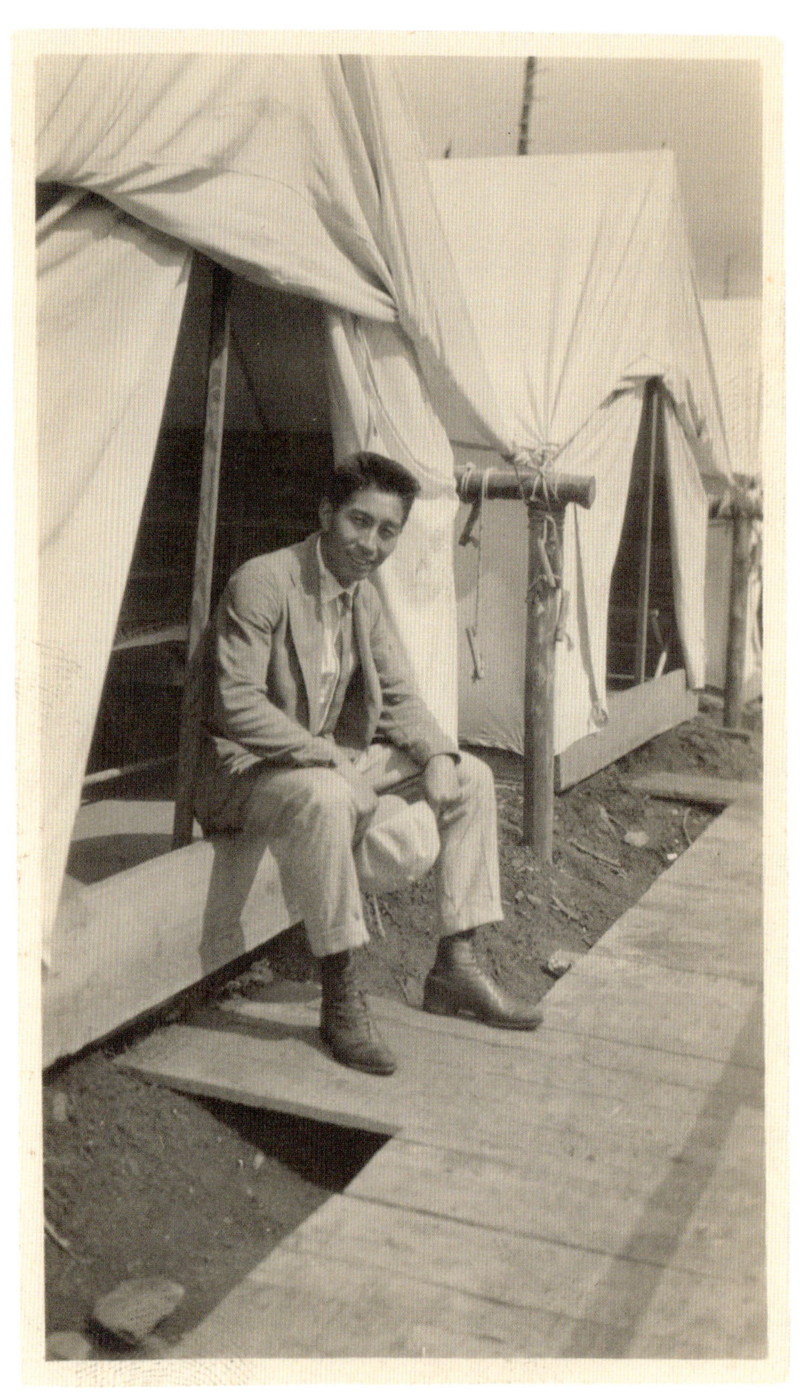

Masa at Camp Alice, c.1923

CHAPTER THREE

MOUNT MITCHELL/ BLACK MOUNTAINS

MASA SITS WELL DRESSED at the entrance to a tent cabin at Camp Alice, the end of the line for the Perley and Crockett railroad at the summit of Mount Mitchell. The year is 1924, and he is in his early forties. He looks youthful, happy, and content, unaware of how rapidly he will age and die early in the next decade. Mount Mitchell, the highest peak in the Black Mountains and eastern North America, was on its way to becoming a state park, named after botanist, geologist, professor, and Presbyterian minister Elisha Mitchell, whose controversial legacy has lingered into the twenty-first century. Mitchell, a nineteenth-century slave owner and avowed racist, was highly critical of mountain people, whom he considered degenerate and under the negative influence of the untamed wilds of western North Carolina. As a native of New England, Mitchell envisioned a similarly developed and pastoral future for the landscape. His lonely death in 1857 came from exploring the headwaters of the Cane River while trying to disprove the highly controversial claim that he was wrong in his altitude calculations of the Blacks. This claim was launched by his former student, the North Carolina congressman and successful amateur geologist Thomas Clingman. Both men envisioned development for the area, though Clingman foresaw a more industrial model largely based on mining and extraction. While much more could be said about this controversy and these two ambitious individuals, the author is grateful that they both, in large part, came out losers in their dispute.

Masa's mission at the proposed state park was to create a promotional piece—yet another project he took on while running a busy photography business, working as the official photographer for the Asheville Chamber of Commerce, exploring, promoting, and documenting the Smokies, and serving the Carolina Mountain Club in its Appalachian Trail efforts. The man is testimony to apparent boundless energy and a personal and creative life fully integrated with work. He wrote to his friend Margaret Gooch in 1931 that he "worked like hell, studied like hell, and got good reputation at present." Financial pressures seem to have been present always, particularly in the years before his death, yet he stayed true to his wild vision. When the pressures became too great, he would take off for the Smokies and lose himself in the beauty and wildness he seemed to crave, an inner drive that was well documented among his closest comrades. The map of the Smokies that hung in his office with its pinhead place markers of his travels was legendary, and testimony to his greatest love and commitment. The degree to which this ultimately contributed to his declining health is a good question.

Though his images of the Black Mountains reveal a cutover and roaded landscape, they nonetheless transcend this destruction with their power and light. Just a little over a decade earlier, logging companies had begun buying up the remaining old-growth spruce-fir in the high elevations surrounding Mount Mitchell. All of those companies were from the North and had participated in logging out the northeastern United States before turning their eyes south. Dickey and Campbell Company owned the forest surrounding the summit and in 1911 began construction of the first logging railroad in the Blacks. In 1913, Perley and Crockett Company, one of several Pennsylvania companies invested in the Blacks, purchased Dickey and Campbell and expanded the railroad up the eastern slopes of Mount Mitchell. Others followed suit, and the forests of the Black Mountains began to fall. Yet while numerous supporters of these enterprises praised the economic development that was simultaneously decimating the remaining spruce-fir forests, others began questioning the short- and long-term effects on watershed health and on the rapidly developing tourism industry.

State forester John Simcox Holmes helped pass a resolution for Mount Mitchell State Park in 1913 at the annual meeting of the North Carolina Forestry Association. The park was to be a demonstration forest where sustainable forestry and reforestation could be practiced in line with the utilitarian forestry principles of Gifford Pinchot at the Vanderbilt Estate in Asheville. North Carolina governor Locke Craig

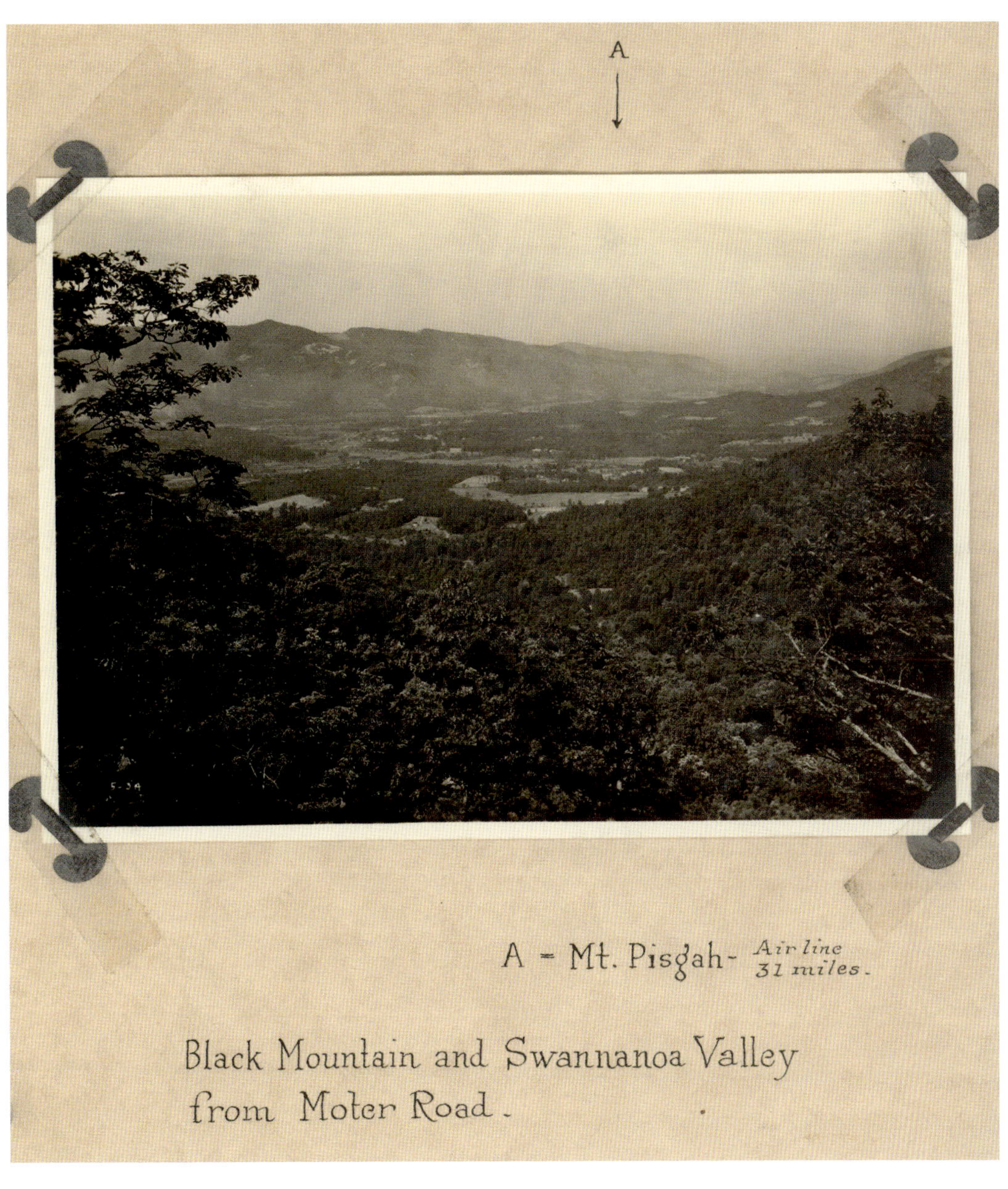

Page 1 from Masa's 1924 publication Mt. Mitchell and Views Along Mt. Mitchell Motor Road

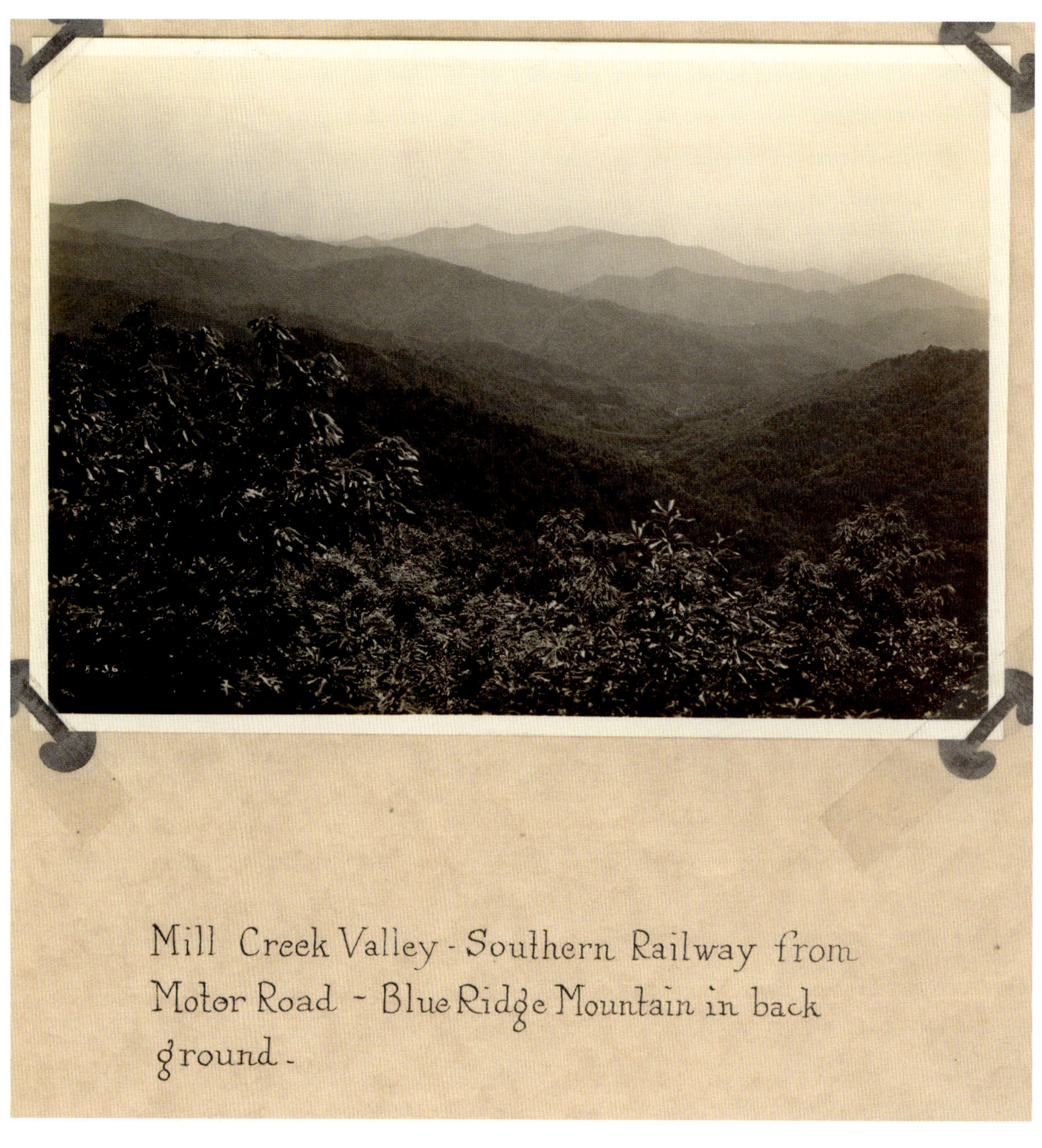

Page 2 from Masa's 1924 publication Mt. Mitchell and Views Along Mt. Mitchell Motor Road

supported the idea and, along with Holmes, brought the Asheville Board of Trade into the campaign. In 1915, the state legislature passed legislation creating the park but could not acquire timber rights. Appropriations were meager, and logging, though dwindling, continued into the twenties. At the same time, interest in the park grew. Also growing was America's automobile industry, and Perley and Crockett wasted no time in building a motor road to accommodate and create demand. Completion of the road allowed Perley and Crockett's Camp Alice to become a popular draw in the teens and twenties. Ironically, Black Mountains historian Timothy Silver points out, the camp was advertised as a respite from the modern industrial world that the railroads had brought to the mountains.

Masa's photos of the Blacks capture the totality of this transition. Though these are arguably some of his best renderings of Appalachian landscapes and light, a closer look shows devastated mountainsides, railroad lines, and motor roads. Only his views to the northeast show exceptions to this. The logging companies were pulling up stakes, having logged out most of the old growth, and a new tension was now at play between park supporters and those who saw the park's tourist infrastructure as a threat to what wildness remained. Did Masa have opinions on this? He was working on a promotional brochure for the new state park, then on its way to completion, and he appears to have been content with his progress. Here again is the indefatigable Masa, pursuing a photographic argument for a place's magnificence and preservation. The publication he completed contains some of his most striking and awe-inspiring images. Perhaps, as with the Smokies, he felt the urgency, the immediacy of the moment, and left those tussles to the public discourse he likely felt on the outside of.

When I visit Mount Mitchell State Park in November 2020, it is open to visitors, but, excepting the toilets, none of the facilities are open. At one in the afternoon, the car thermometer says thirty-five degrees, and the parking area that will easily hold a few hundred cars is empty but for a dozen or so, almost all of them with out-of-state tags—Florida, South Carolina, Illinois, Indiana, Alabama, Georgia, Wisconsin, Virginia. The sky is cloudless and exceptionally clear, with an occasional stiff breeze. A few small groups of young people mill about the parking area, along with an assortment of couples, preparing either to leave or to hike. I climb the three hundred yards from the closed visitor center to the summit in anticipation of what will be incredible views of the Black Mountains on this rare and clear autumn day. At the viewing platform, I am alone but for a group of four young women who are cutting up and huddling against the cold. A few minutes later, a young couple arrives. Although we are all sharing a special place and a special moment, no one communicates or makes eye contact. It's like the pandemic has created communication distancing as well as social. The young white male in the couple is wearing a black hoodie that says, "No Lives Matter." Behind the expression on the shirt is what appears to be a hockey mask from a horror scene. I have no idea what in the hell this means, but it doesn't feel right. I look at them, but they never look at me. I'm feeling pretty lonesome in this bare place and would love to chat, but they take selfies, then head down the ramp to the actual and physical summit.

Elisha Mitchell's large stone grave lies upon the summit, and another group of young people is hanging out there, also taking selfies and laughing among themselves. They see the NO LIVES MATTER guy and ask him to take a photo of them. I'm wondering what the sole African American male in the group is thinking when the NLM guy stands before them. When I get home and do an internet search, I see that NO LIVES MATTER is a song by the hip-hop group Body Count. It's about class and the fact that, when it comes to poor people, no lives seem to matter. I feel better. But I'm also wondering if he knows much about Elisha Mitchell. It has been only a few months since the Elisha Mitchell Audubon Chapter for this area dropped his name because of his racist views, renaming itself the Blue Ridge Audubon Chapter. The park was whites-only for many years, a racist move made by the North Carolina legislature in the 1920s. Masa would have been here during that time, and I can't help wondering how he was able to pull it off. He had plenty of white friends, and his photography was unparalleled—I'm sure that helped.

I consider hiking the trail down to old Camp Alice, where Masa stayed while photographing Mount Mitchell and the Blacks, and where the Perley and Crockett road once ended. I'd rather take the crest trail out to Mount Craig, though, so I depart the parking area into the cold spruce-fir forest. I see a few hikers when I start out but no one else on the rugged one-mile hike to the Mount Craig summit. As for birds, there are only red-breasted nuthatches making their tinny songs, and I watch two of them scrambling up and down the spruce trunks for a few minutes. Red squirrels are active, a few of them chattering and scolding me along the path. No clear-cuts or large industrial mining operations are visible in any direction. There are only forested mountains and clear, cold, blue late-afternoon skies, merged into a fantastic depth of light that only an artist such as George Masa could capture and render into magic.

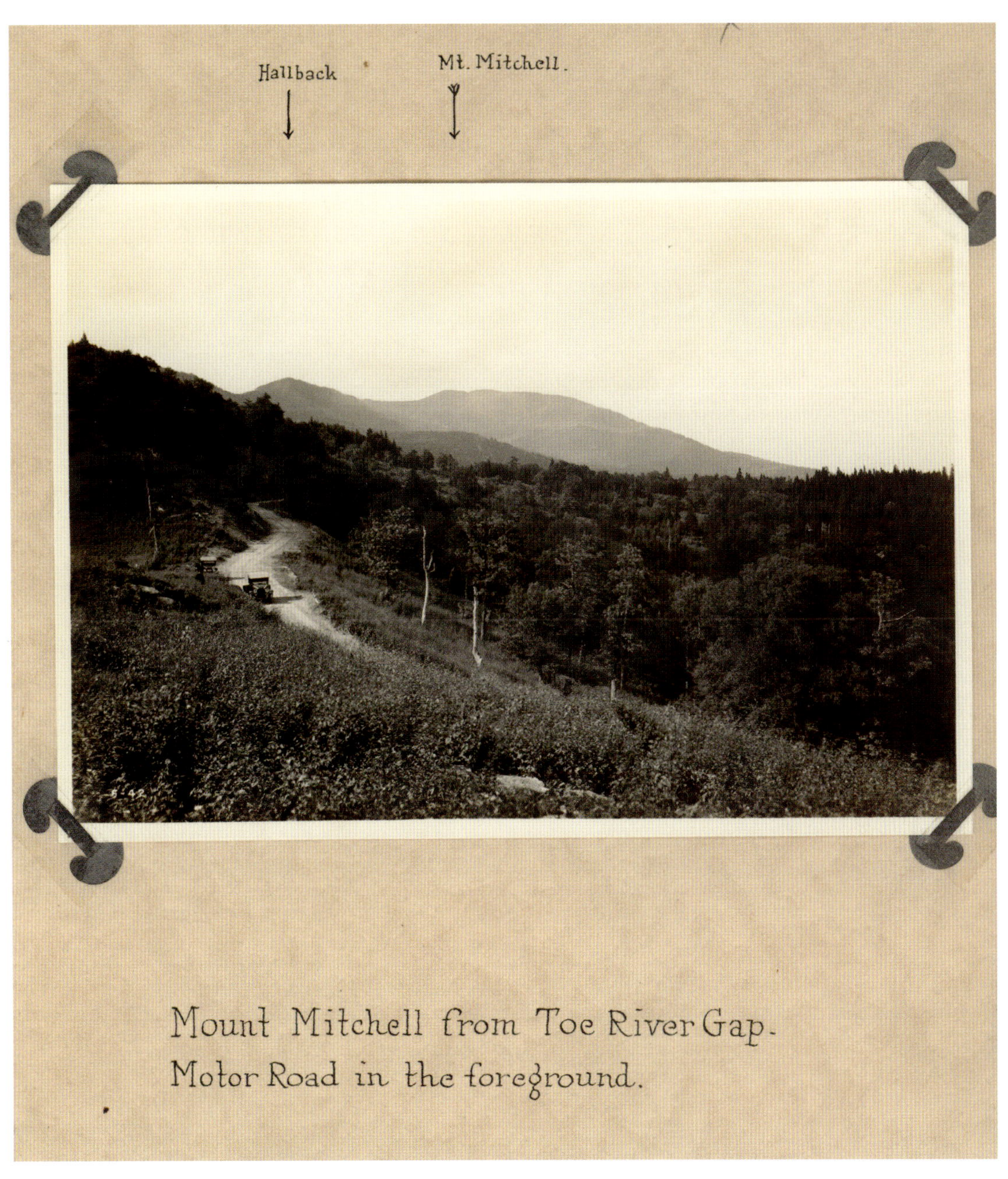

Page 3 from Masa's 1924 booklet Mt. Mitchell and Views Along Mt. Mitchell Motor Road

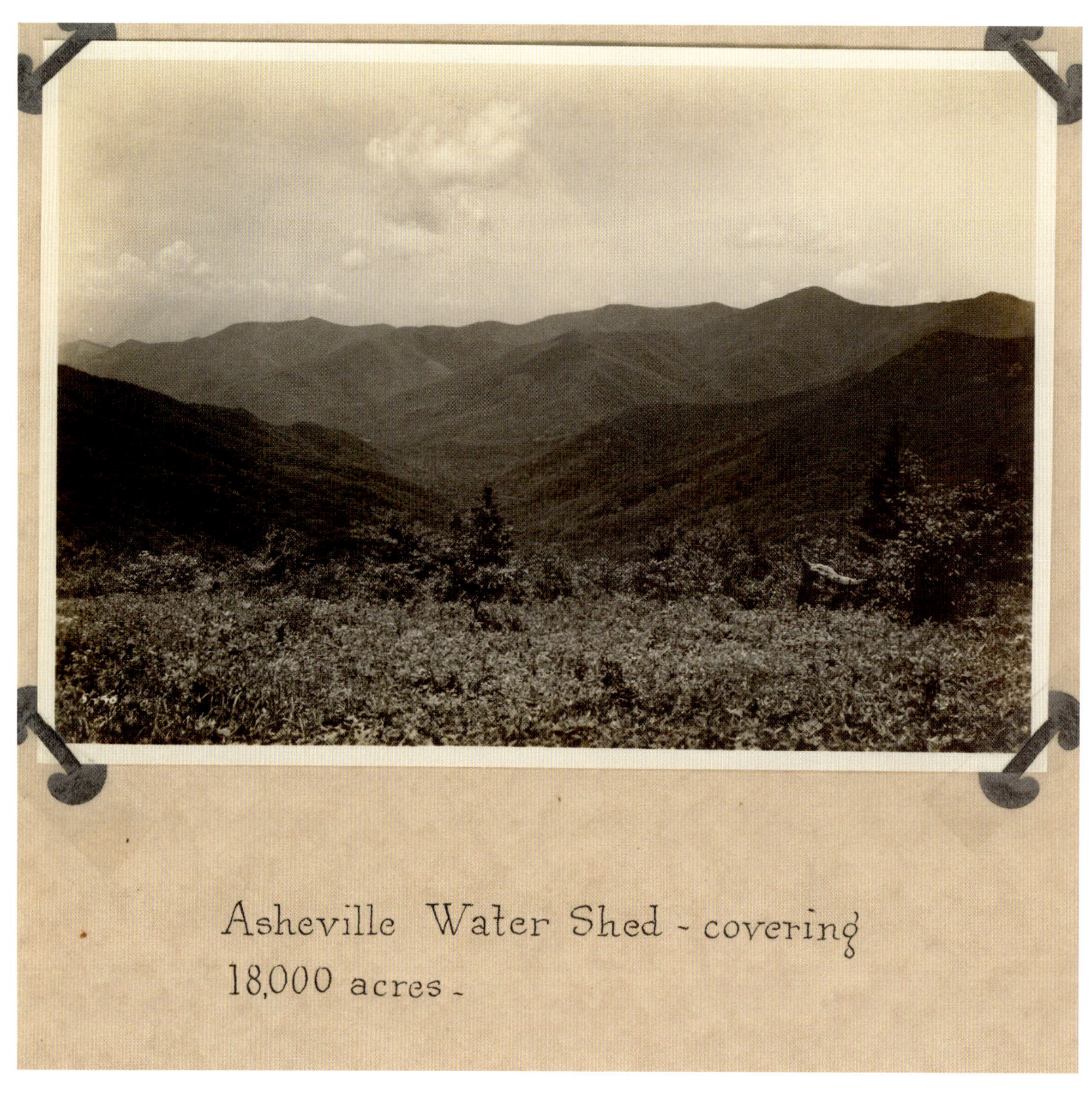

Page 5 from Masa's 1924 booklet Mt. Mitchell and Views Along Mt. Mitchell Motor Road

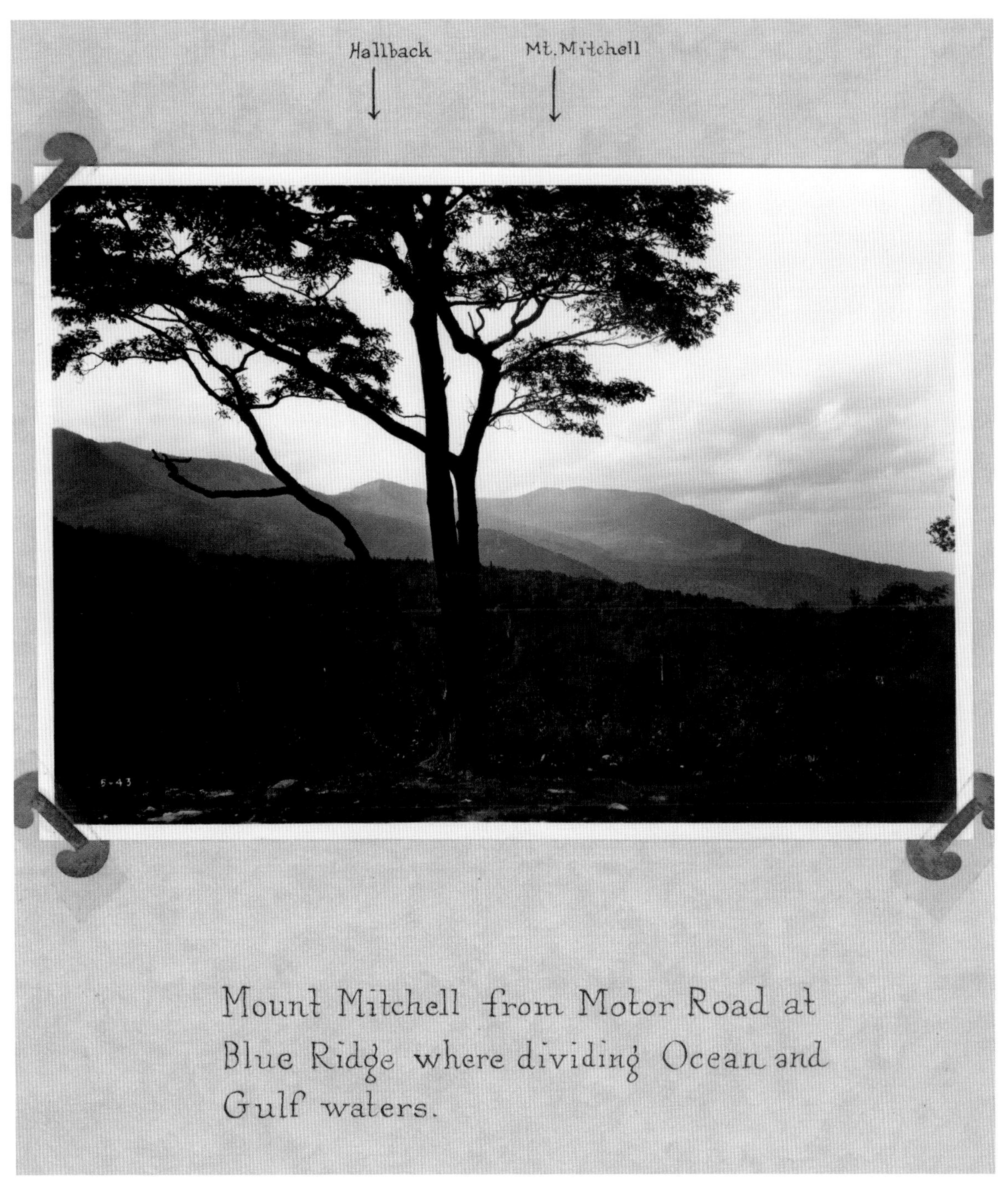

Mount Mitchell from Motor Road at
Blue Ridge where dividing Ocean and
Gulf waters.

Page 6 from Masa's 1924 booklet Mt. Mitchell and Views Along Mt. Mitchell Motor Road

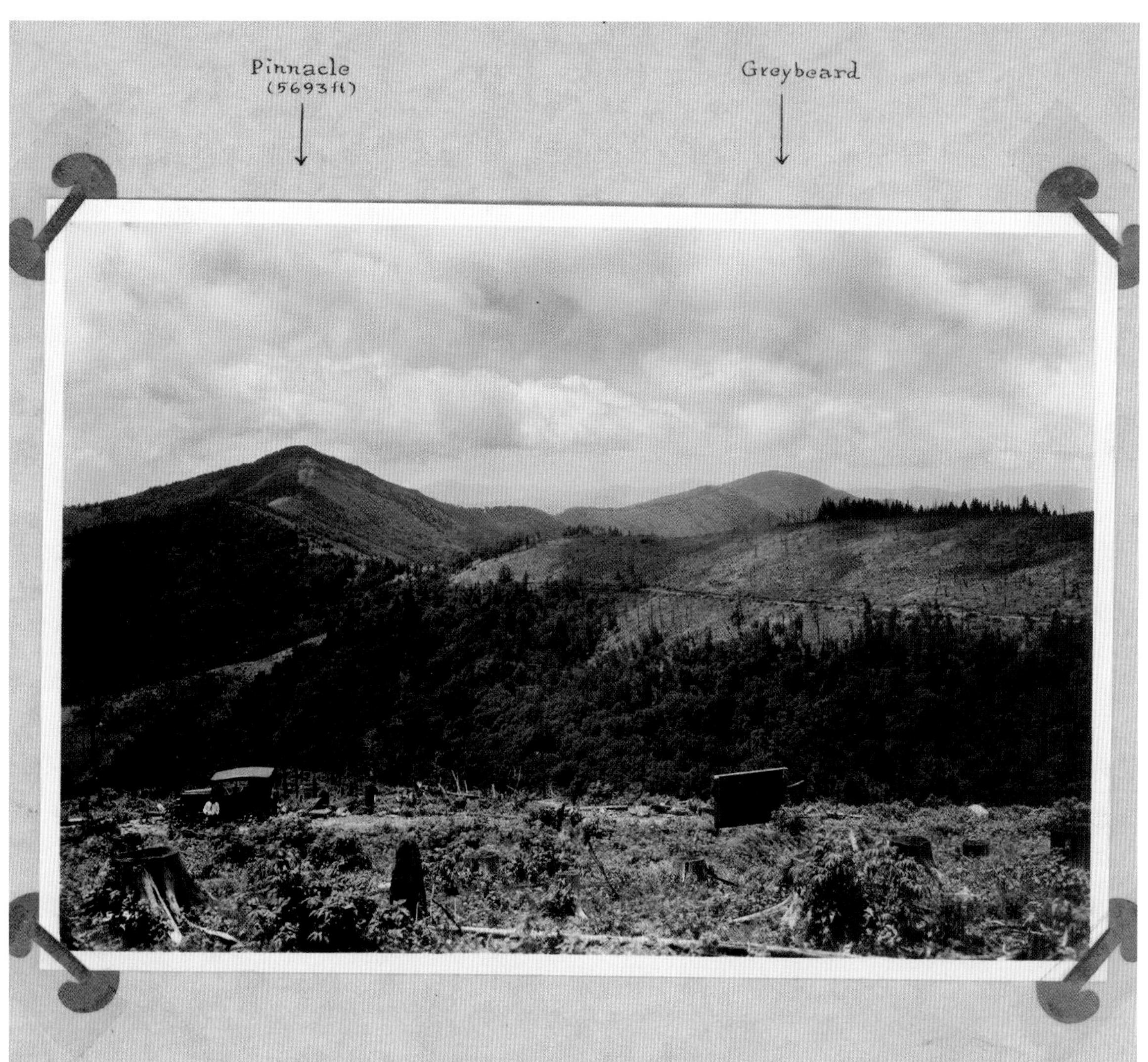

Looking toward South from Re-forest Area of
U. S. Forest Service.   Motor Road in the foreground
also in the first ridge.

Note :- The top of Pinnacle, meets three County
Line - Buncomb, McDowell and Yancey.

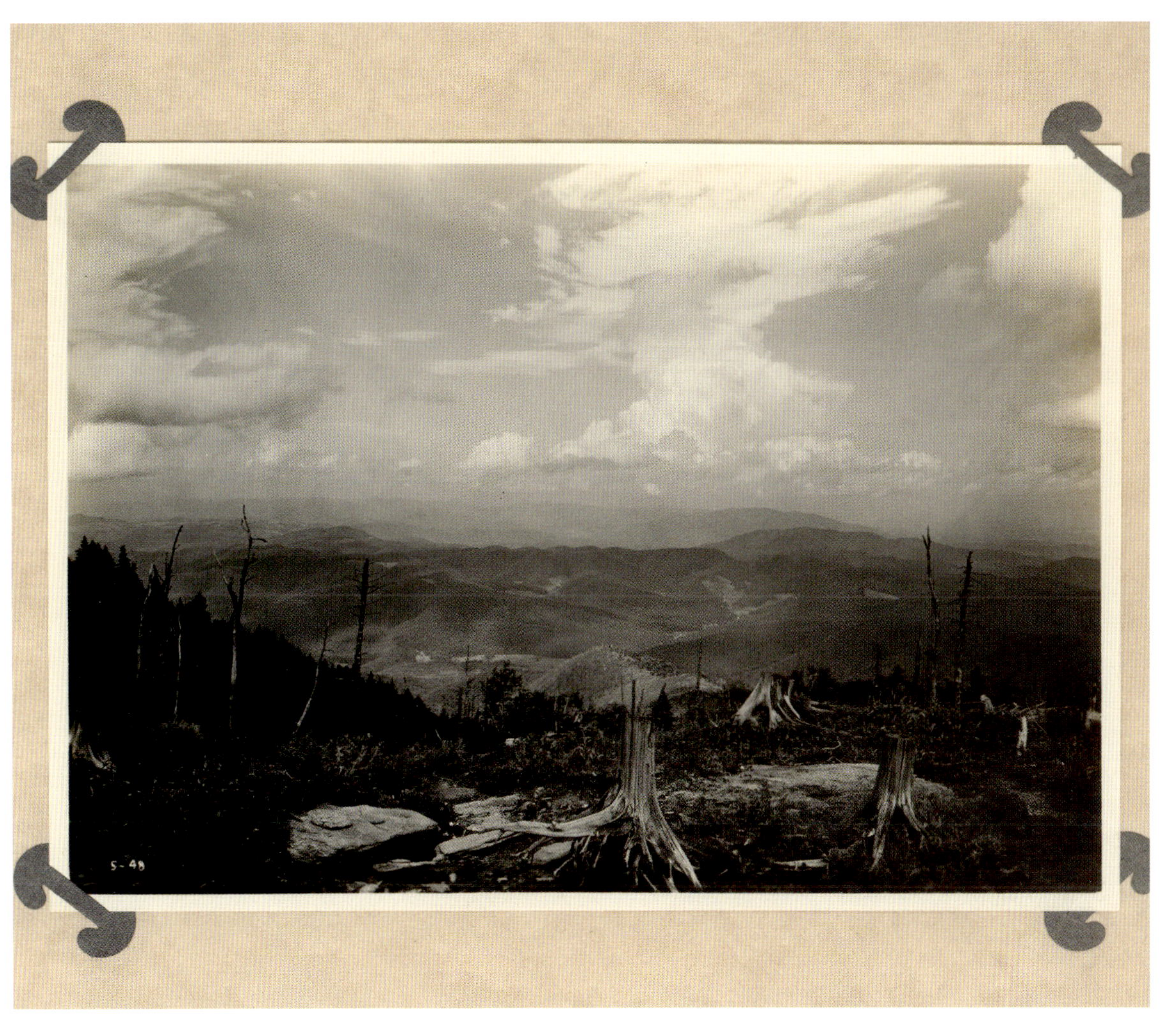

OPPOSITE AND ABOVE: *Pages 8 and 13 from Masa's 1924 booklet*
Mt. Mitchell and Views Along Mt. Mitchell Motor Road

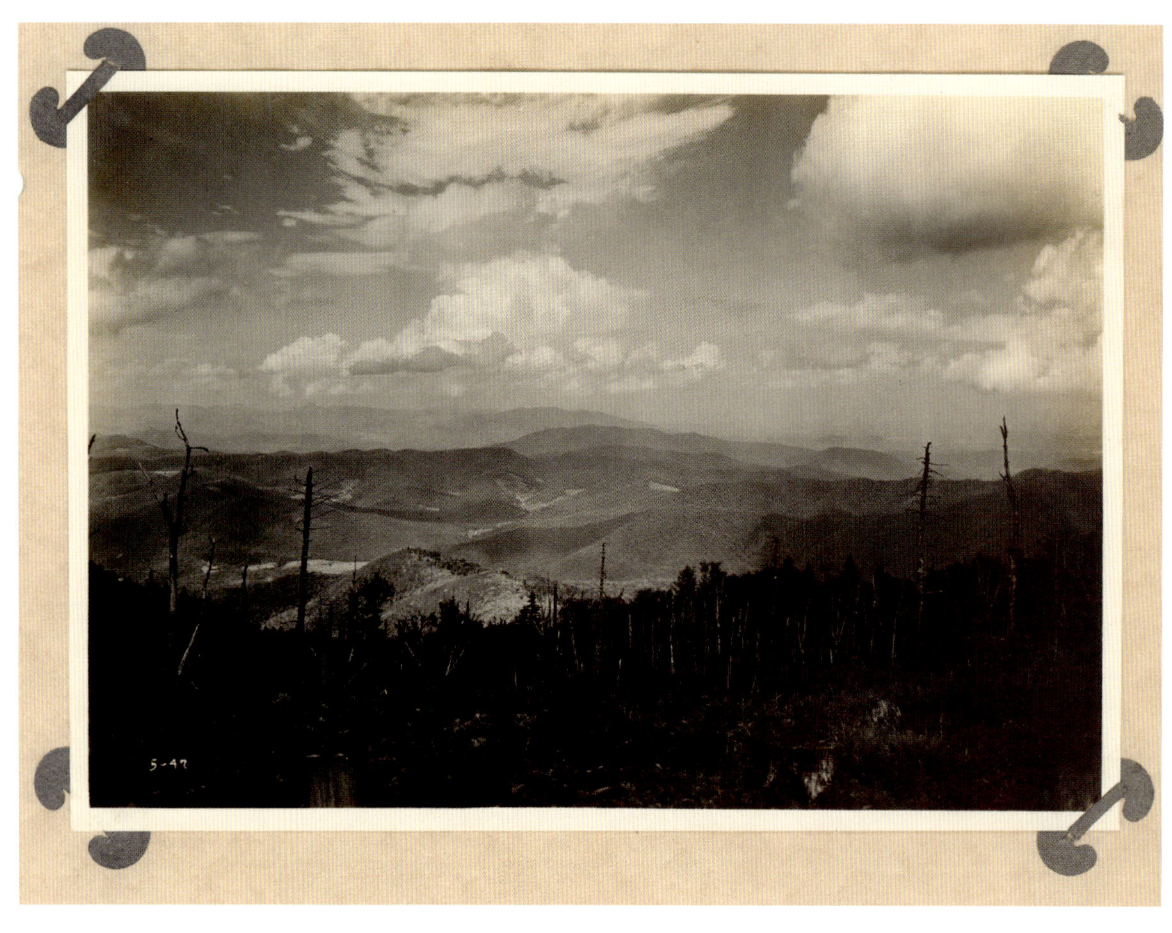

ABOVE AND OPPOSITE: *Pages 14 and 15 from Masa's 1924 booklet*
Mt. Mitchell and Views Along Mt. Mitchell Motor Road

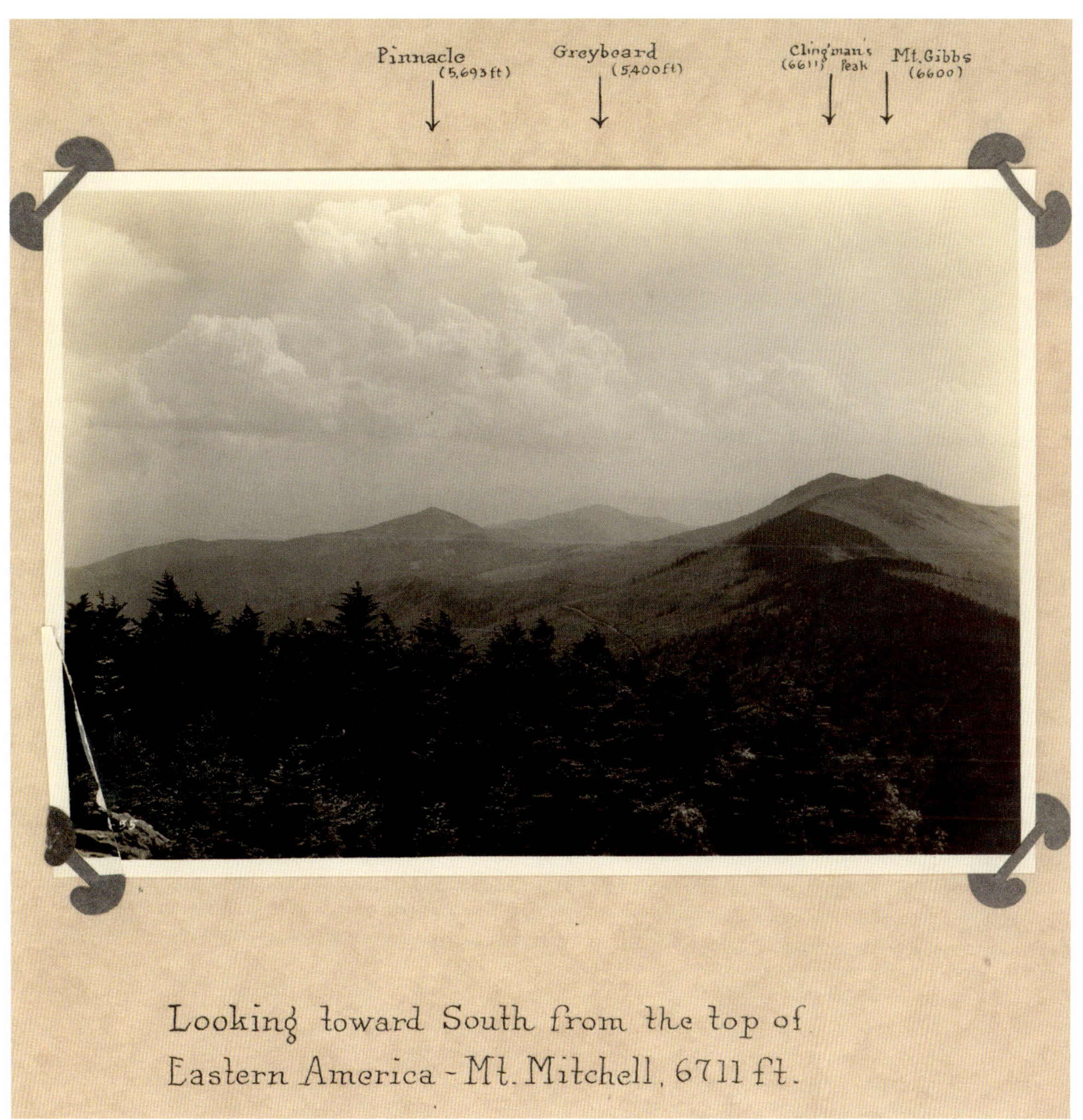

Looking toward South from the top of Eastern America - Mt. Mitchell, 6711 ft.

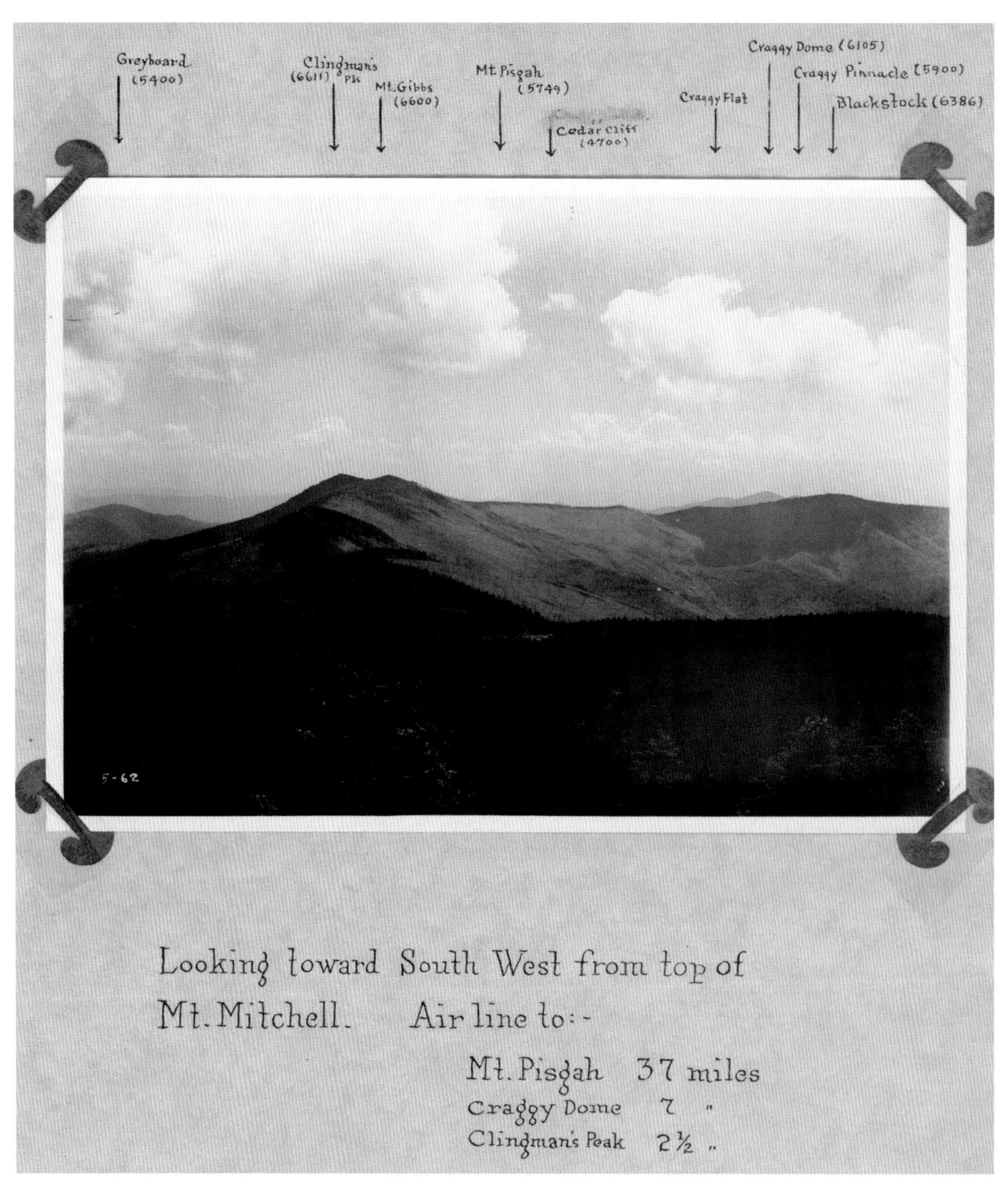

ABOVE AND OPPOSITE: *Pages 16 and 21 from Masa's 1924 booklet*
Mt. Mitchell and Views Along Mt. Mitchell Motor Road

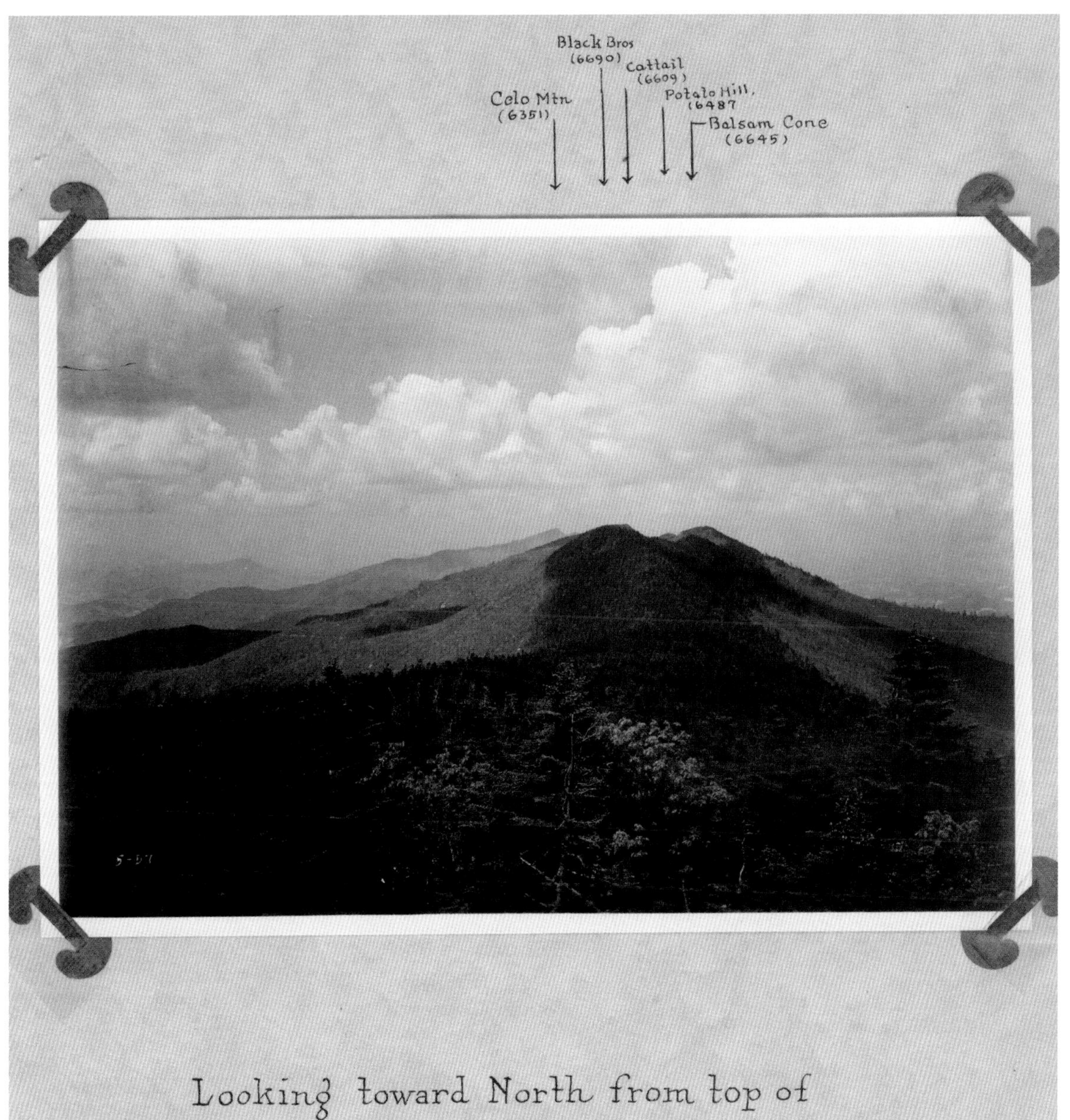

Looking toward North from top of
Mt. Mitchell.   Black Bros - (6690-6620) only
21 feet lower than Mt. Mitchell.

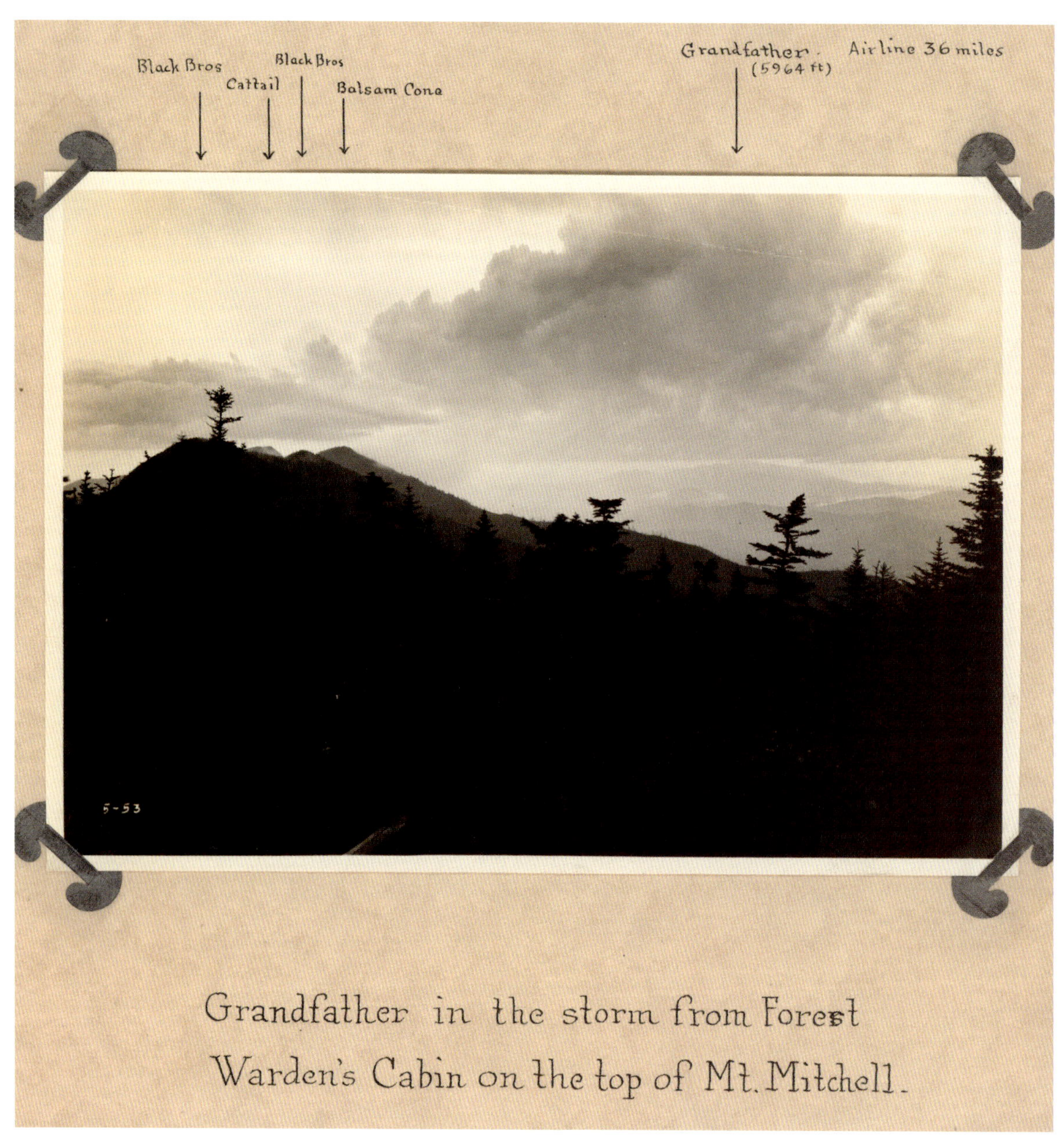

Grandfather in the storm from Forest Warden's Cabin on the top of Mt. Mitchell.

ABOVE AND OPPOSITE: *Pages 23 and 25 from Masa's 1924 booklet*
Mt. Mitchell and Views Along Mt. Mitchell Motor Road

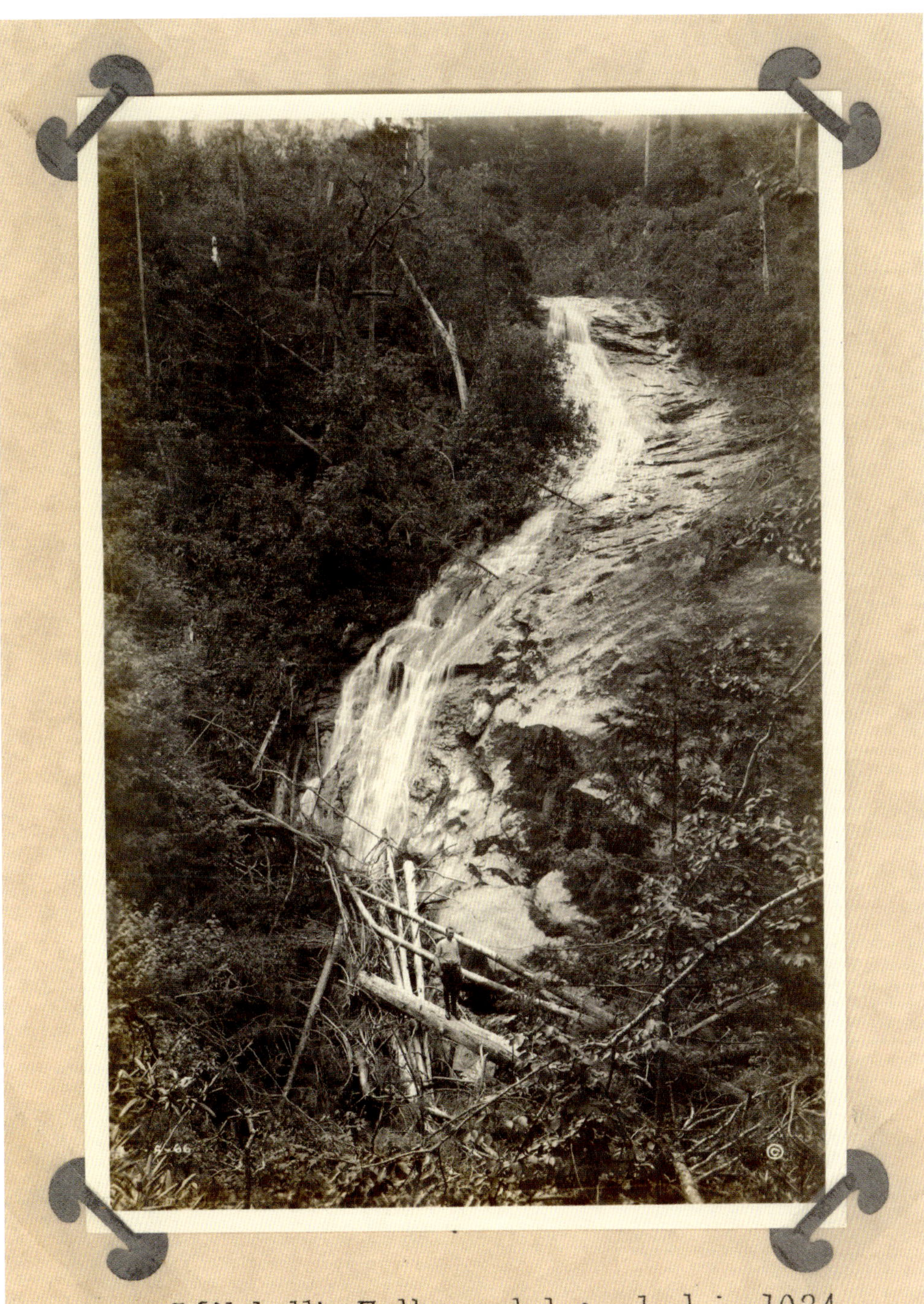

Mitchell's Falls - photographed in 1924,
67 years after Dr. Mitchell lost his life.

CAROLINA MOUNTAIN CLUB

TRIP REPORT

Trip Name ___Mitchell Falls.___________________________ Date __March 27, 1932.__

Mileage of round trip; By car___99.7___miles; Afoot___4.8___miles; X By wheel By Pedo Estimated

Time required: By car___2.___hours one way; Afoot___4___hours (total)

Departure: From Asheville__8;15 A.M.___ From car __10:15__ reach Fall 12:

Arrival: At car __2:30________ At Asheville __6:00 P.M.___

Members___________Visitors _____________

Trip register: (get signature if possible) LEADER___George Masa,_____________

Jewel King,	Barbara Ambler,	Margret Allen,
Lydia Beck,	Sue Latimar,	Julia Nevercel,
Dorthy Collin	Dr. O. C. Barker,	Roger Morrow,
L. D. Roger,	Marion Roger,	

Motor Log: (Asheville to point of leaving car)   Leaving Arcade Bldg follows N.C. 20 - 69, at 6.3 N.C.20 turn to left, follow N.C.69 thru Weaverville at 9.3m. At 13.9 junction N.C.695 turn to right follow N.C.695, at 20.5 m Barnardsville, at 30.35 Little Cane River Gap on county line, at 35.9 m highway sharp turn to left, make right turn leave highway follow dirt road at 38.5 m. Wilson's toll gate, follow Motor Road, at 39.2 leave motor road turn in left at 39.6 m. parked car.

Return:- 0.0 Wilson's toll gate, at 2.6m junction #695, follows highway at 3.9 m Pensacola, at 6.2 m Dixen P.O. right, at 13.65 m. junction # 69 turn to left, follows # 69, at 14.3 m. Burnsville, at 25.9 Ivy Gap, at 38.1 County line Big Ivy, at 40.6 junction #695, at 54.9 Asheville.
Note: Highway 695 not recommend wet or rainy day.

Trail Log: Parking place at 0.0 m. at 0.3 one trail at right, go straight following logging railroad grade, at 0.4 m. cross Oges Creek, at 0.52 railroad grade turn to right, at 0.72 old shack at left, at 1.0 m. cross Timber Creek, trail quite steep going up, not so well beaten, watch blazed marks on trees, at 1.73 cross Branch, at 1.94 cross Branch again, at 2.4 Mitchell Falls.   Big Poplar Tree - from Parking place cross Sugar Camp Creek about ¼ m. Datas obtained from Appalachian Forest Experiment Station as following;-

Circumference at breast height on the contour	25.3 ft
Height to point where broken off	105.0 ft
Total height	132.0 ft
Height to forks	75.0 ft.

Comparing to Reems Creek Big Poplar.

Masa's Carolina Mountain Club trip report, Mitchell Falls, March 27, 1932.
OPPOSITE: *Original stone observation tower on Mt. Mitchell.*

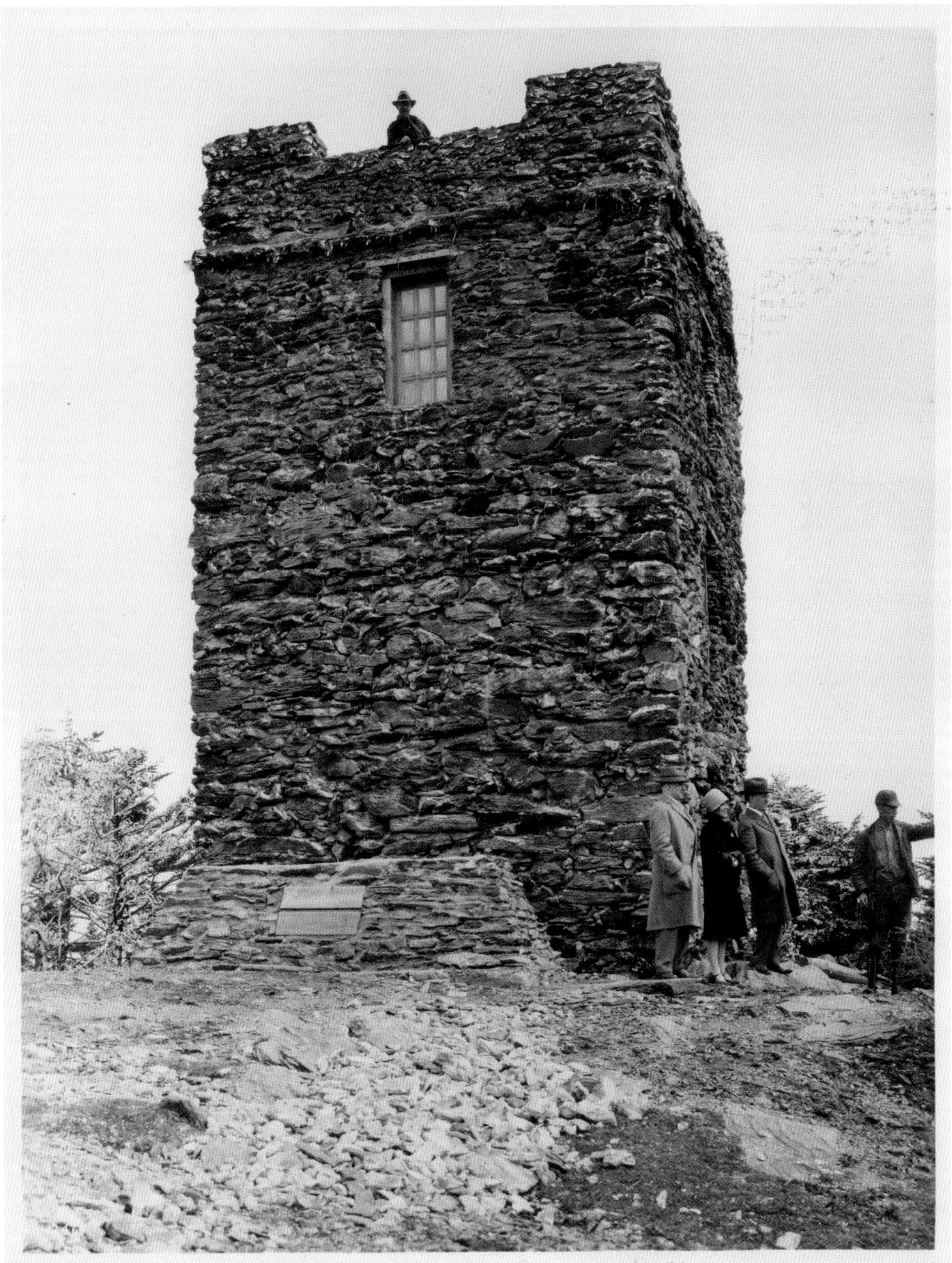

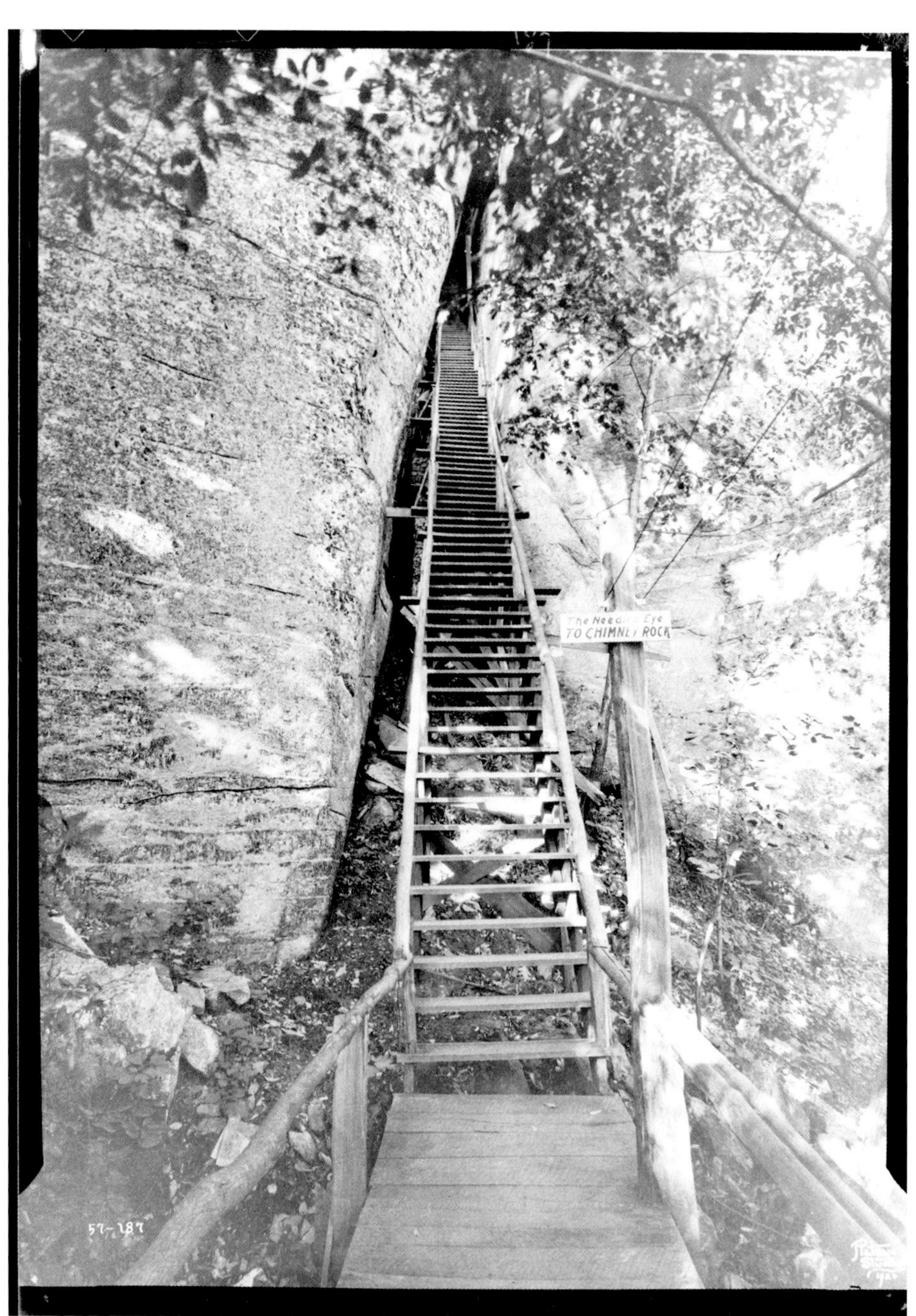

The Needle's Eye to Chimney Rock

CHAPTER FOUR

CHIMNEY ROCK/ HICKORY NUT GORGE

LIKE ALL OTHER western North Carolina landscapes that Masa photographed, Hickory Nut Gorge in 1921 was a place of transition. This remote and rugged gorge had fascinated the public for many years with its fabled ghost stories and Cherokee legends, along with its many stunning natural features, and was well on its way to becoming a major tourist destination and resort when Masa arrived. The route up the gorge, a major Native American trade path, was considered sacred ground by the Cherokees and Catawbas, who forbade killing and warfare there. It became the Rutherford Trace after the brutal suppression and removal of native people and the arrival of early American settlers in the eighteenth century. Nineteenth-century travel writer Charles Lanman published one of the earliest known written descriptions of the area in 1848, remarking that the gorge seemed destitute of its namesake tree. Lanman noted the numerous cliffs and waterfalls but added that "leaving these remarkable features entirely out of the question, the mountain scenery in this vicinity is as beautiful and fantastic as any I have yet witnessed among the Alleghanies [*sic*]. At a farmhouse near the gap, where I spent a night, I had the pleasure of meeting an English gentleman and tourist, and he informed me that, though he had crossed the Alps in a number of places, yet he had never seen any mountain scenery which he thought as beautiful as that of the Hickory Nut Gap."

The area is loaded with old ghost stories, one of the most famous dating back to July 1806, when members of the Reaves family and others saw thousands of angel-like shining beings around the summit of Chimney Rock, from which they eventually ascended into the heavens. The story was big enough to make the *Raleigh Register and Gazette.* Several years later, in 1811, numerous witnesses saw two large opposing armies of cavalry circling one another high in the sky for several evenings, until the armies clashed in battle and vanished into the sky. In February 1874, a series of loud rumblings began to plague the area, a phenomenon that lasted for six months. Scientists theorized that rocks were shaking loose from a series of underground cave systems during this time, but local people feared it was the end of the world, due largely to claims a local minister made that he had prayed for the mountain to rumble to wake sinners from their godless stupor.

In 1902, tuberculosis patient Dr. Lucius B. Morse purchased the iconic Chimney Rock and the surrounding sixty-four acres from Jerome Freeman for five thousand dollars, having fallen in love with the place after traveling there by horseback from Hendersonville. Freeman had purchased the tract as part of a four-hundred-acre parcel a decade earlier for a mere twenty-five dollars from a land speculator. Morse's purchase included the primary attractions of today's park, which became the anchor for growing his vision into a private park and creating Lake Lure and the town of that name. With the financial backing of his brothers, Morse formed Chimney Rock Mountains Inc. During the early 1900s, the company purchased eight thousand acres of what was to become the town of Lake Lure and the lake of that name. Carolina Mountain Power Company, of which Chimney Rock Mountains Inc. owned all the stock, began construction of the lake in 1925. In the process, the town of Buffalo, a stopping point on the old drovers' road to Asheville, was flooded over, and residents of what was known as Whiteside Valley were relocated. The town of Lake Lure was incorporated in 1927, and the development of the resort community continued in earnest until the market crash of 1929. The two mortgage companies that backed the effort foreclosed on Chimney Rock Mountains Inc., forming Lureland Realty and selling off all of Chimney Rock's eight thousand acres over the next decade.

When Masa first visited the area, there was little in the way of infrastructure, and his images are startling contrasts to the park and valley today. The bridge across the Rocky Broad River to access Chimney Rock was only five years old, and the trail system and stairways that allowed him to access the various lookout points on the tract had only recently been built by a local, Guilford Nanney. Over the years, Morse and his brothers purchased almost a thousand acres to add to Chimney Rock Park, which remained private until 2007, when the state of North Carolina purchased it

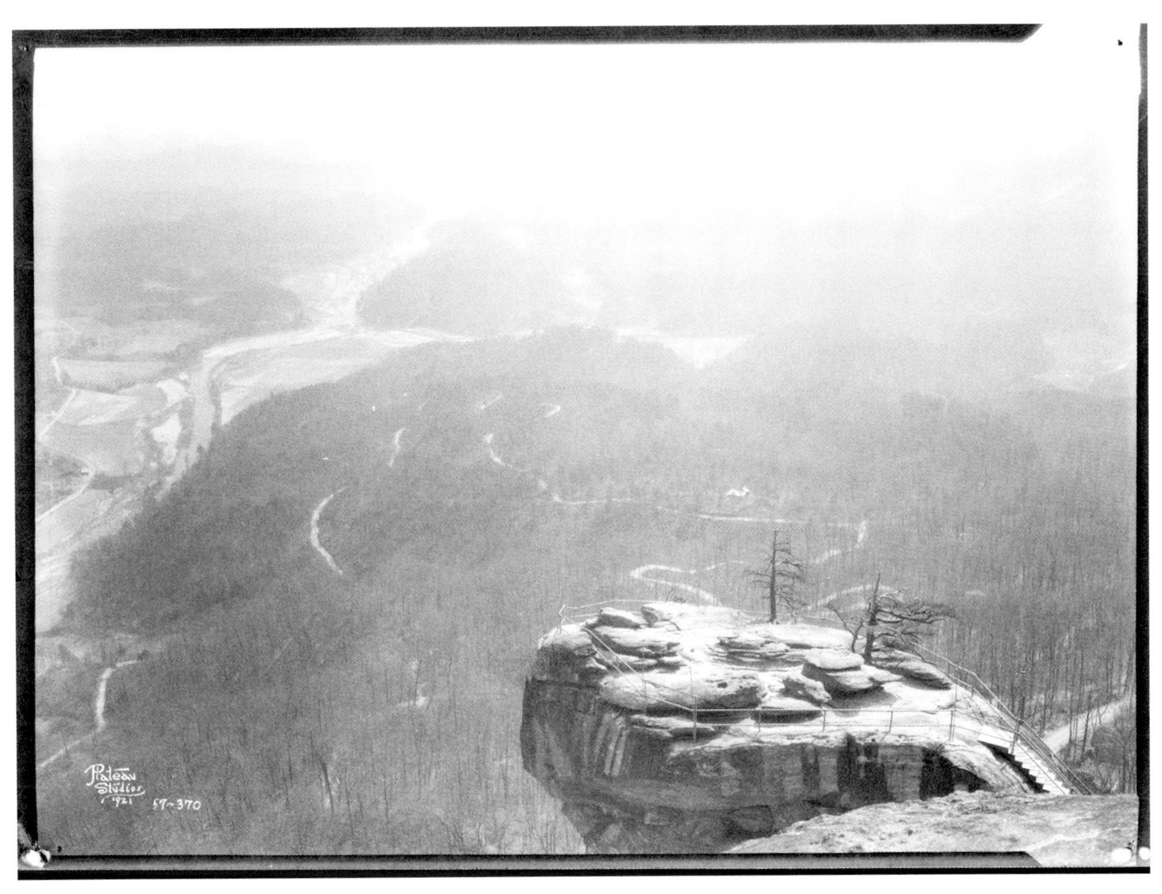

Chimney Rock, 1921

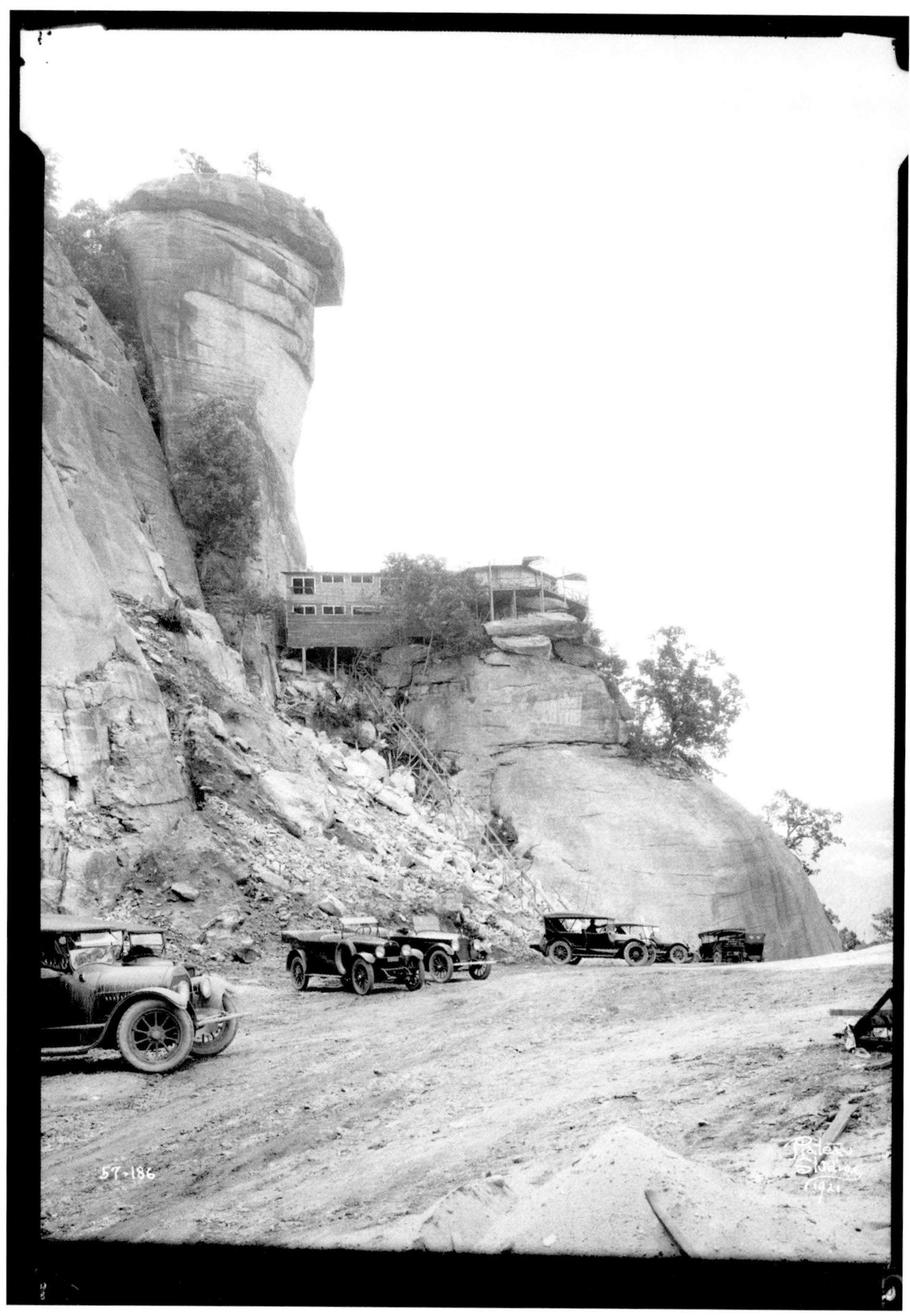

Original unpaved parking area, Chimney Rock Park

for $24 million and made it part of the newly christened Chimney Rock State Park. The Morse family began an extensive development plan in 1946 with the blasting of a 198-foot-long tunnel to create a 258-foot-tall elevator shaft, an effort that required eight tons of dynamite and eighteen months. The elevator to Chimney Rock opened to the public in 1949, followed soon by the Sky Lounge snack bar and gift shop and a three-mile-long paved road and parking area. Morse's descendants continued the improvements over the decades, and today—due largely to the efforts of the Carolina Mountain Land Conservancy, the Nature Conservancy, and other partners—the park is over eight thousand acres.

We are left to wonder over Masa's visit, or visits, to Chimney Rock and Hickory Nut Gorge. Was he seeking work to promote the park, or was he only visiting due to his innate sense of curiosity and wonder? Maybe it was his postcard business, as hand-colored photos of the area, including post-impoundment Lake Lure, were printed by Asheville Postcard Company. These are currently housed at Pack Memorial Library in Asheville.

IT'S APRIL 2021, and I cannot believe it costs seventeen dollars per adult to get into a state park. I grumble a bit to my wife, Angela, pay the price, collect my small, folded map of the park, and drive the paved three miles that Masa would have traveled back when it was a rough gravel road. The gravel parking area that Masa photographed in 1921 is now much larger, paved, and fuller than I expected it to be. It's spring break for a lot of kids, though, and as we prepare to exit the car, we watch layered and fleece-clad families marching toward the gift shop and bathroom area, a crowded gauntlet we must pass through to access the trails and views. A blast of cold weather has arrived after a week of paradisal warmth, and it's thirty-seven degrees at ten in the morning as we begin our walk up the multiple flights of stairs from the rapidly filling lot. I thought we'd be the only fools out walking at these exposed elevations on April Fools' Day, when gusts of up to fifty miles per hour and highs in the forties were predicted. The cold wind that greets us is as stunning as a Masa photograph, making this one day from the past year when I am happy to be wearing a mask. The sky is perfectly clear as we proceed up the more than eight hundred stairs that will take us to Chimney Rock and beyond it to Exclamation Point.

As at all of the popular park settings I've been in during the pandemic, I'm struck by the variety of languages I hear from groups and couples. I'm guessing that many of these people are from European and Asian countries. The CDC's only requirements at present are that a COVID test be taken three days prior to entering the United States and that a negative test result be shown upon arrival. Numerous Hispanic families are also here, going between English and Spanish with their children, and this diversity of people lifts me up. The other pandemic—anti-immigrant and racist—is far from over, and perhaps all of us are here in some way because nature seems like a safe place from such insidious behavior. There's been an increase in violence against Asians and Asian Americans in recent weeks, beginning with the massage parlor shootings in the Atlanta area. Masa's Japanese heritage is not lost on me as we encounter a Japanese family outside the bathroom. Despite what I consider to be overdevelopment, I'm glad there is such access and freedom and a measure of security in such a place.

When we get to Chimney Rock, the wind is fierce, but we climb the stairs out to it anyway. A bit of vertigo hits as I look down between the slats to the distant ground. Several people are bumping around in the wind, and I find a large rock to sit down in front of while Angela wanders the perimeter. It feels dangerous. Below me is all of Lake Lure, the busy tourist town and the blue-green lake spread like a flattened serpent upon the land. Neither of these is in Masa's photographs, only the free-flowing Rocky Broad River making its unimpeded course toward the Atlantic and a few small communities spread down the valley. I wonder if he ever tried to forecast the future as he stood in these vast wild places so quickly and easily tamed. His photograph from the summit of the rock is in winter, a forest of bare trees revealing the three-mile gravel road that wound its way to the parking area. I have found no reference by Masa to Chimney Rock in the sources I've accessed at the University of North Carolina Asheville and Western Carolina University and am left to wonder who he was here with, if anyone, and why.

After Chimney Rock, we climb toward Exclamation Point, losing people by the dozens as we ascend. The elevator is shut down, and the climb to Chimney Rock is more than enough for most folks. We can now stop to look at blooming plants and shrubs and listen to black-throated green warblers singing in the cedars and Table Mountain pines. We stop to talk to a trail guide along the way, and she tells us there is a chance we can see peregrine falcons from Peregrine Point, another half-mile past Exclamation. She also tells us that the occasional small trees blooming with brilliant pink flowers, which I am thinking are some rare endemic not native to my local mountains, are peach trees growing from tossed pits. At Exclamation Point, where I think Masa must have photographed Hickory Nut Gorge, the wind is so strong and

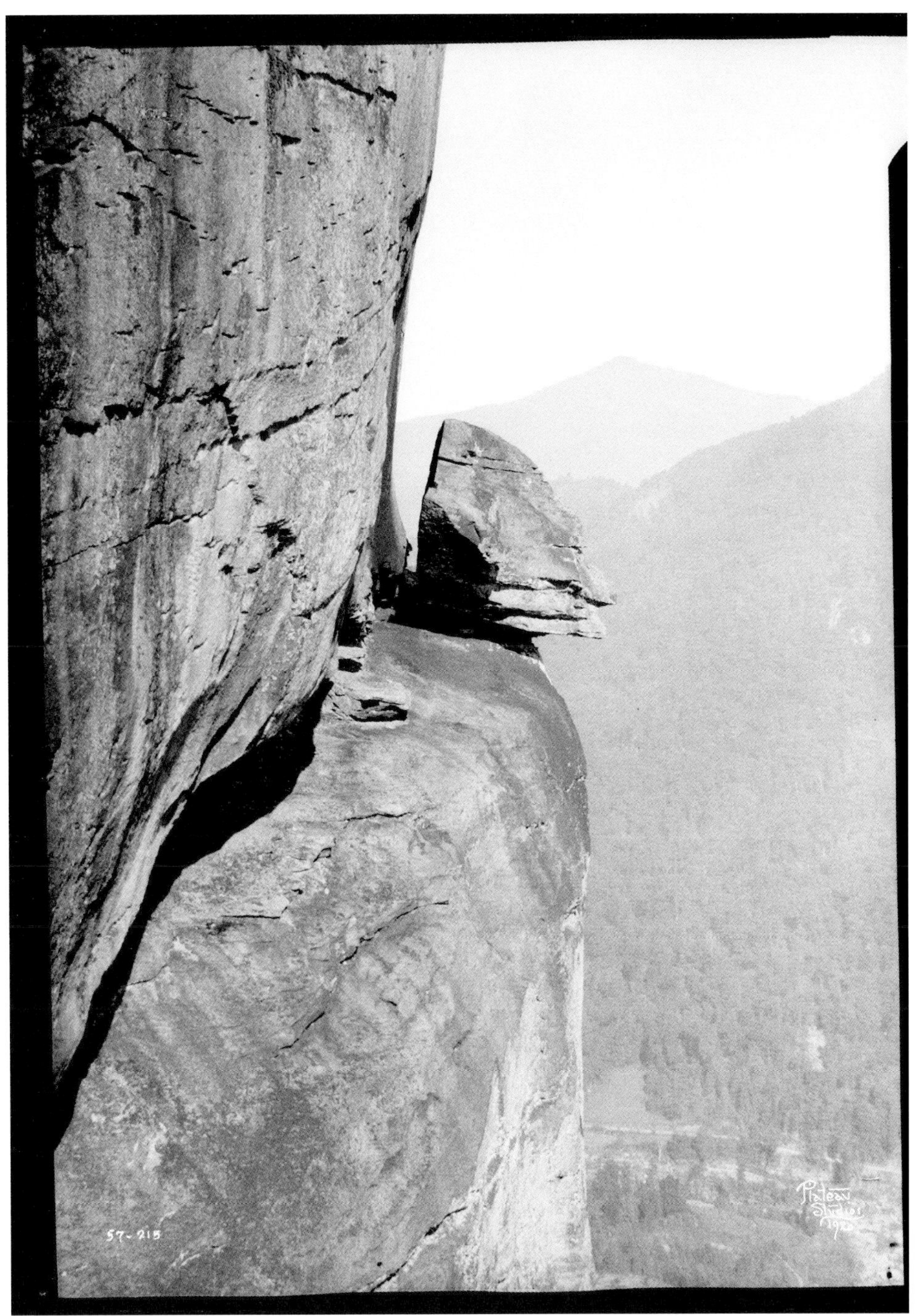

Devil's Head, Chimney Rock Park

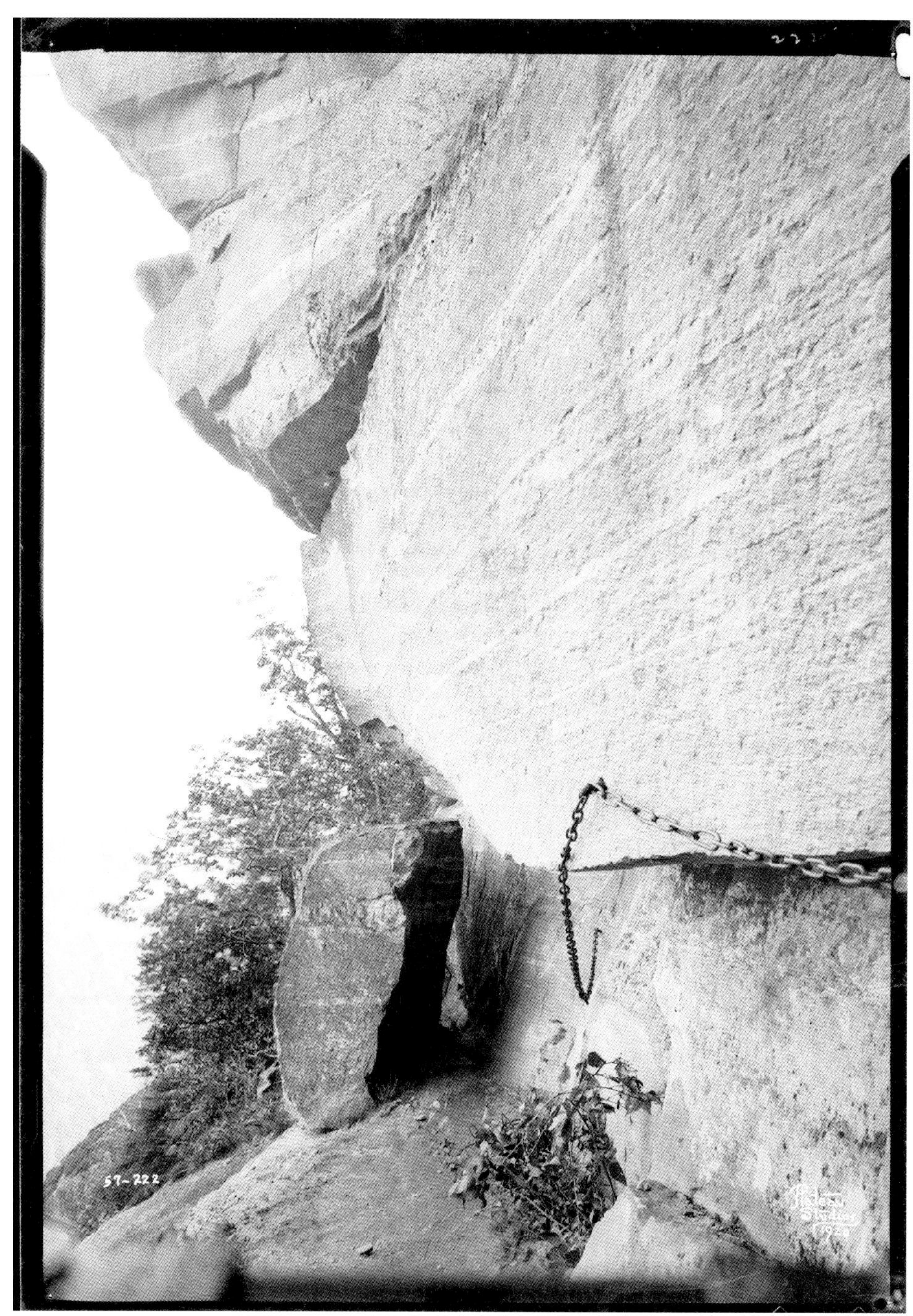

Before there were guardrails, there were chains.

cold that we cannot stay exposed more than a few minutes, so we move on into the forest and toward Peregrine Point. At Peregrine Point, no peregrines. The wind is ferocious here as well, and instead of walking another mile to the top of Hickory Nut Falls, we decide to walk back down to the Sky Lounge for a windy and cold outdoor lunch. People are sitting outside, but it's closed.

We head back into town, but Lake Lure is crowded with tourists, and after waiting at an outside table for forty-five minutes in a stiff, cold breeze, we decide to leave town and head for the Hot Dog King in Fairview, where there are no tourists and where a vegetarian like Angela will find little to nothing for lunch. For the forty-five minutes we wait, though, we enjoy a view of Hickory Nut Falls that is spectacular. The emerging forest leaves are electric with clear skies and spring light, and I wonder what Masa would think of this town now, its tourism vision complete, and the wild and free-flowing Rocky Broad he photographed now tamed and held captive by an impoundment.

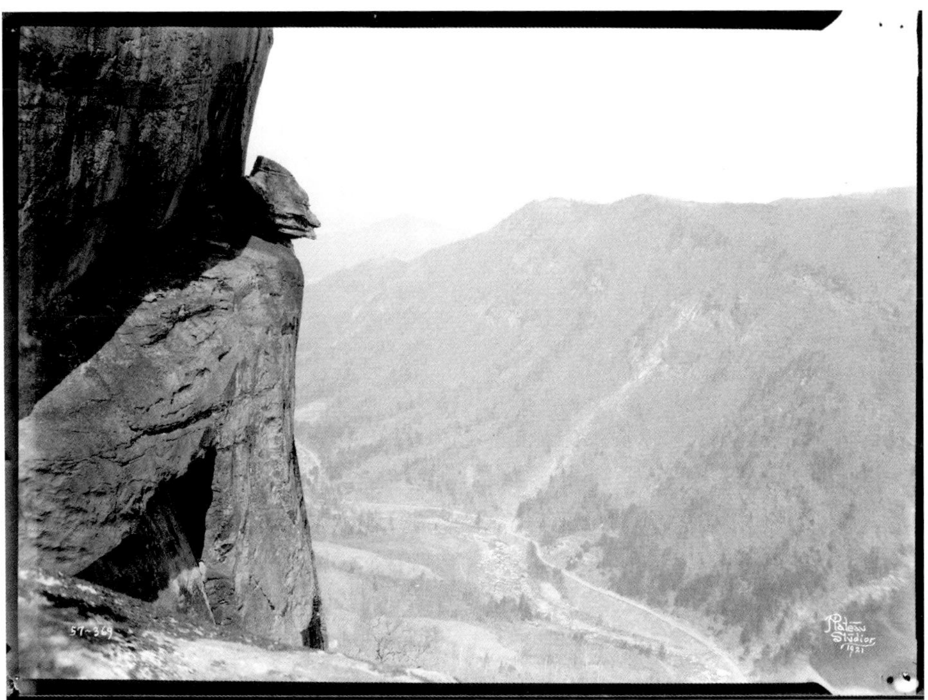

Devil's Head, Hickory Nut Gorge

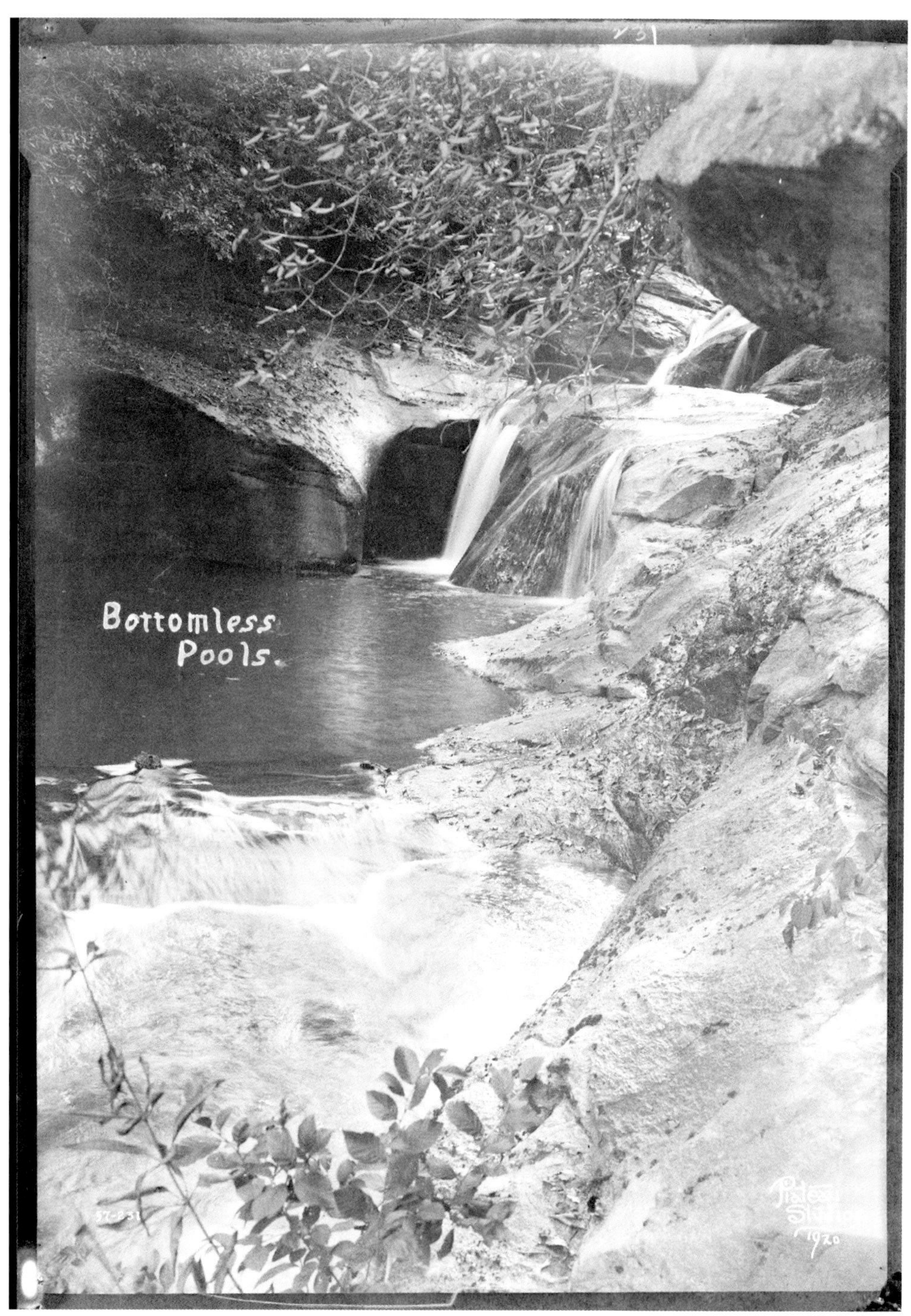

Rocky Broad River, Hickory Nut Gorge

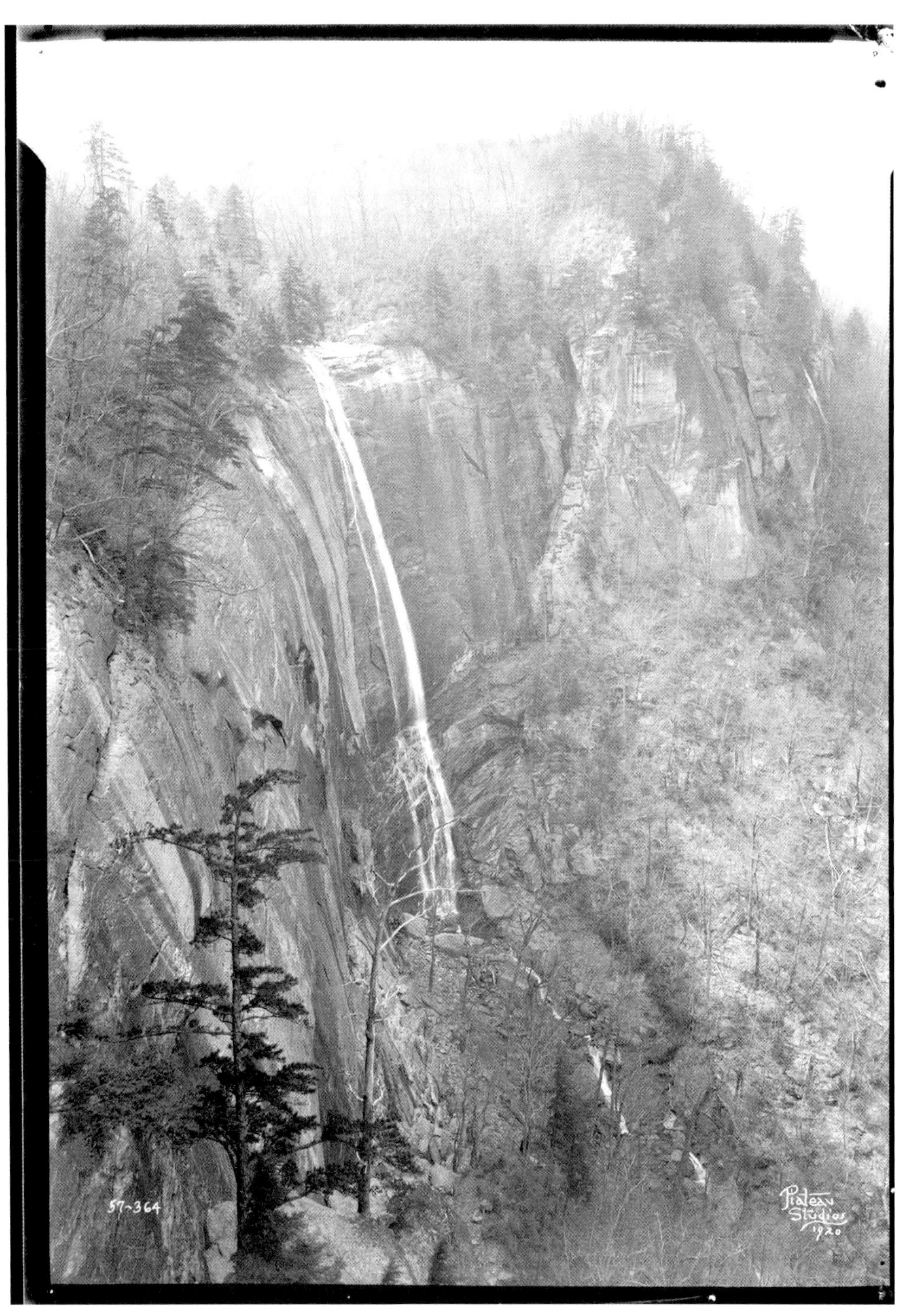

Hickory Nut Falls

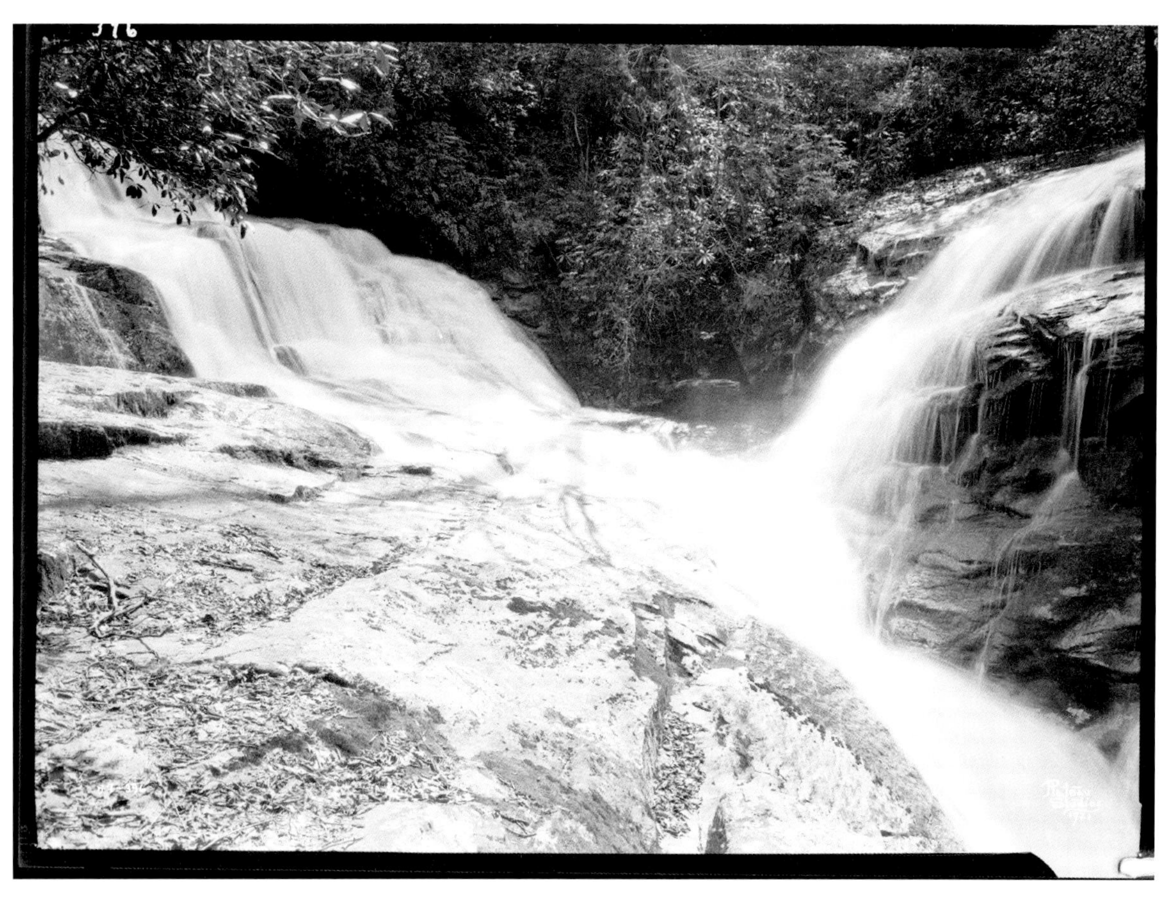

Rocky Broad River, Hickory Nut Gorge. OPPOSITE: *Rocky Broad River, Hickory Nut Gorge.*

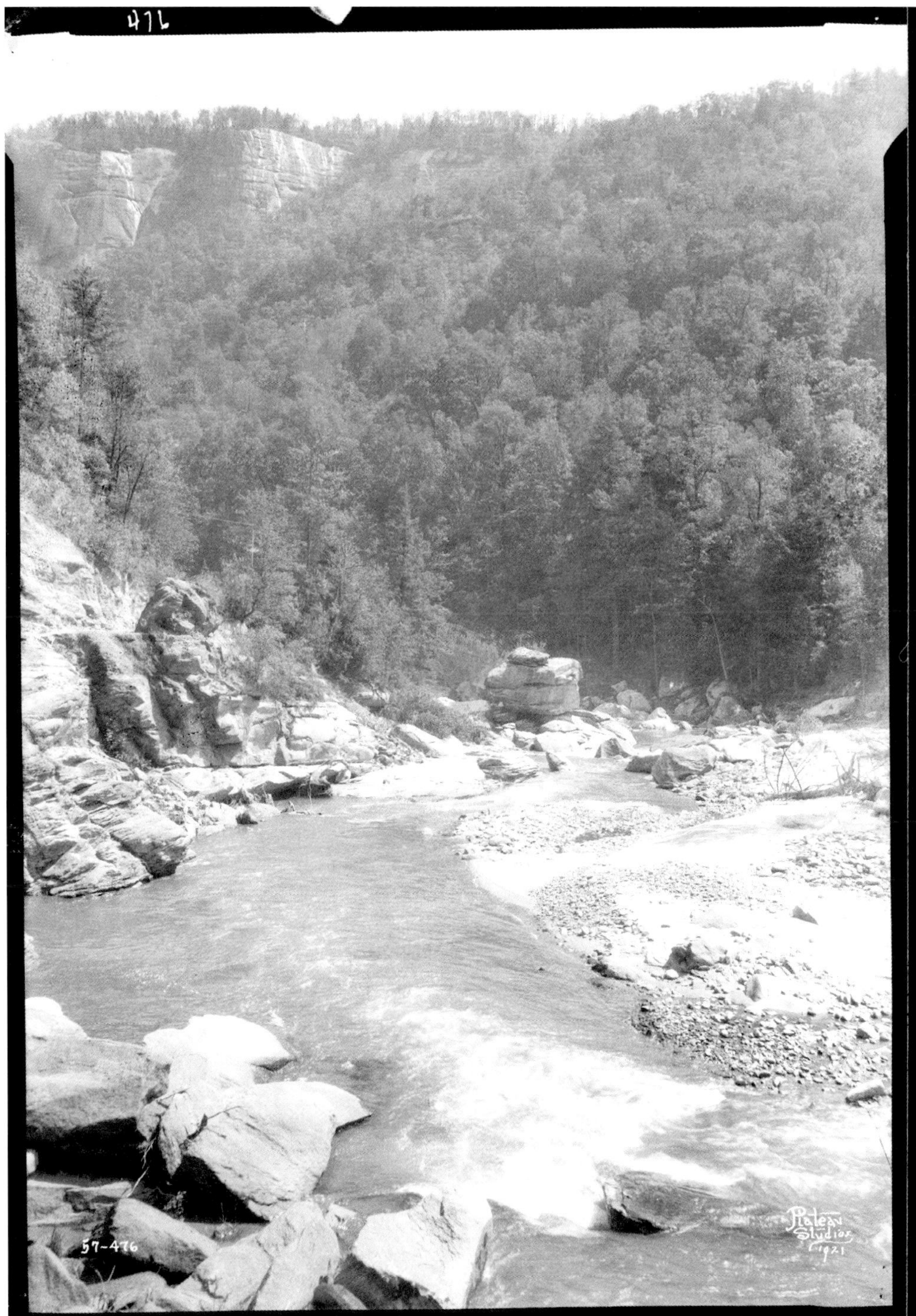
57-476
Plateau
Studios
1921

RIGHT: *Entrance Station at Nose Rock, Chimney Rock Park*

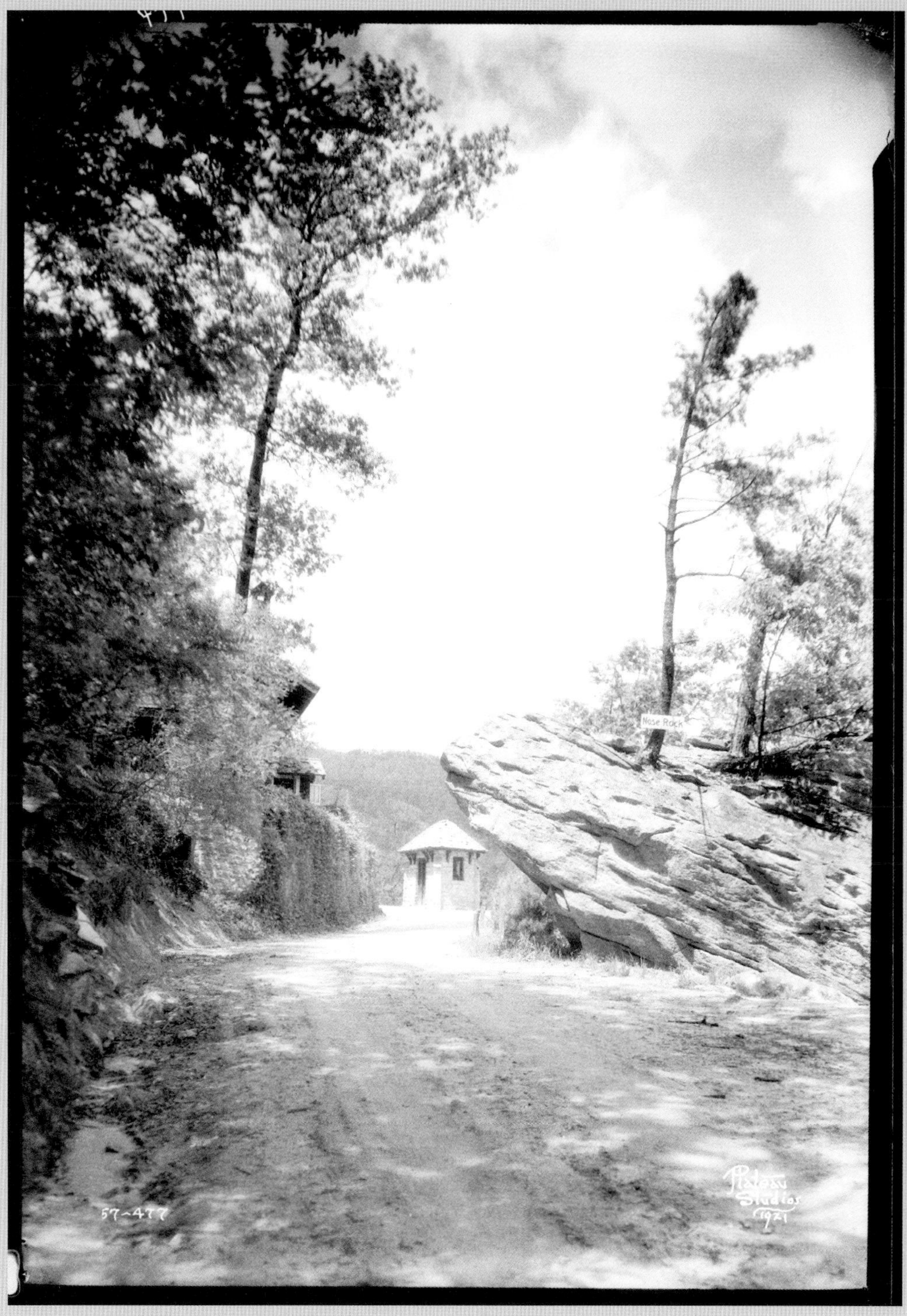
Nose Rock

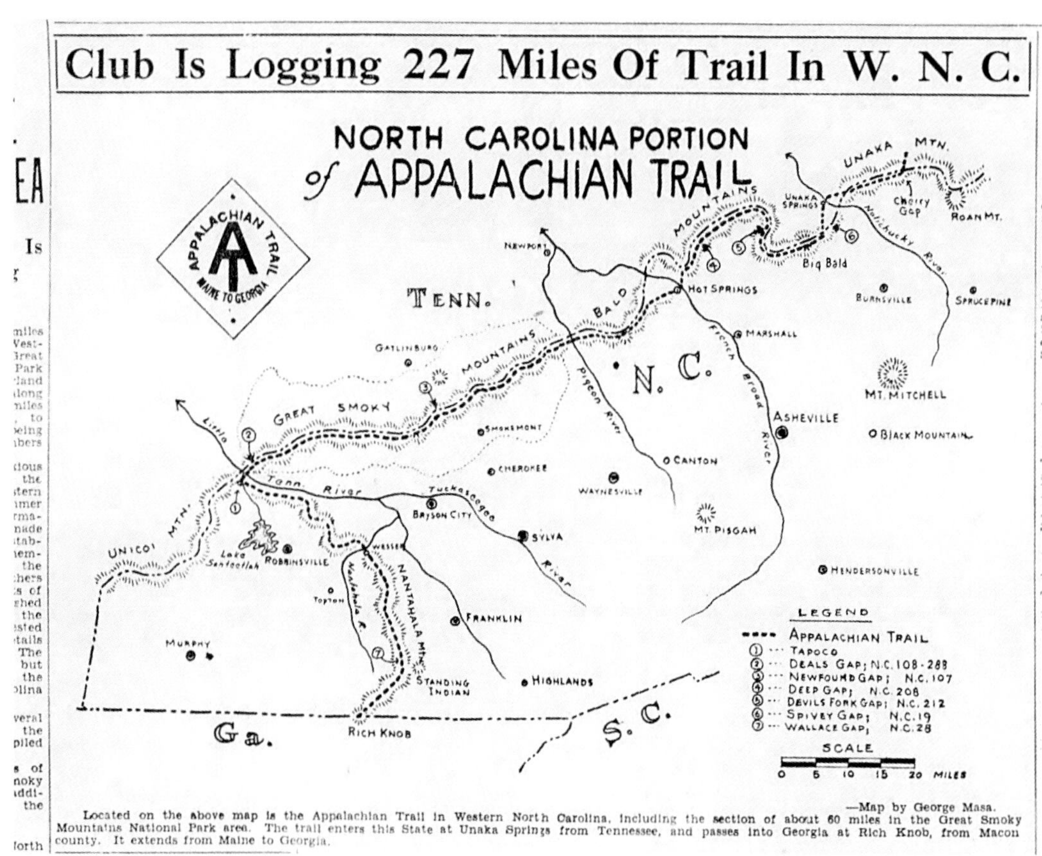

Masa's map of the North Carolina section of the Appalachian Trail,
Asheville Citizen Times, *August 7, 1932*

CHAPTER FIVE

OUTLIERS

ALTHOUGH THE MAJORITY of Masa's surviving work focuses largely on the Smokies and other iconic places such as Mount Mitchell and Chimney Rock, he photographed in many other locations, and his subjects were often equally iconic places, such as the Nantahala Gorge, Shining Rock, and Linville Gorge. He also photographed people, plants, trees, buildings, caves, and objects. A lifetime could be spent searching for his locations and for the stories that exist within them. Some are easily identifiable; others are mysteries left to the imagination. The identifiable legacy includes a photograph of John D. Rockefeller that ran in the *New York Times*. Rockefeller later made a critical $5 million gift to the park.

Others are identifiable, yet nonetheless mysterious, such as Stone Mountain, Georgia. At some point, Masa traveled to Stone Mountain, likely on his way to a meeting with Appalachian Trail folks to determine the route of the trail through the North Georgia mountains. His photos of Stone Mountain are intriguing, though they are nothing more than snapshots and obviously not part of his normal creative process. Perhaps he took them during the late twenties, when he and Kephart were highly engaged in the trail's route through the southern mountains. Stone Mountain was proposed as an alternative terminus for the trail so he was probably there for this reason. His photos are likely some of the last examples of the yet undefiled, stupe-fying hunk of granite that would soon be carved into one of the largest testimonies to racism that has ever existed. Stone Mountain, owned by Ku Klux Klan member Samuel Venable, was the site of the Klan's rebirth in 1915. The United Daughters of the Confederacy approached Venable with the monument idea, to which he agreed. They then contacted sculptor and Klansman Gutzon Borglum. Borglum didn't work out, moving on to create Mount Rushmore, but President Calvin Coolidge and the 1926 U.S. Congress supported the U.S. Mint in creating a Stone Mountain commemorative silver half-dollar to raise funds for the effort. Venable gave the Klan an easement on the property, and they held annual cross burnings there for over forty years until the state of Georgia condemned the property after acquiring it for a park in 1958, thus ending the Klan's access. Venable and his fellow Klansmen primarily targeted African Americans, but they also targeted Jews, Catholics, and foreigners in their hatred.

Perhaps Masa had been warned of this, and it is why his photographs are from a far-removed distance. But was the geological wonder of Stone Mountain a destination he went out of his way for, perhaps on his way to Mount Oglethorpe, the original southern terminus of the Appalachian Trail? Or was Stone Mountain yet another location he sought out of his own innate curiosity? It makes sense that he might have traveled there while also visiting Jasper, Georgia, the town near the terminus. His photo of the thirty-eight-foot marble obelisk at Mount Oglethorpe, named after the first Georgia governor and donated by local marble magnate Sam Tate, would have been taken around the time that this location was officially designated the southern terminus of the trail in 1930. Tate donated money to build structures for the trail and allowed it to pass through his property. The dozen or so people milling about in the photo were likely participants in the Appalachian Trail Conference's meeting that year. Masa would not have foreseen the relocation of the trail's terminus to Springer Mountain over two decades later, due to overdevelopment that was occurring around Mount Oglethorpe from country clubs such as Bent Tree and Big Canoe.

NANTAHALA GORGE

SEVERAL DECADES BEFORE Masa traveled through this area, writer and lawyer Wilbur Ziegler and fellow attorney Ben Grosscup, authors of *The Heart of the Alleghenies: Or Western North Carolina* (1883), explored this once-wilder landscape, writing that, "in Macon County, North Carolina, is a section of country so seldom visited by strangers, that few persons living beyond its limits are aware of its existence. In pomp of forest, purity of water, beauty of sky, wildness of mountains, combining in a wealth

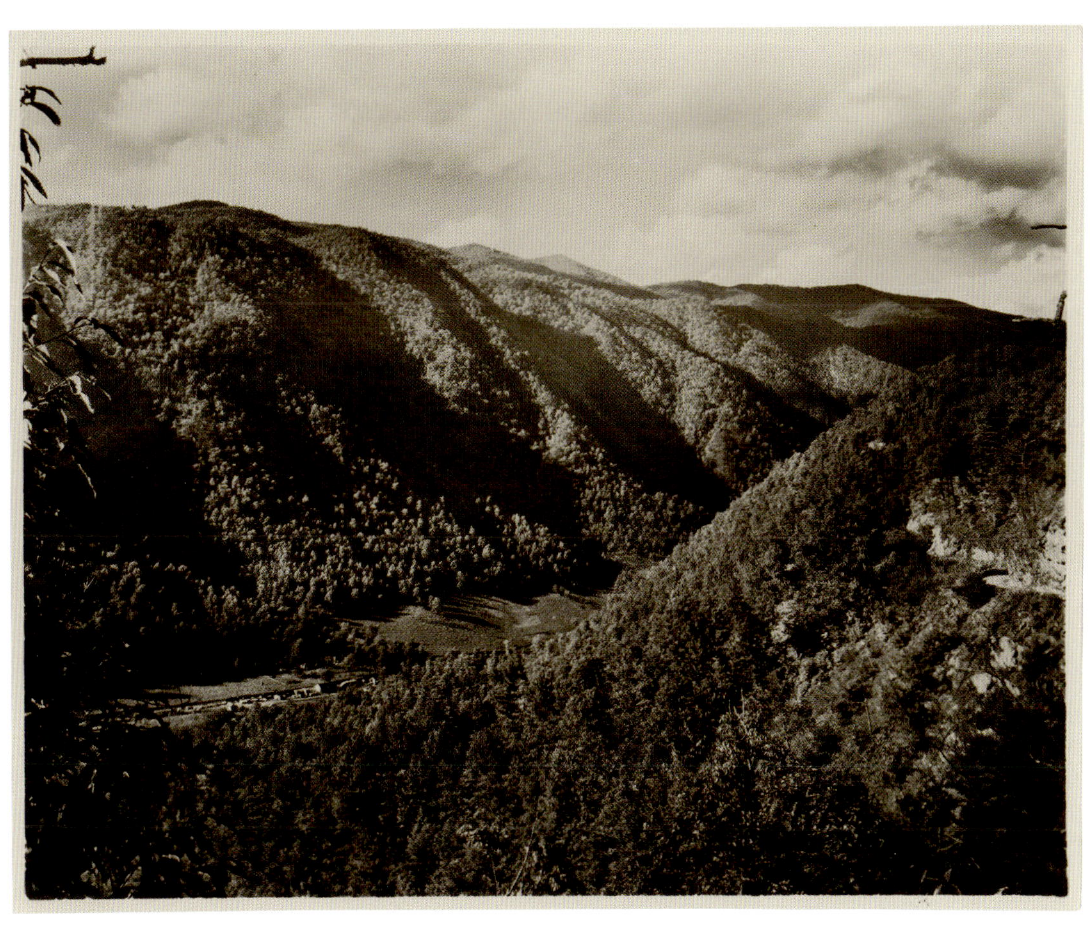

*Looking down from the old Winding Stairs road into what is likely
the Beechertown community, Nantahala River Valley*

of sublime scenery, the valley of the Nantihala [*sic*] is not surpassed by any region of the Alleghenies." This is a strong superlative from two individuals who traveled the western North Carolina mountains—or the Alleghenies, as they were then called—so extensively, and though anyone living in this varied mountainous landscape could challenge them today on the merits of this statement, this remains one of the region's most remote mountain communities, and one that can still be described by any number of such superlatives. Masa would have been a true oddity in this landscape, and one is left to wonder over what his encounters with the mountain people were like, and what his impressions were. One is also left to wonder, given the area's features as outlined by Ziegler and Grosscup, why only two known photographs of Masa's exist of the Nantahala Gorge—or three, if the one of the adjacent Snowbird range is included. Perhaps he was obsessed with the Smokies at the time, his vision and intention a guiding star that led him toward the goal of park creation and protection and rendered him unwilling to allow further distraction. He was a busy man.

THE NANTAHALA RIVER descends from the Nantahala Mountains through a long series of precipitous drops and cascades, is then blocked from its wild descent by the confines of Lake Nantahala, and is finally freed to drop again through craggy sluices to form the popular and now well-tamed Nantahala Gorge. When Masa explored the area with Horace Kephart in 1930, searching for the best route out of the Smokies for the Appalachian Trail, the gorge was pastoral and dotted with small and remote self-sufficient communities such as Aquone, Beechertown, Little Choga, Otter Creek, and others. Remnants of old Cherokee communities survived in the anglicized names of churches, lumber mills, schools, and stores. These human landmarks are mostly relics now, but for the hulls of abandoned buildings and old roadbeds. Nantahala Power and Light began removing some of these communities in 1929 for the construction of Lake Nantahala, and Masa would have been here at the time of this upheaval.

One of these old roadbeds is now part of the Bartram Trail, named for the eighteenth-century naturalist and artist William Bartram, who traveled into the Nantahala Gorge in May 1775 by horseback. Bartram followed an ancient trading path here from Cowee Town, and his descriptions of the gorge, later published in his 1791 *Travels,* are tinged with drear and gloom, emotions that Bartram experienced

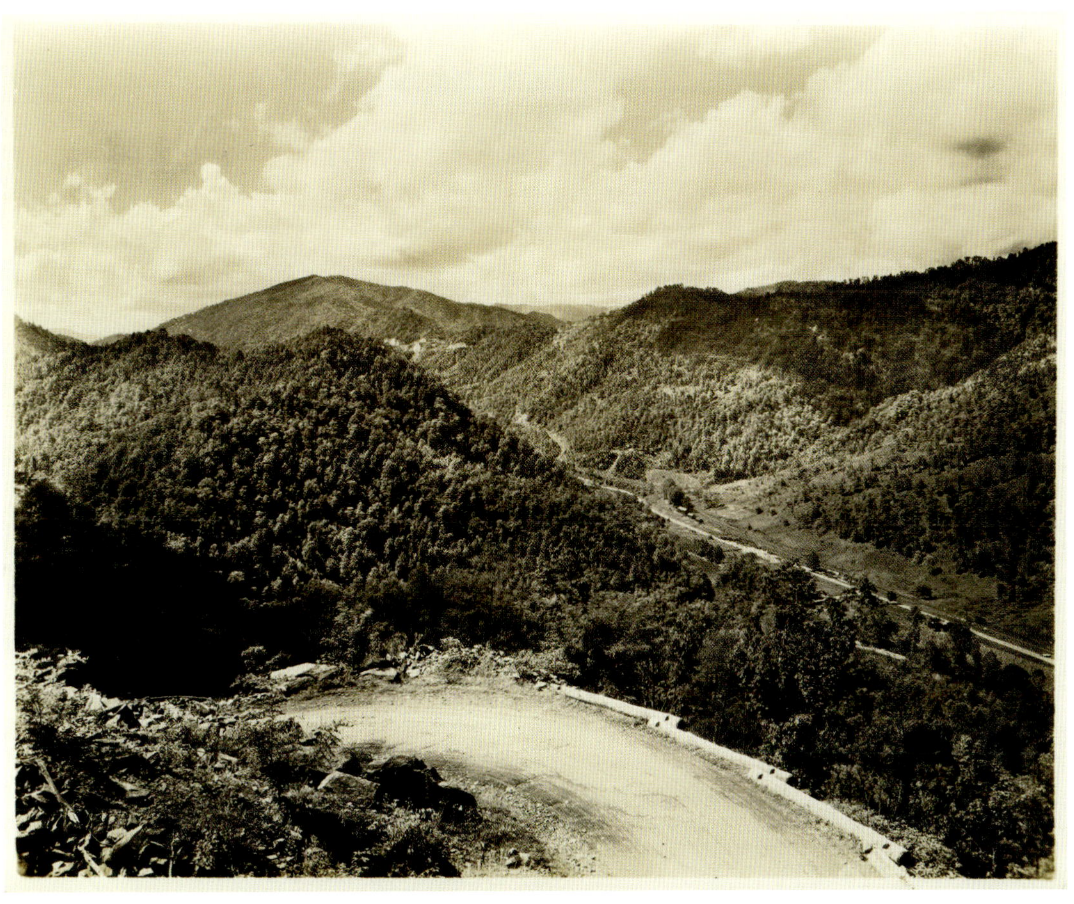

View west toward the Snowbird Mountains from the old Winding Stairs road

more than once while journeying through our southern mountains. Fearless William Bartram turned around here after encountering the Cherokee chief Attacullaculla, who warned him of troubles between Cherokees and white settlers in the Overhill towns, where Bartram was intent on going. He did not turn around for much, so was it his fear of these troubles, or the melancholy exuded by these haunted, exquisite mountains? The name Nantahala is Cherokee and translates as "Land of the Noonday Sun," due to the gorge's brief period of sunlight as it passes over the high Nantahala and Snowbird mountains. Masa would have felt this gorge's gloom and beauty.

I believe I am standing near the exact spot where he took these two photographs, but I'm not positive. These are the only known photographs that Masa took of the gorge, or the only two I can locate. One of these was produced as a postcard by the Asheville Postcard Company and was colored to dramatic effect. The card is stylized and bright, with reds, greens, and yellows and fake rays of sunlight streaking across the empty Nantahala sky. The location is high on a mile-long gated road that is maintained by Duke Energy to access a surge tank. The road also serves as a connector for the Bartram Trail between Beechertown and its entry/exit into the national forest. I am intrigued by the idea that Attacullaculla, William Bartram, and George Masa might have stood on the same spot. When I return home, a friend and expert on ancient trails and roads confirms this location. This was once the old Winding Stairs road, built by one of the area's most notable settlers, Nimrod Jarrett. Jarrett lived at the old Cherokee village site of Appletree, which is now a forest service campground. Part of the ten miles of road he constructed is the footpath now known as the Bartram Trail. The Appalachian Trail location that Masa and Kephart would determine is several miles east of here, where the sprawling Nantahala Outdoor Center dominates the landscape, serving as the biggest employer in Swain County.

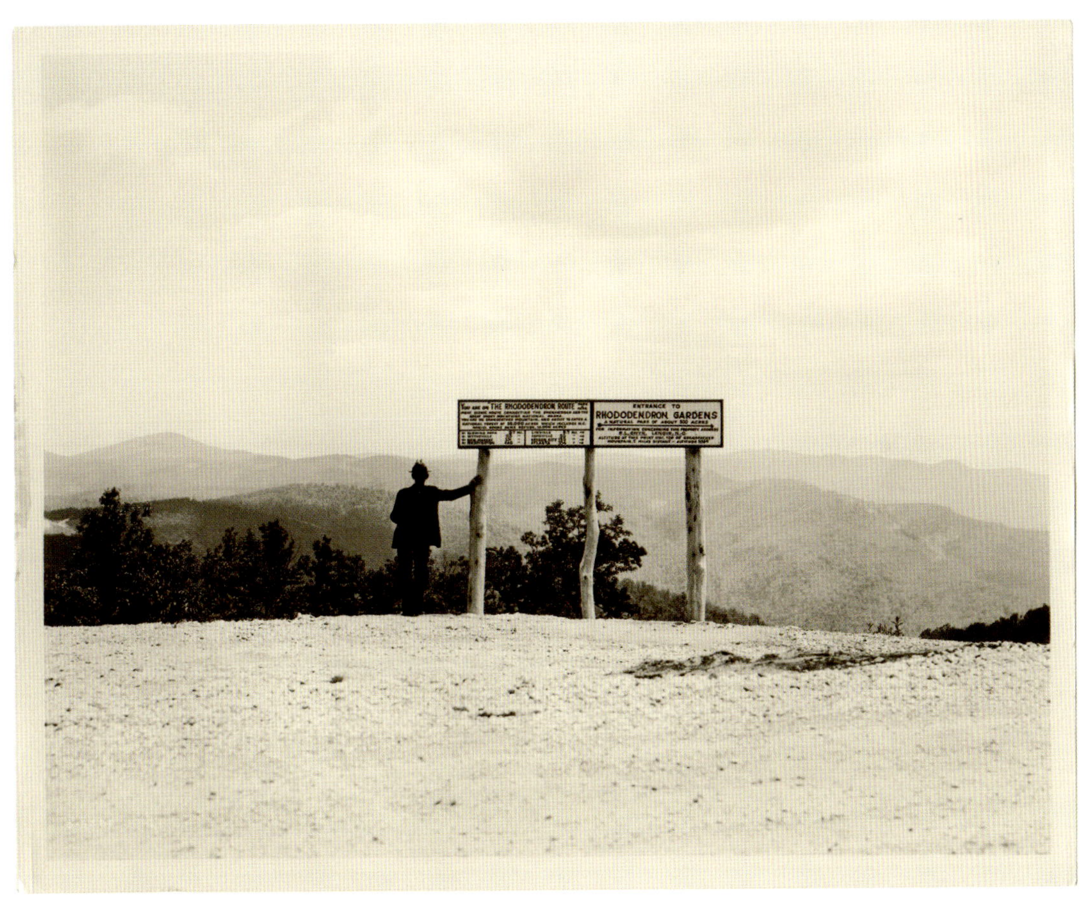

The Rhododendron Route, Grandfather Mountain. This appears to be part of the route that was to become the Blue Ridge Parkway. Note its connection to the Great Smoky Mountains and Shenandoah National Park. Figure is possibly Horace Kephart.

OVER: *Masa among the recovering spruce fir forest of what is now Shining Rock Wilderness. The area was heavily cut over by Champion Fiber in the early 1900s.*

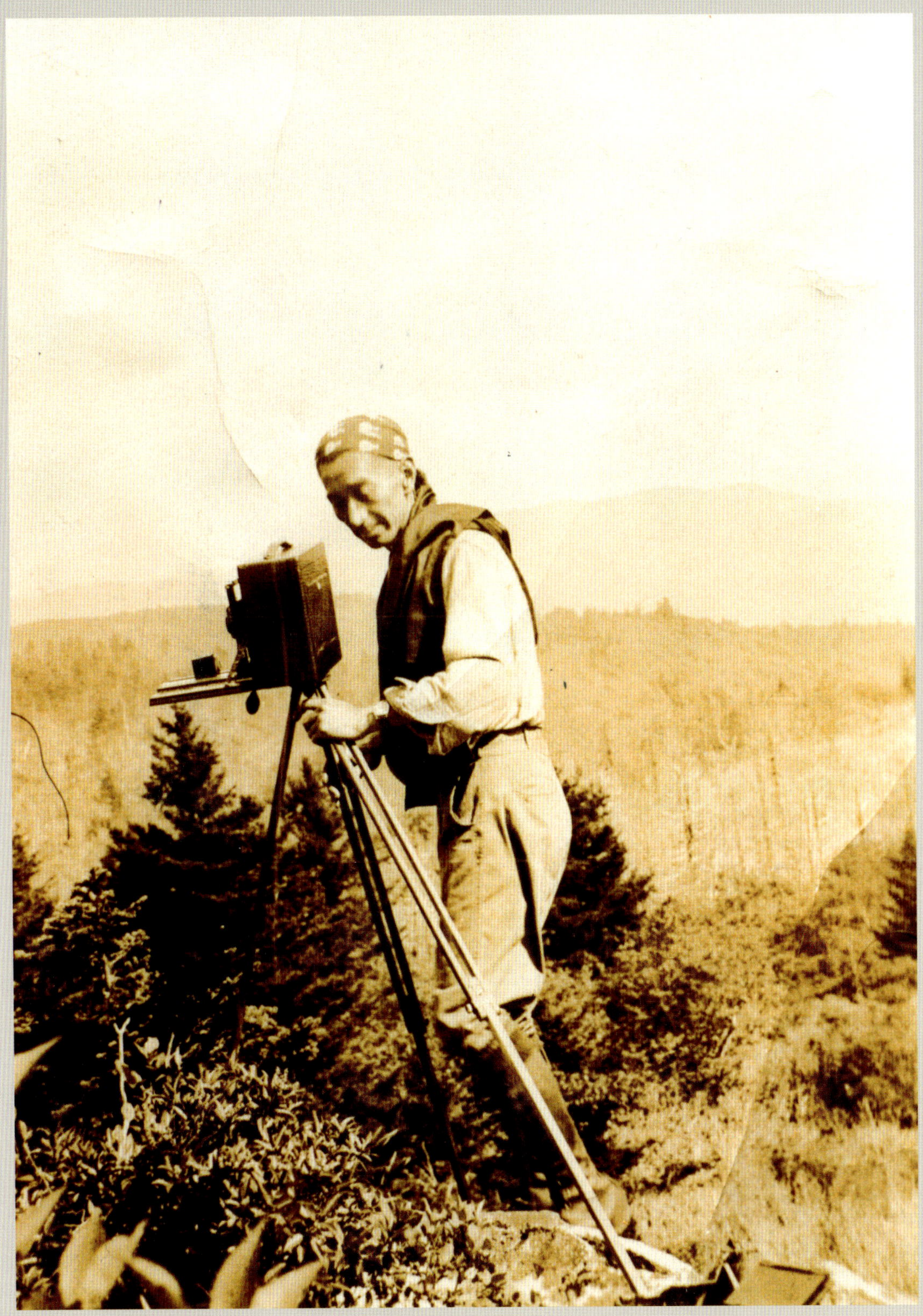

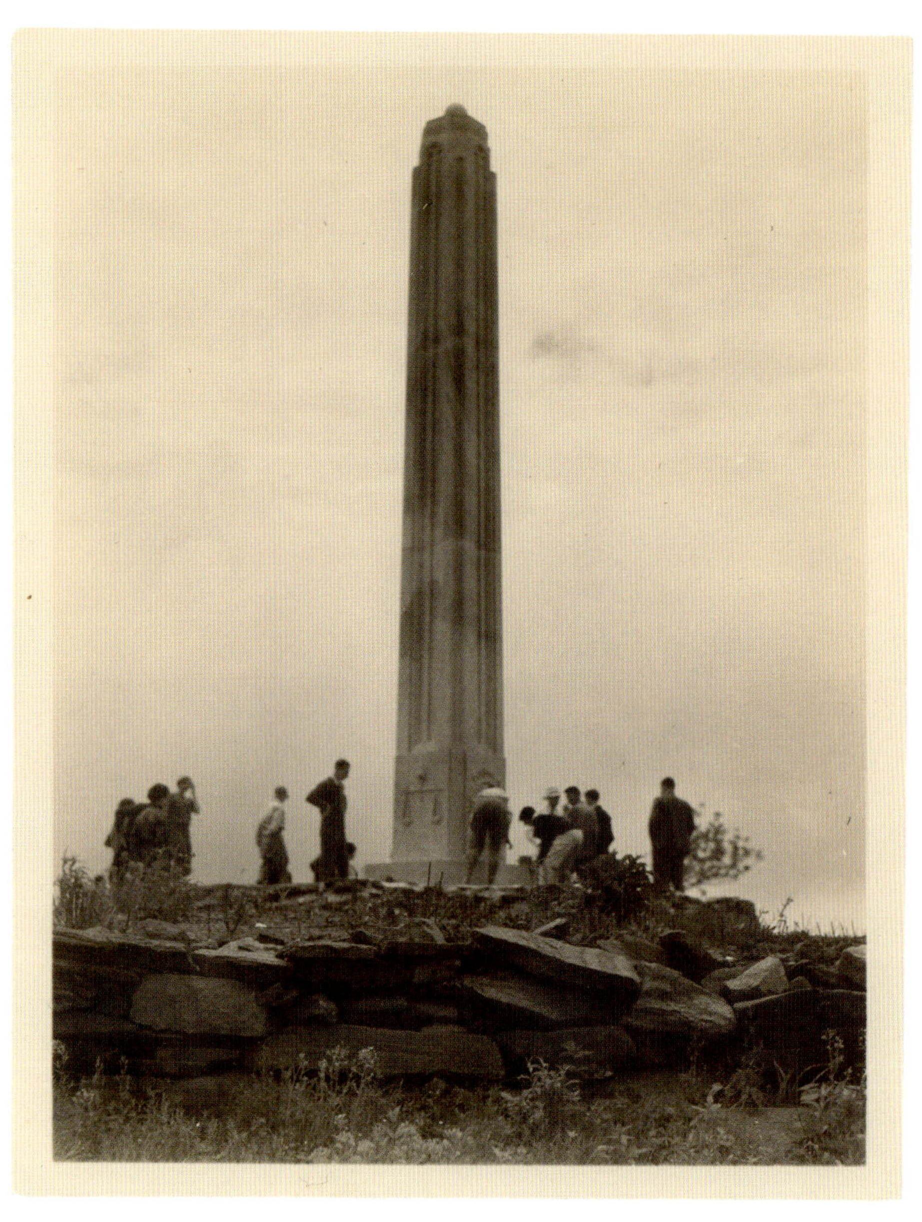

*Marble obelisk at Mt. Oglethorpe, Georgia, once proposed as
the southern terminus of the Appalachian Trail*

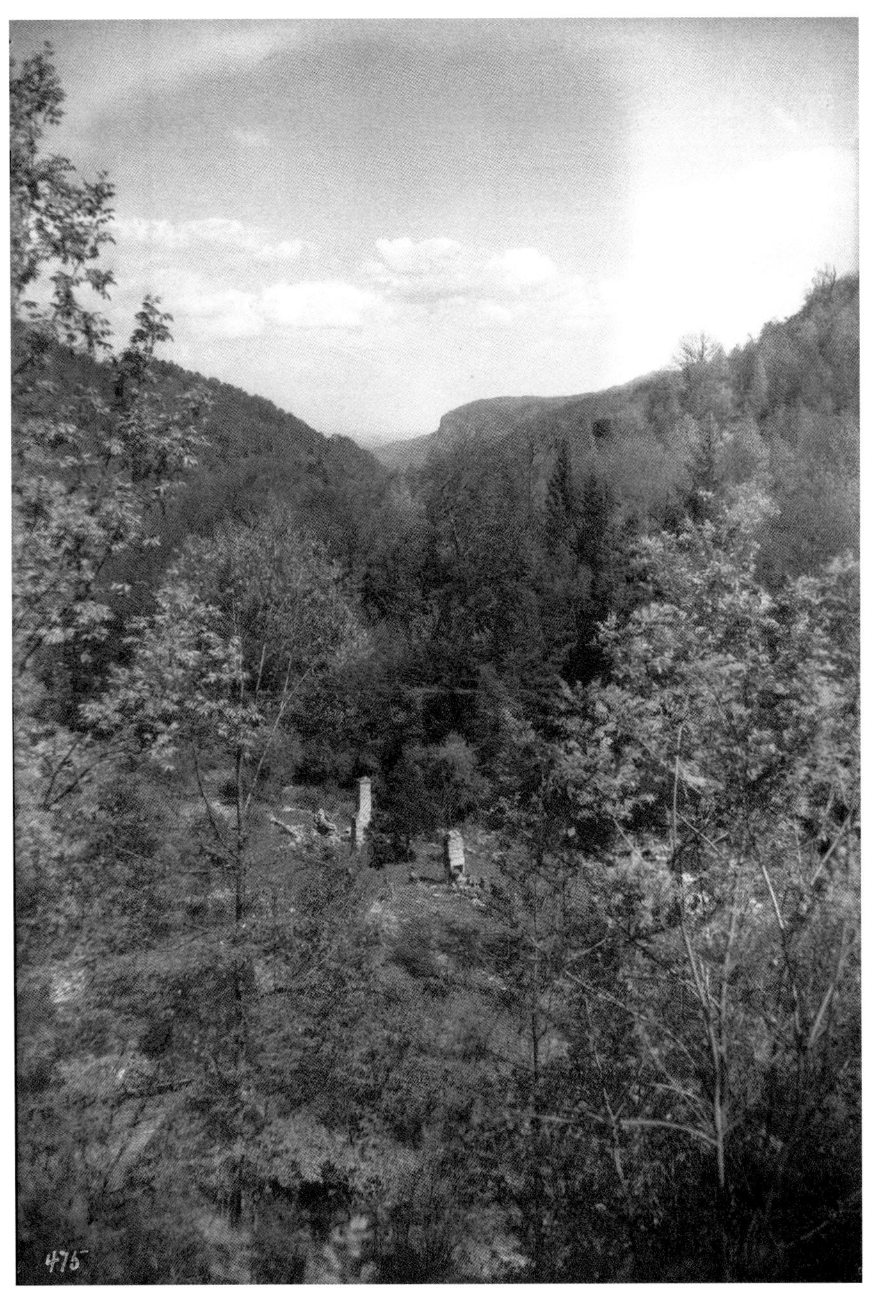

View of Chimney Rock from Hickory Nut Gorge

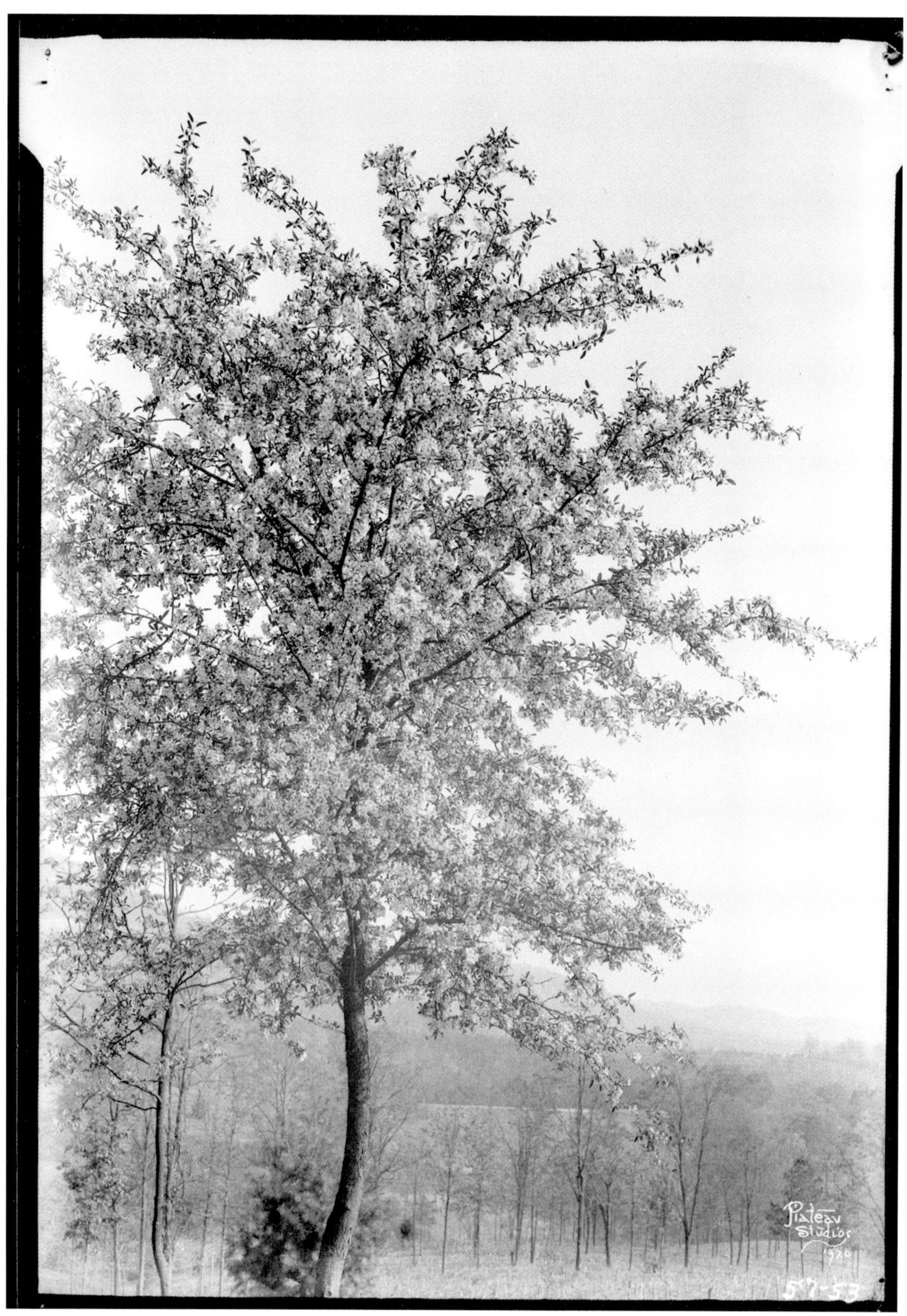

Black cherry in full bloom, 1920

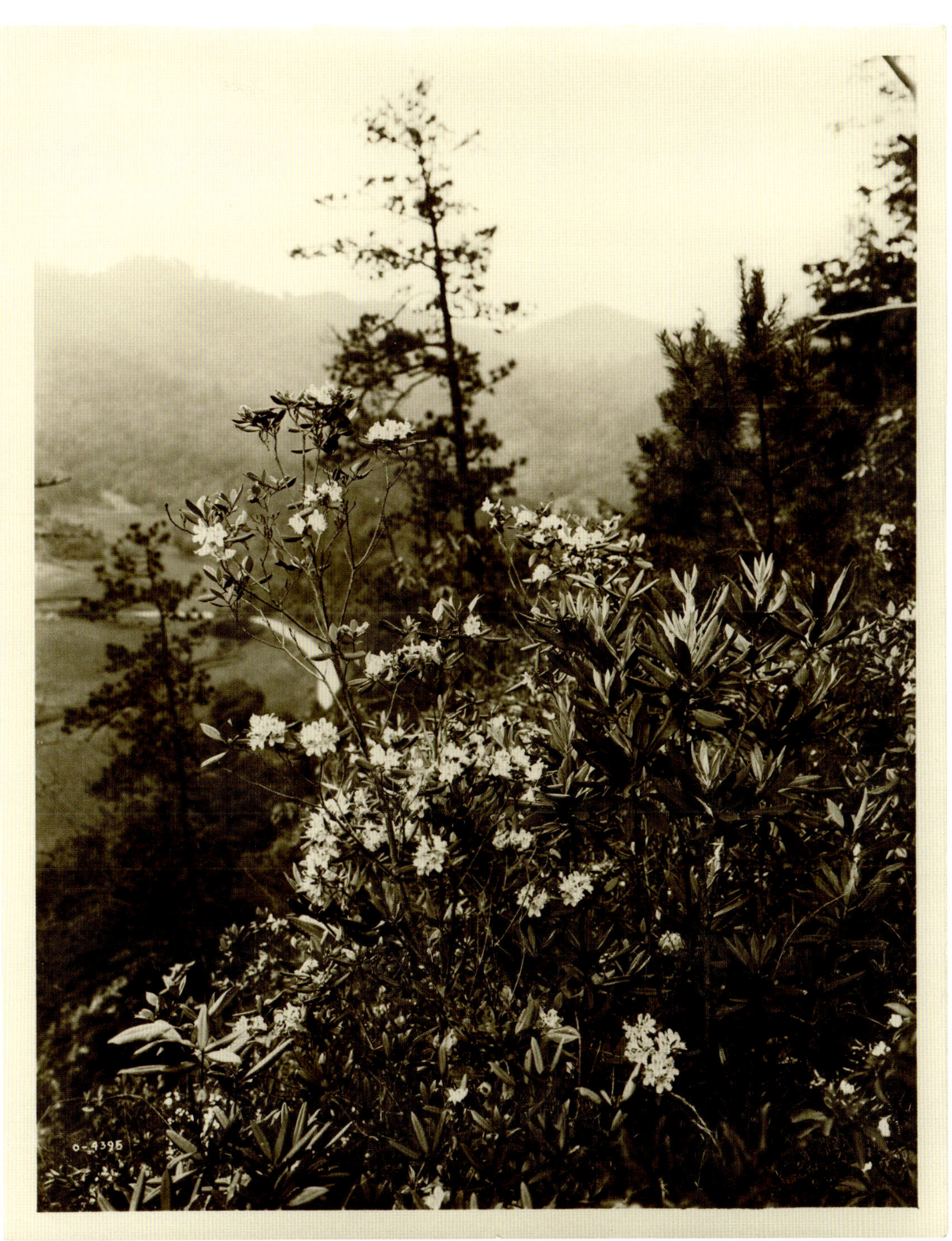

Rosebay rhododendron, location unknown

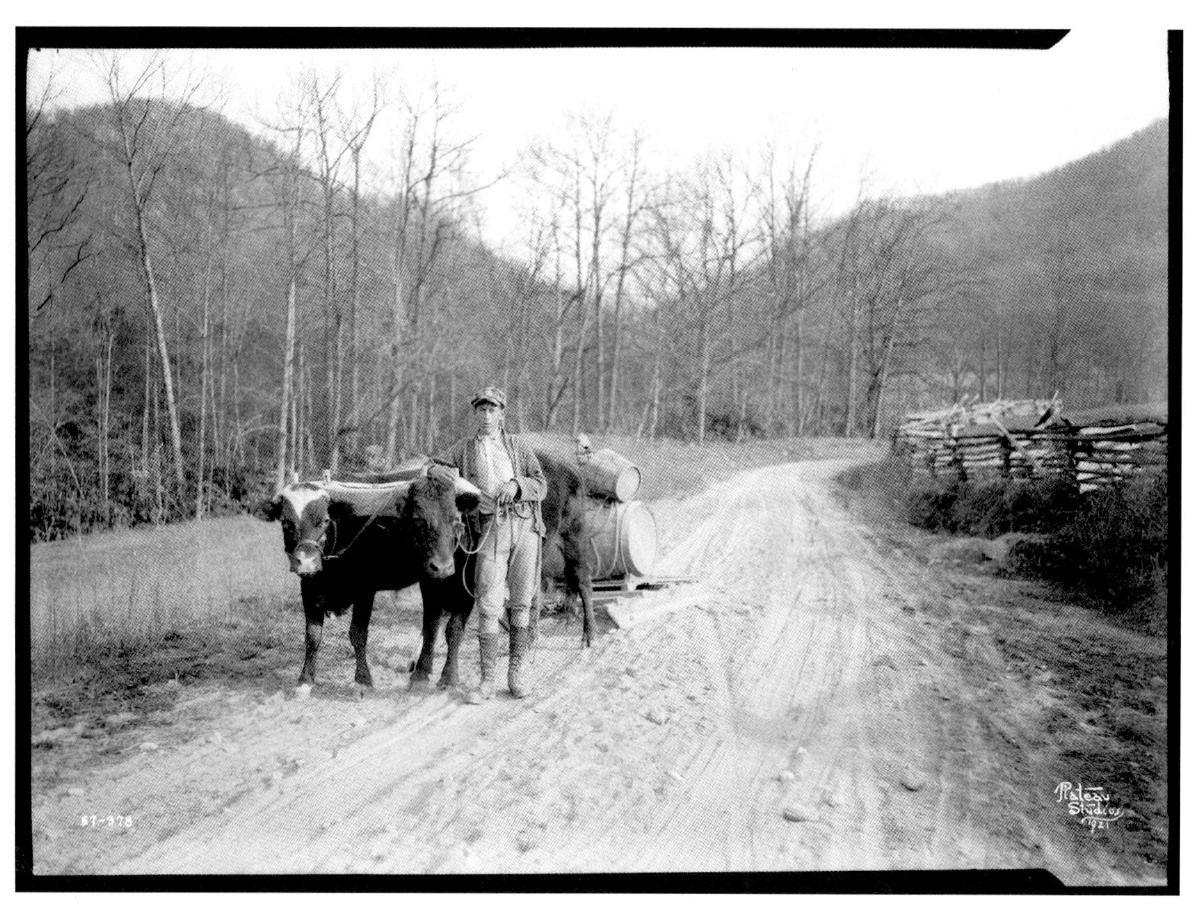

Boy with oxen and sled, 1921

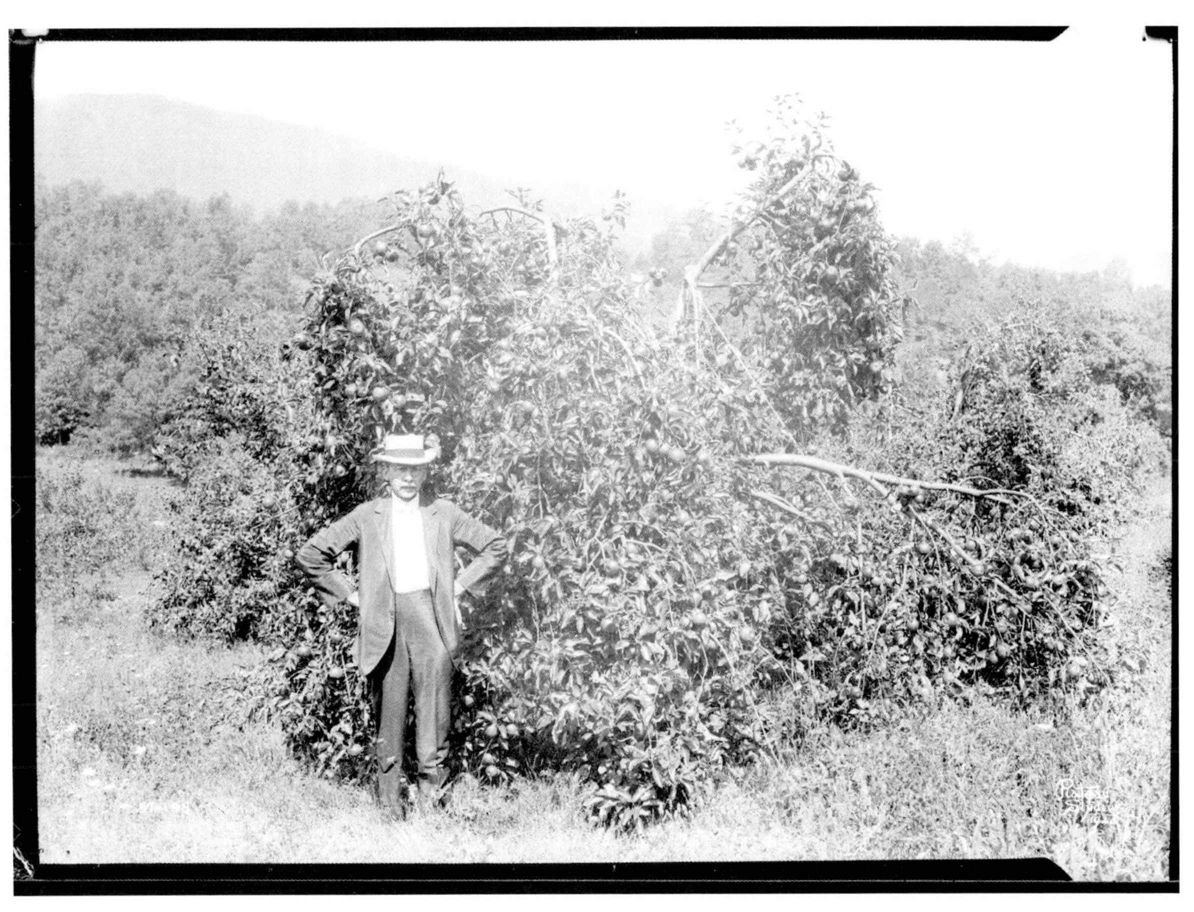

Well-dressed man with heavily laden apple tree, 1920

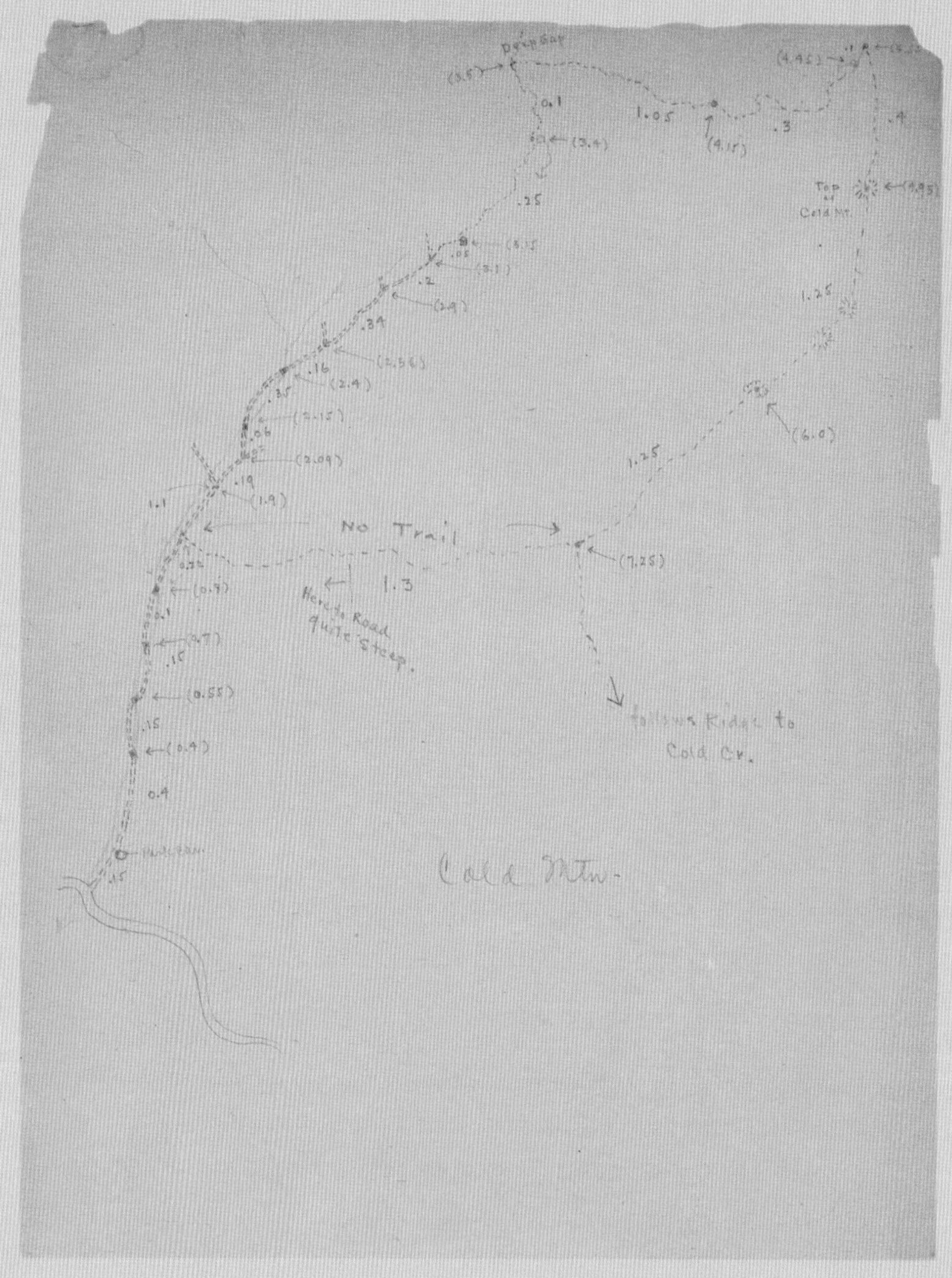

Masa's map to Cold Mountain. OPPOSITE: *Masa's New Year's Day report to Carolina Mountain Club on outing to Cold Mountain, 1933*

CAROLINA MOUNTAIN CLUB

TRIP REPORT

Trip Name ______Cold Mountain - Elevation 6,000a ft.______ D a te__Jan. 1, 1933.__

Mileage of round trip; By car __72.8 m.__ miles; Afoot __9.45 m.__ miles; X By wheel / By Pedo / Estimated

Time required: By car __1½__ hours one way; Afoot __8__ hours (total)

Departure: From Asheville__7:15 A.M.__ From car __8:45__

Arrival: At car__4:30 P.M__At Asheville__6: P.M.__

Members____________Visitors ____________

Trip register: (get signature if possible) LEADER__George Masa.__

Jewel King,	Dr. O. C. Barker,	Roger Morrow,
Marcus Book,	Charles Book,	William Schwartz,
Boby Gottlieb.		

Motor Log: (Asheville to point of leaving car) Drove N.C.No. 10 West from Federal
Building, at 19.6 m first signal lights at Canton off No.10 to left
thru Canton, at 19.8 m. turn left onto No. 110, at 25.3 m. junction
No.284, take left followed No. 284, at 34.2 m. Cruso P.O. at left,
before crossing Crawford Creek Bridge at 36.1 m. off highway turn
to left follow dirt road and at36.25 parked cars in pasture.

Trail Log: Follow wagon road toward upstream of Crawford Creek, at 0.4 m
cross bridge, at 0.55 m. cross bridge, at 0.7 m. cross bridge
0.8 m. cross bridge, at 1.9 m. road at left, at 2.09 m. road forks
take left, at 2.15 m. cross bridge, at 2.4 cross bridge, at 2.56 m.
road forks take right, at 2.9 m. road forks take right, road from
here on washed out bad shape, better call trail, at 3.1 m. trail
forks take right toward cabin, at 3.15 Cabin, this cabin very small

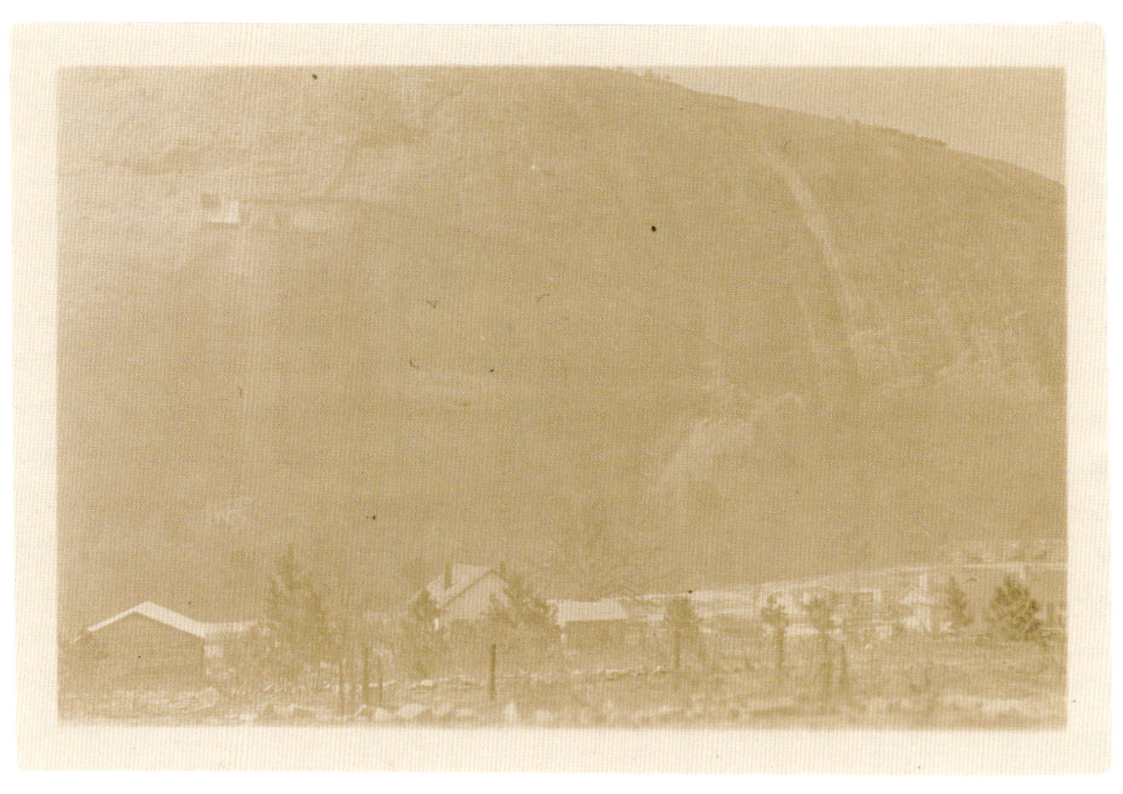

Stone Mountain, Georgia. Site of proposed southern terminus of Appalachian Trail. Note what appears to be the beginning of the Confederate Memorial carving on the upper left side of the mountain's face.

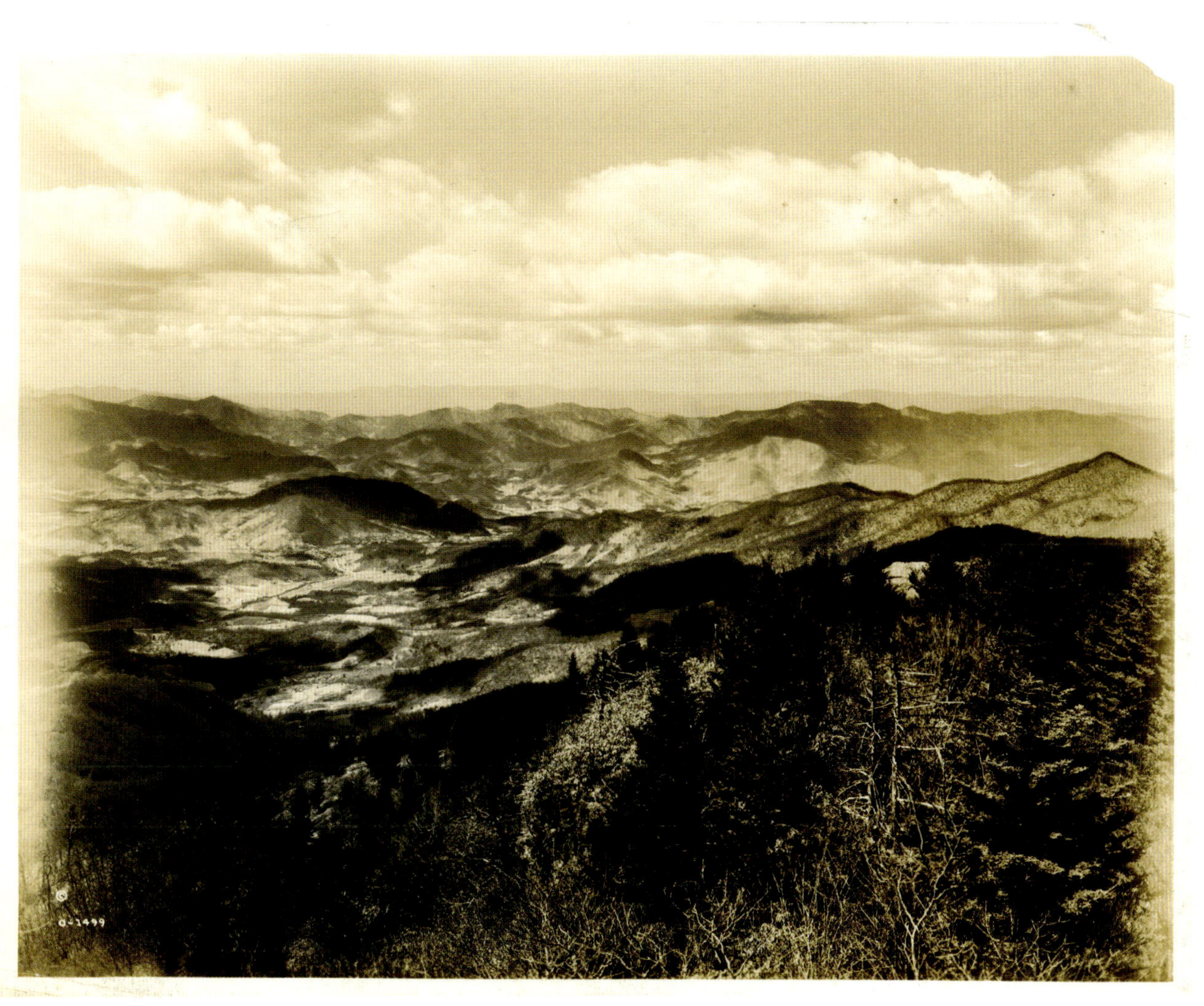

View from Table Rock

George Masa Will Rest In Grave At Riverside

Funeral Services Will Be Held At Church This Morning

Following simple funeral rites, George Masa, for many years an ardent outdoorsman and photographer in Western North Carolina, will be laid to rest in Riverside cemetery this morning.

Dr. W. A. Lambeth, pastor of Central Methodist church, will officiate at the service which will be held at 10 o'clock. The body, sealed in a steel casket with a simple name plate, will probably be removed later into the Great Smoky Mountains National Park—that vast area of forested mountains and quiet coves where Mr. Masa for many years was wont to travel with his camera, to capture the beauty and picturesque grandeur of the peaks, and to live in the outdoors alone, or on many occasions with his close friends. Close associates of Mr. Masa, including members of the Carolina Mountain club and the national Appalachian Trail association, of which he was a member, already have in mind a plan to bury him in the Smokies. However, it will be necessary at first to confer with park authorities.

Ill Several Weeks

Mr. Masa, whose real name was Masahara Iuzuka, died Wednesday in a local sanitarium after an illness of several weeks of influenza and complications.

Pallbearers, close friends of Mr. Masa, will be George M. Stephens, Roger Morrow, Blake Creasman, Dr. H. M. May, L. D. Rogers and Anthony Lord.

So far as can be learned Mr. Masa had no relatives in America and it is believed that his only surviving relative is a brother living somewhere in Japan. Because of this, arrangements for the funeral and burial have been taken in charge by the Carolina Mountain club officers and members and other close friends.

Troubles in Germany have been reflected in North China, dealers there

MIDWEST STATES SIZZLE UNDER SCORCHING SUN

(By The Associated Press)

The June heat wave settled with sizzling intensity on the right bank of the Mississippi river and part of the Atlantic Seaboard Thursday, more than making up for relief that came with cooling showers of breezes to other parts of the country.

A group of states including Oklahoma, Texas, Kansas, Iowa, Nebraska, and Missouri comprised one of the "heat belts." The center of it appeared to be at Bartlesville, Okla., where a reading of 108 degrees was made.

A portion of the Atlantic Seaboard likewise was uncomfortable. It was 98 at Washington and 94 at Baltimore.

Except for those two sections, reports generally were of temperatures several degrees lower than for several days. In the states surrounding the Great Lakes, including Illinois, Wisconsin, and Minnesota, showers and lower temperatures halted crop damage which experts said was serious.

A survey indicated the death toll from the four-day heat wave had passed 20, and it was increasing.

24 ITALIAN PLANES READY FOR FLIGHT ACROSS ATLANTIC

ORBETELLO, Italy, June 22. (AP)—General Italo Balbo, Italian air minister, who will lead a flight of 24 Italian seaplanes on a flight by stages to the Century of Progress exposition in Chicago, said tonight departure was practically certain Saturday.

He and eight fellow fliers came here by bicycle tonight from the airport in flying togs.

With weather improving over the Alps, the general added that the

Asheville Citizen Times, *June 23, 1933*

CONCLUSION/CODA

MY EDITOR SUGGESTED the title of this book. I was taken by it immediately, as I found it intriguing and full of questions. There is no doubt about his enthusiasm for wild places, but did George Masa have a vision, and how did his imagination underpin this vision and his work? The word *vision* has many meanings. At its most literal interpretation, we can define it as sight—someone has poor vision and needs glasses to perceive the world clearly. Or vision can be a goal someone aspires to, an ideal or a life mission. Or it can be a mystical vision, something spiritual or supernatural. Imagination is the image-making power of the mind, a process of creating an image or object based on an ideal of that image or object. Vision and imagination can work in tandem, a symbiosis, with one underpinning the other. So what was George Masa's *wild vision*, and how did he *imagine* the western North Carolina landscape?

The word *wild* is generally taken to mean undomesticated or untamed, something not controlled by humans but instead left to its own devices in its natural environment. It could be a place, an animal, or a plant. Given the trajectory of humanity, it could also be a word on its way to obsolescence. Masa certainly had a fascination and obsession with wild places, whether real or perceived. Some of them were truly wild, such as Three Forks, and some were losing their wildness and in the midst of being tamed, such as the Cullasaja and Nantahala gorges and the falling old-growth forests of the Black Mountains. Much of the Smokies remained wild, and his tireless pursuit of protection for them, as well as his tireless pursuit of photographing them in perfection, makes me think his vision for them was clearly a wild one, or a vision informed by the idea of wildness. His vision for the park was one that encompassed protection of a place in its natural condition. And though he and Horace Kephart both understood that the park needed access and infrastructure, I cannot imagine

Asheville Citizen Times,
May 16, 1933

George Masa Is Still Ill At Residence Here

The condition of George Masa, well known photographer and outdoorsman, who has been ill at his home, 144 Mount Claire avenue, for several weeks, was reported unimproved yesterday. Mr. Masa rested well Sunday, friends said, but his condition became worse yesterday.

that Masa would have envisioned a park in the future overrun by millions, bookended by two tourist towns packed with tacky gift shops, water slides, caged bears, sky lifts, helicopter rides, and casinos. Nor could he have imagined a park that is now dependent upon humans to preserve its wildness by removal and treatment of invasive exotic species, or one where coal-fired power plants would wreak havoc on its high-elevation spruce-fir forests, ruining the views Masa captured in their magnificence. One is left to wonder if his work was celebration, lamentation, plea for help, or all of the above. Or was it simply art—an obsession with craft and quality, born of ambition, that made the most mundane of landscapes at once magical and full of light?

Regardless, we can consider the internal landscape of George Masa as wild. He was wild in his passion, pursuits, photography, and love for hiking and exploring western North Carolina's forests and mountains. He took wild risks, abandoning his family and native land to pursue dreams in a country unfriendly to his ethnicity, venturing into difficult and pathless terrain, living on faith and passion, traveling in an often hostile and racist rural South. The courage required for such a pursuit is intimidating and inspiring, yet this passion for life seemed to be his internal natural environment, essential to his wild vision. It makes me think of the Mary Oliver poem "The Summer Day," and her poetic question, "Tell me, what is it you plan to do with your one wild and precious life?" Masa's life embodies how one might answer.

ASHEVILLE, N. C. JUN 23 1933 _______ 193___

M⌀ Anthony Lord

To **Asheville Cemetery Company** Dr.

LOT NO.	SECTION		
JUN 23 1933	FOR Interment Fee Geo Massa	15	00
	Single Grave Geo Massa	5	00
		20	00

PAID
Asheville Cemetery Co
JUN 23 1933

*Payment from Carolina Mountain Club's Anthony Lord to
the Asheville Cemetery for Masa's internment, June 23, 1933*

ON APRIL 27, 2021, my wife and I travel to Asheville to visit Masa's grave. It's a brilliant spring day, clear, mild, and intoxicating as an Appalachian spring can be. We have the coordinates to locate it but still have difficulty as we drive around the sprawling cemetery attempting to get our bearings. Along the way, we see large burial monuments, family mausoleums, and obelisks for local politicians, business leaders, artists, writers, and Confederate generals, and we wish we had more time to explore. These were the types of people Masa and Kephart had to ingratiate themselves to for their park dream to come to fruition, and as a career conservationist, I can only say that some things never change. The power structure in conservation, then and now, is class-based, though in recent years mainstream conservation organizations have felt pressure to change. The product of a working-class family, I was nonetheless determined to have a career in conservation, and I witnessed and experienced this power structure to a degree that I often found sickening. Kephart at least enjoyed the privilege of being a highly educated, well-respected white male from an upper-class family. Masa had to transcend class, ethnicity, language, and anti-Asian attitudes that were being codified and institutionalized across the country at the time. Given these factors, his level of artistic commitment and creative perseverance is staggering.

We at last settle on the area we think he's buried in and walk toward a large white oak that is just beginning to leaf out. A nearby fir is spreading its shade across the area, and it is suddenly much cooler as we move beneath it. Then Masa's simple, flat grave marker appears, standing out among the adjacent headstones with pebbles, rocks, sticks, and a small artificial bouquet of flowers that fans have laid as elemental tokens of respect.

It somehow seems appropriate that this diminutive, intense, and gifted immigrant who knew more about the Smokies than anyone alive at the time lies here in such a humble setting. The Carolina Mountain Club and his many friends wanted his body moved to Bryson City to be interred next to his close friend Kephart, but lack of funds at the time made this prohibitive. His grave remained unmarked for two years until funds could be raised for a proper headstone. Lying on the headstone today is an image of Masa at Shining Rock, the one that is on the cover of this book, printed on a durable and waterproof material, with the inscription, "To George Masa, F32 to Infinity, Forever," written on it. I don't know much about F stops on a camera lens or why this particular number in the range of possibilities was important to the inscriber, but I somehow get it. I do know that the F stop controls the amount of light entering the camera, and that Masa was obviously a genius at the process. "F32 to Infinity"—let the light Masa captured come infinite and forever, his great spirit an aperture without bounds.

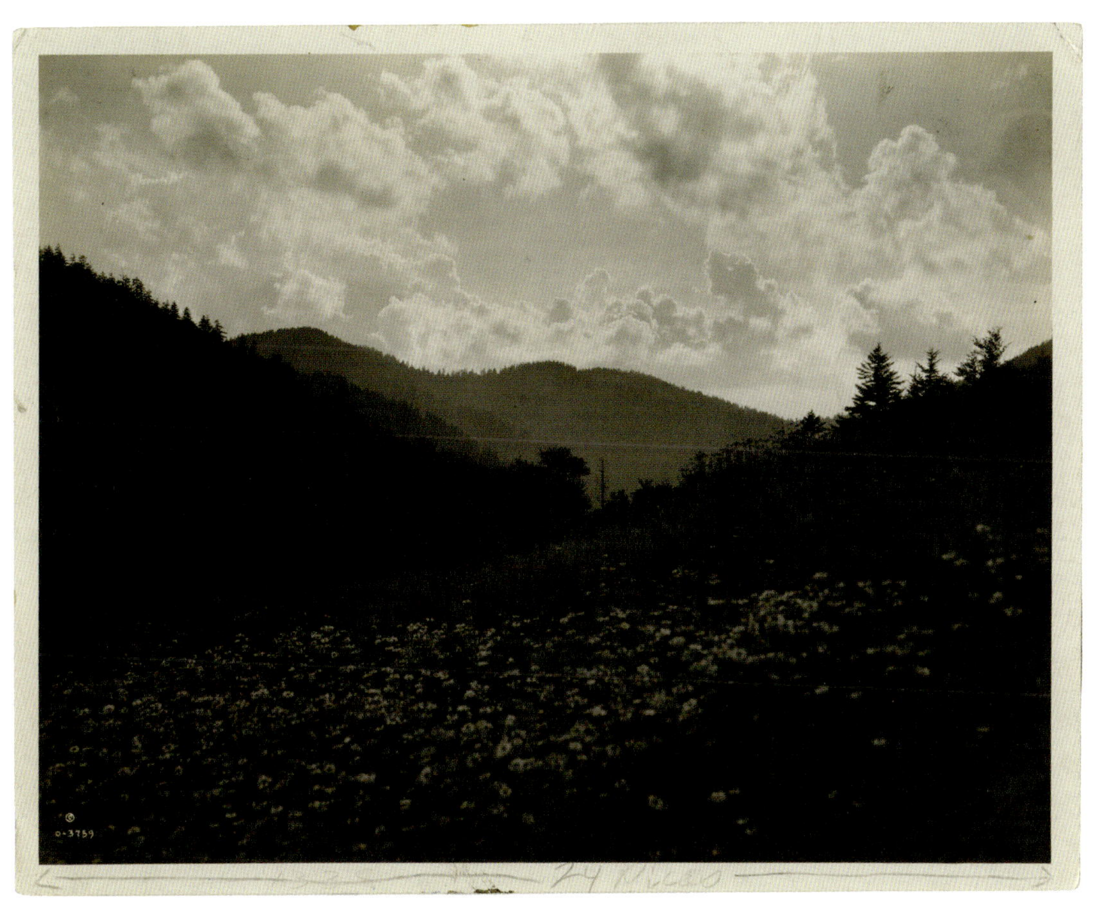

Great Smoky Mountains National Park, location unknown (WCU)

Letter from Asheville realtor R. J. Morrow regarding funds from the sale of Masa's estate to cover the cost of a headstone for Masa's grave. Kenneth Lee, the administrator of Masa's estate, sold Masa's collection to I. K. Stearns, president of the Carolina Wood Turning Company in Bryson City, who in turn donated it to the Great Smoky Mountains National Park museum.

March 2, 1939.

Dear Miss Hale,—

I enclose check for one hundred dollars,—payable to the Carolina Mt. Club—from Kenneth Lee, Adm. of estate of George Masa. We are to use such part of it as is necessary to erect a suitable marker at Masa's grave. The balance,—if any—goes to the Mountain Club in reimbursement of Mr. Masa's funeral expenses.

I think it would be better to cash this check as soon as possible, and deposit the one hundred dollars in the savings account of the Club, since we do not have a checking account of the Club.

Very truly yours,

R. F. Morrow.

P.S. It may be several months before we use this money for the marker.

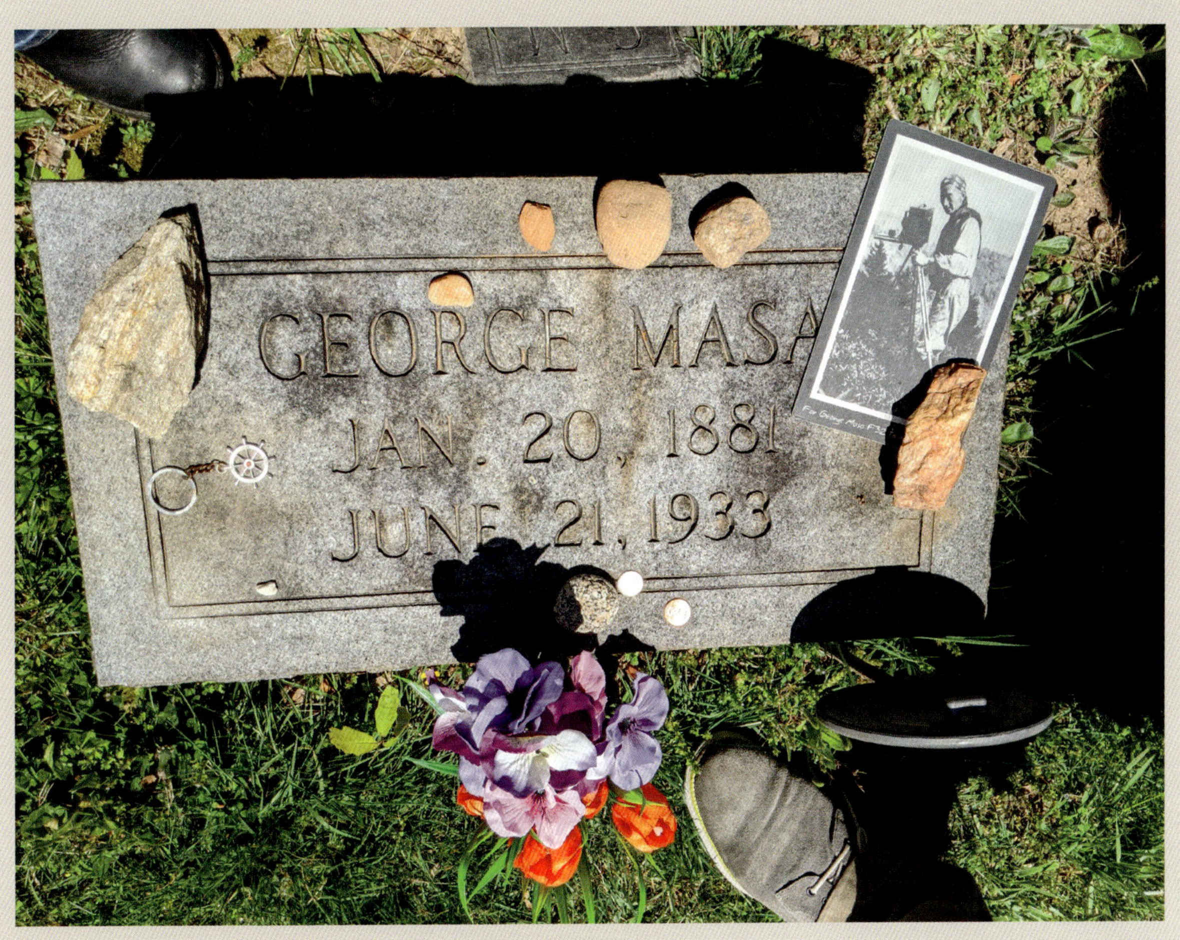

Masa's grave, April 27, 2021 (photo by Angela Martin)

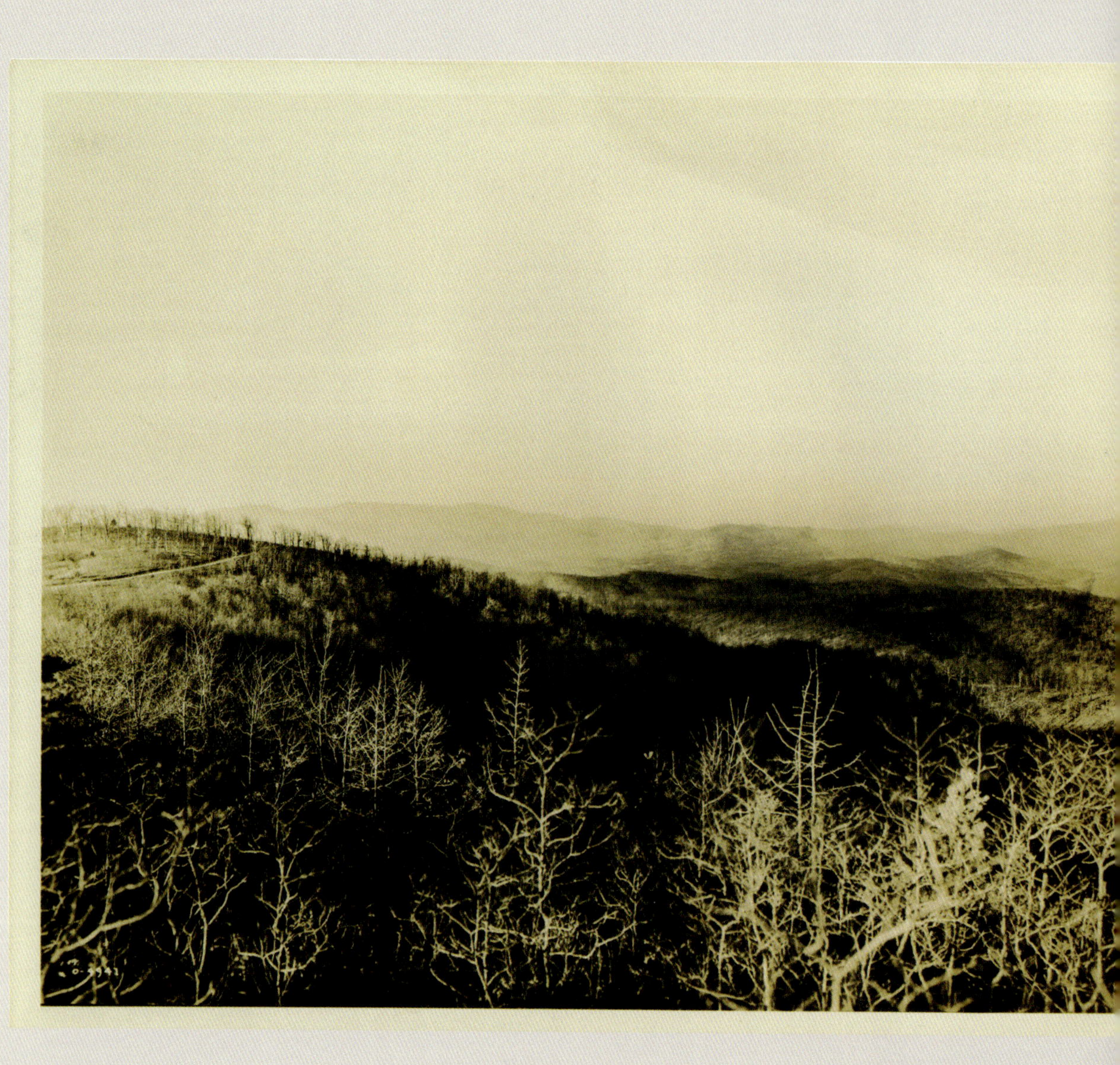

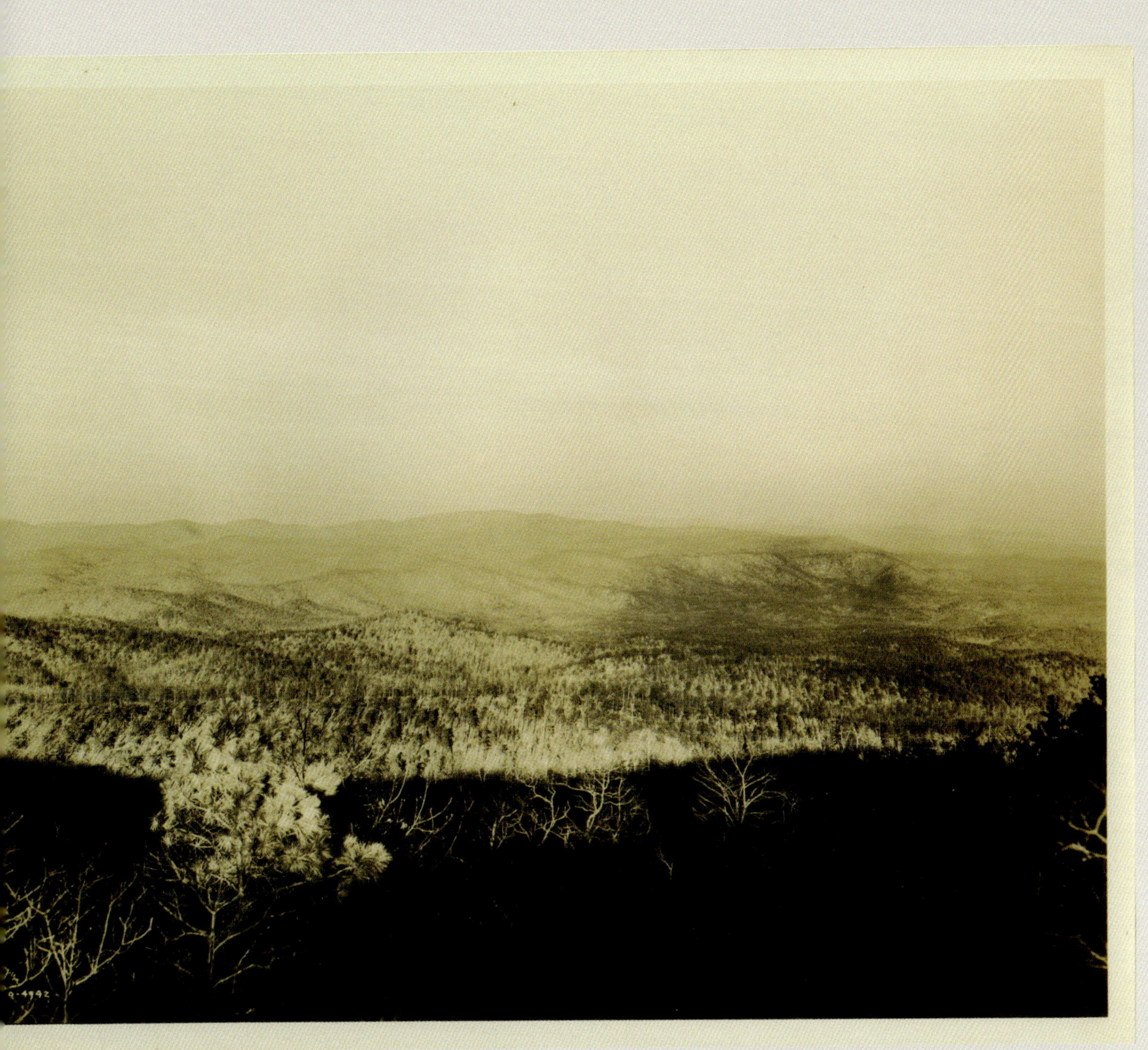

Mountain Panorama, location unknown

ACKNOWLEDGMENTS

SPECIAL THANKS GO TO John Lane and Betsy Teter, who encouraged this project and trusted me to complete it, and to Meg Reid at Hub City Press for her creativity and professional abilities with the book's direction and completion. John and Betsy's friendship, porch sittings, and kayak trips were a blessing during the long century known as 2020. Thanks also to Paul Bonesteel for reviewing this manuscript, and to George Ellison, William Hart, and Janet McCue for offering encouragement and support and for their dedication to keeping George Masa's memory alive through research, publication, and film. Jason Brady, head of Special Collections at Hunter Library, Western Carolina University, provided invaluable assistance with their Masa collection of photographs, journals, maps, and clippings, and went beyond the call of duty during the pandemic by scanning a large quantity of these materials so that I could review them during lockdown in the months when the Collections closed to the public. Gene Hyde, head of Special Collections at the University of North Carolina Asheville, performed a similar effort during lockdown, going so far as to have interns scan their Carolina Mountain Club collection of Masa correspondence, hike reports, and more and to organize them online—a resource now available to the public. Frances Figart and Lisa Horstman of the Great Smoky Mountains Association provided me with over two hundred PDFs of Masa images in their collection and granted permission and high-resolution images for those used in this publication. Obie Oakley, Ran Shaffner, and Stuart Ferguson of the Highlands Historical Society were more than accommodating and helpful by providing images and insights on their Masa collection. Eternal gratitude goes to my closest friend, unswerving critic, and partner in pursuit of all things wild for almost thirty years, Angela Faye Martin.

REFERENCES

Alexander, Tom. *Mountain Fever*. Fairview, NC: Bright Mountain Books, 1995.

Bennett, Terry. *Photography in Japan: 1853–1912*. Singapore: Tuttle Publishing, 2006.

Bonesteel, Paul, dir. *The Mystery of George Masa*. Bonesteel Films, 2002.

Claxton, Mae Miller, and George Frizell, eds. *Horace Kephart: Writings*. Knoxville: University of Tennessee Press, 2020.

Ellison, George, and Janet McCue. *Back of Beyond: A Horace Kephart Biography*. Great Smoky Mountains Association, 2019.

Hart, William. "George Masa: The Best Mountaineer." In *May We All Remember Well*, vol. 1, edited by Robert Brunk, 249–75. Brunk Auction Services, 2001.

Schwarzkopf, Kent S. *A History of Mt. Mitchell and the Black Mountains: Exploration, Development, and Preservation*. Raleigh: North Carolina Division of Archives and History, 1985.

Shaffner, Randolph P. *Heart of the Blue Ridge: Highlands, North Carolina*. Highlands, N.C.: Faraway Publishing, 2001.

Silver, Timothy. *Mount Mitchell and the Black Mountains*. Chapel Hill: University of North Carolina Press, 2003.

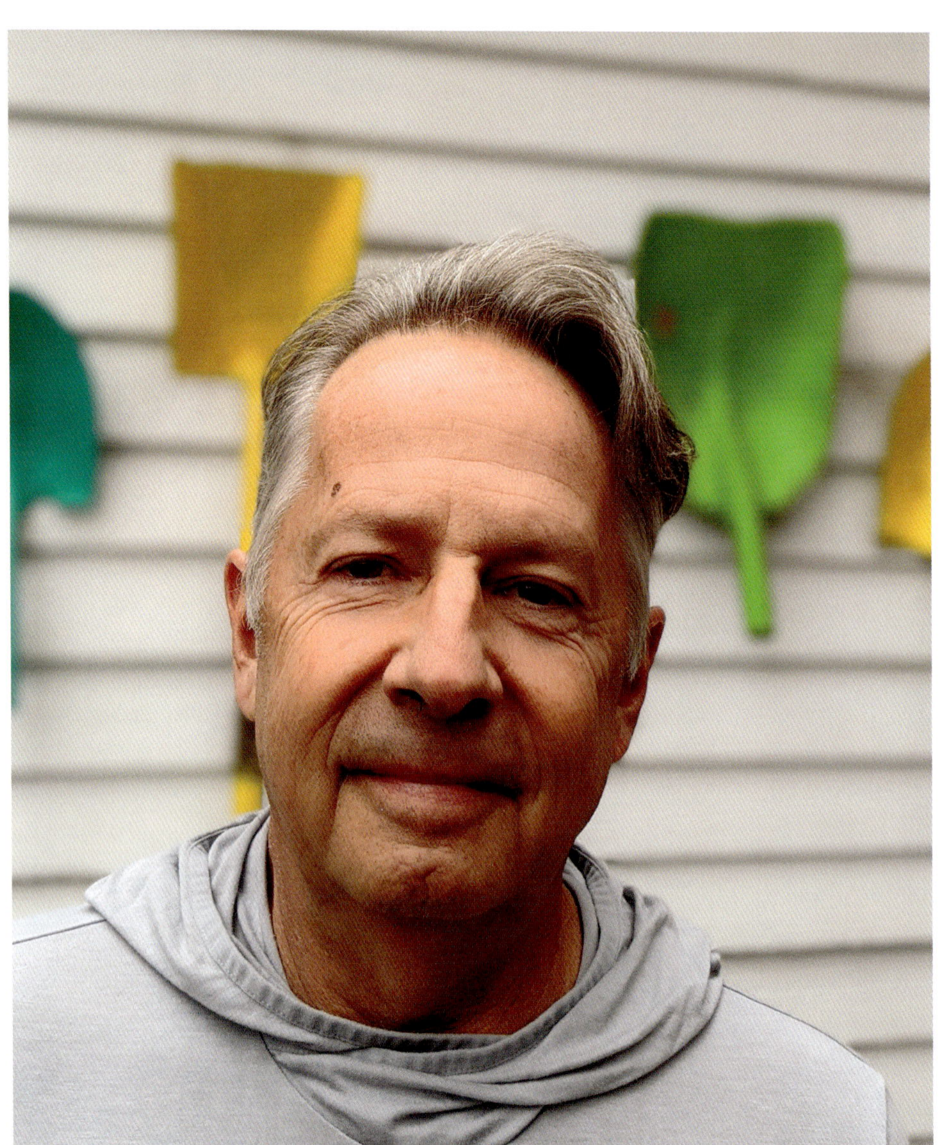

ABOUT THE AUTHOR

BRENT MARTIN lives in the Cowee community in western North Carolina, where he and his wife, Angela Faye Martin, run Alarka Institute, a nature-, literary-, and arts-based business that offers workshops and field trips. He is also the executive director of the Blue Ridge Bartram Trail Conservancy. He has served as the southern Appalachian regional director for the Wilderness Society, executive director of Georgia ForestWatch, associate director of the Land Trust for the Little Tennessee, and executive director of the Armuchee Alliance. He has an MA in history from Georgia State University and worked for several years on a dissertation on historical land-use patterns in the northwest Georgia mountains. He is a recipient of the Southern Environmental Law Center's Southern Environmental Leadership Award. In his spare time, he writes poetry and essays. Martin is the author of three chapbook collections of poetry—*Poems from Snow Hill Road* (New Native Press, 2007), *A Shout in the Woods* (Flutter Press, 2010), and *Staring the Red Earth Down* (Red Bird Press, 2014)—and is the coauthor of *Every Breath Sings Mountains* (Voices from the American Land, 2011) with Barbara Duncan and Thomas Crowe. He is also the author of *Hunting for Camellias at Horseshoe Bend*, a nonfiction chapbook published by Red Bird Press in 2015. His poetry and essays have been published in *North Carolina Literary Review, Pisgah Review, Tar River Poetry, Chattahoochee Review, Eno Journal, New Southerner, Kudzu Literary Journal, Smoky Mountain News*, and elsewhere, and he has served a two-year term as Gilbert-Chappell Distinguished Poet for the West.

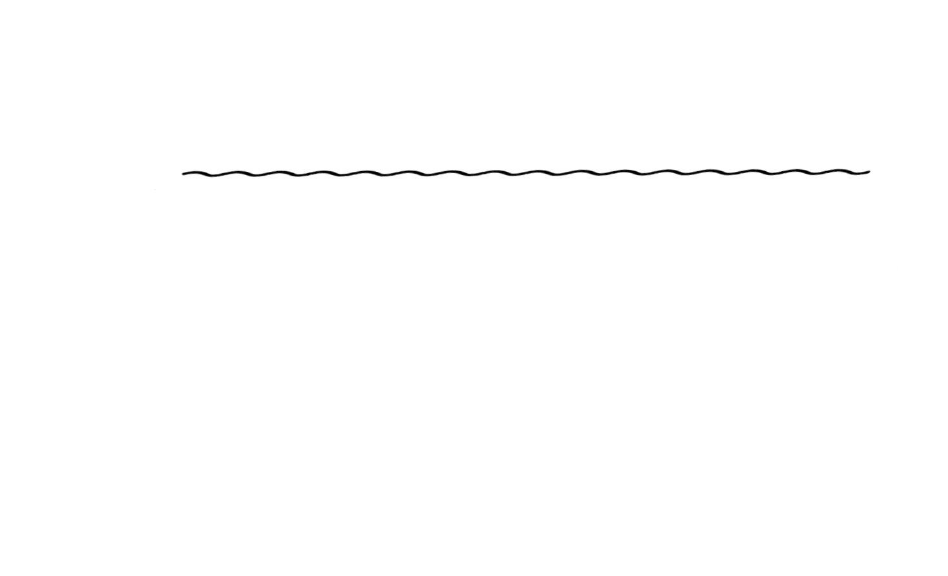

*Hub City Press and Brent Martin gratefully acknowledge our friends
who made contributions in support of this book.*

Ken Adams

Dusty Allison

City Lights Bookstore

Phyllis Bowen

Wayne Caldwell

Catherine Carter

Thomas Clairborne Jr.

Cheryl Clever

Helen Conley

Jim and Leslie Costa

Mr. and Mrs Thomas L. Davis

Caleb Enloe

Walter Enloe

Severin/Woodward Family

Jim Ward and Rachel Fraser

Michael Gillen

Jane and Tom Hatley

Kathryn Hendricks

Curtis Hertwig

Laurence Holden

Jean and Ronald Hunnicutt

Betsy Teter and John Lane

Jennifer and Jason Love

Eddi Minche

Marion Norwood

Jeremy Peach

Stanley Polanski

Don Russ

Vernon Skiles

Kathleen Stilwell

Mary Catherine Temple

Trent Bouts and Deborah White

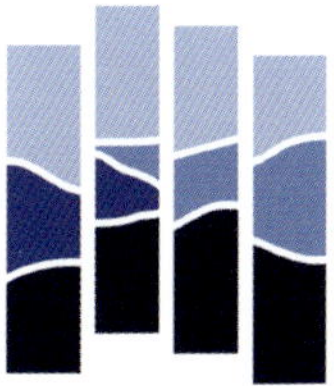

The **COLD MOUNTAIN** *Fund*
S E R I E S

NATIONAL BOOK AWARD WINNER Charles Frazier generously supports publication of a series of Hub City Press books through the Cold Mountain Fund at the Community Foundation of Western North Carolina. The Cold Mountain Series spotlights works of fiction and nonfiction by new and extraordinary writers from the American South. Books published in this series have been reviewed in outlets like *Wall Street Journal, San Francisco Chronicle, Garden & Gun, Entertainment Weekly,* and *O, the Oprah Magazine*; included on Best Books lists from NPR, *Kirkus Reviews,* and the American Library Association; and have won or been nominated for awards like the Southern Book Prize, Crooks Corner Book Prize, and the Langum Prize for Historical Fiction.

The Crocodile Bride • Ashleigh Bell Pedersen

Child in the Valley • Gordy Sauer

The Parted Earth • Anjali Enjeti

You Want More: The Selected Stories of George Singleton

The Prettiest Star • Carter Sickels

Watershed • Mark Barr

The Magnetic Girl • Jessica Handler

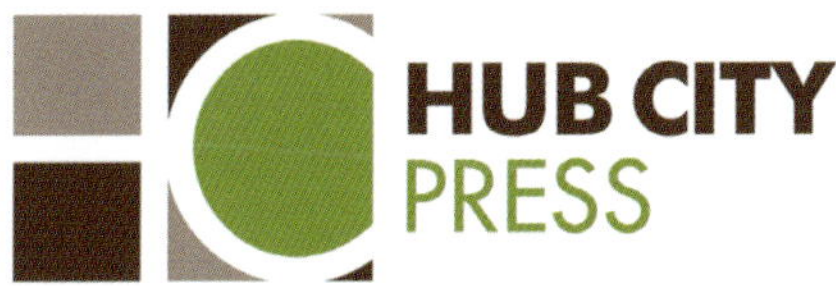

FOUNDED IN SPARTANBURG, South Carolina in 1995, Hub City Press has emerged as the South's premier independent literary press. Hub City is interested in books with a strong sense of place and is committed to finding and spotlighting extraordinary new and unsung writers from the American South. Our curated list champions diverse authors and books that don't fit into the commercial or academic publishing landscape.

George Masa's Wild Vision was designed by Blue Egg Design Studio
in Durham, North Carolina. The text is set in Garamond.